SECOND EDITION

Workplace Sexual Harassment

Anne C. Levy
Michigan State University

Michele A. Paludi
Paludi & Associates
Consultants in Sexual Harassment

Prentice
Hall

Upper Saddle River, NJ 07458

For George Cattermole, my father
Anne Levy

For Rosalie Paludi and Lucille Paludi, my sisters,
Michele Paludi

Levy, Anne
  Workplace sexual harassment / Anne C. Levy, Michele A. Paludi. — 2nd ed.
  p. cm.
  Includes index.
  ISBN 0–13–041560–X (pbk.)
    1. Sexual harassment — United States. 2. Sex discrimination in employment —
  United States. 3. Sex role in the work enveironment — United States. 4. Sexual
  harassment — Law and legislation — United States. I. Paludi, Michele Antoinette. II.
  Title

  HD6060.3 .L486 2002
  331.13'3'0973 — dc21

                                                                            2001016421

Acquisitions Editor: Elisa Adams
Assistant Editor: Jennifer Surich
Editorial Assistant: Virginia Sheridan
Media Project Manager: Michele Faranda
Marketing Manager: Debbie Clare
Marketing Assistant: Jessica Pasquini
Production Manager: Gail Steier de Acevedo
Production Editor: Maureen Wilson
Permissions Coordinator: Suzanne Grappi
Associate Director, Manufacturing: Vincent Scelta
Manufacturing Buyer: Natacha St. Hill Moore
Cover Design: Kiwi Design
Cover Illustration/Photo: PhotoDisc
Full-Service Project Management and Composition: Impressions Book and Journal
  Services, Inc.
Printer/Binder: R. R. Donnelley & Sons

Credits and acknowledgments borrowed from other sources and reproduced, with permission, in this textbook appear on appropriate page within text.

Prentice
Hall

10 9 8 7 6 5 4 3 2 1

ISBN 0-13-041560-X

Contents

Preface

In 1991 when we first began planning for this book, sexual harassment was a relatively newly recognized phenomenon that had been thrust to the center stage by the Clarence Thomas hearings. Although 10 years have passed since then, the topic continues to be one of the most important personnel issues for business, and, unfortunately, it is still much misunderstood. In one business publication, the author noted that

> sexual harassment is among the most prominent civil rights issues in the workplace. More than 15,500 sexual harassment charges were filed with the Equal Employment Opportunity Commission or state agencies in fiscal 1998, compared to about 10,000 complaints of racial harassment.[1]

Despite many years of advice and warnings from attorneys, even the largest companies find themselves facing large jury verdicts and settlements because employees were subjected to conduct that should have been dealt with long before it became front-page news.

It is obviously a very bad public relations scenario to have your company appear in the media as one of those that allow these conditions to occur. The business suffers in a number of ways, some obvious when looking short-term, others only seen when looking long-term. Certainly the buying public sees and processes the fact that the company has problems, but in addition, those who are looking, in a wide-open labor market, to choose an employer will often take such information into account. Shareholders may become unhappy to be associated with such a company, and future potential shareholders may be dissuaded from becoming part of an organization with negative connotations in their minds.

Thus, it is clear that the ramifications of not dealing appropriately with sexual harassment in the workplace are far-reaching. The purpose of this book is to clarify the issue, create an understanding of what this is all about, and create a dialogue for those who are or will be guiding the course of business in the future. This understanding is important for everyone: employees who may be subjected to or charged with sexual harassment, managers to whom employees may turn to report harassment or ask advice, and everyone involved in the process of setting up policies and procedures, investigating complaints, being witnesses in an investigation, making determinations about complaints, deciding on and carrying out remedies, and monitoring the workplace for illegal behavior at all times, especially after a harassment investigation is completed and a determination made. Consider the following "nightmare" discussed in a recent business publication:

> An employee—one with a good track record and who's generally well liked—comes in to lodge a sexual harassment complaint. The alleged harasser also has a good track record and is also well liked. The alleged victim finishes the complaint with, "I don't want you to do anything—I just wanted to get this out in the open." So for now, you're off the hook, right?
>
> Actually, you're as off the hook as if that same employee came in and told you, "I embezzled $10,000 from the company, but I'm planning to put it back in a couple of weeks, so don't tell anyone."
>
> Despite the widespread publicity that sexual harassment has gotten in the press over the past decade, and despite the fact that companies know how much it can cost if they get hit with a harassment suit, it's amazing to find out how little people understand about sexual harassment. Many managers will say, "Well that's why we have lawyers." No doubt that's a critically important factor—but it's not enough. If the situation escalates to the point where litigation takes place, it means something was overlooked early on.[2]

If sexual harassment is thought of as the important business concern that it is and if it is clearly understood that the effect can be immense on fellow employees, it becomes far easier to make sure that any problems that do occur are given the kind of serious attention that the law requires. Dealing with sexual harassment in the workplace takes time and effort, but the rewards in workplace satisfaction, management of litigation expenses, productivity, loyalty, and public relations are widespread.

Bringing our two perspectives, legal and psychological, together, we hope to give you a more integrated picture of what harassment is, why it occurs, and how to deal with it appropriately. A complete program requires not just a commitment to "keep the company out of court" but also an understanding of all that harassment can take from business and its resources.

This new edition contains all of the new developments in the law and in the psychology of harassment, but one thing has not changed—the focus on the reality that the most successful programs will be those that sincerely commit to encouraging (not just allowing) employees to come forward with complaints, dealing with every incident in an appropriate manner without concern as to whether the "level of legal liability" has been reached, and helping every worker understand its effects. Rhetoric and reality must not be separate. The company must say what it means and mean what it says. A company with no reports is usually a company with problems that have no outlet except the final one—the courtroom.

Consider this . . .

When others harass, now managers lose pay

Supervisors across America take note: How well you promote and enforce your company's sexual-harassment policy could soon impact whether you get that next raise or promotion.

This tough new standard of evaluating supervisors' rigor on harassment is something Ford Motor Co. agreed to as part of its $7.5 million sexual-harassment settlement with federal regulators in Chicago this week. And experts say it will soon become standard practice at most U.S. firms.

The plan is the latest in a new wave of efforts by the courts and government agencies to ensure that harassment policies don't languish unread in employee handbooks—that they're in use everywhere from the corporate suite to the assembly-line floor. "The bottom line for companies is if your supervisors support the policy then it will work, but if not, chances are it won't," says Jon Zimring, who handles harassment law at the firm Duane, Morris & Heckscher in Chicago. And having a policy that doesn't work can cost employers big.

Ford had an antiharassment policy. But it will pay $7.5 million in damages, and spend about $10 million more on training, because 19 women at two Chicago-area plants complained to the federal Equal Employment Opportunity Commission (EEOC), saying male workers routinely used sexually degrading names for them, put explicit materials in the workplace, and even groped some of the women. Furthermore, the EEOC said some managers threatened to fire the women who complained.

The settlement is the fourth-largest of its kind in U.S. history—and comes just over a year after the biggest settlement, also in the auto industry. Last year, Mitsubishi Motor Manufacturing of America agreed to pay $34 million in harassment claims at its Normal, Ill., plant. Before the complaints against Mitsubishi were filed, it had fired 15 employees on sexual-harassment grounds. But that was not enough. Investigators documented a pattern of harassment—and unwillingness to stop it among supervisors and managers.

"We're continuing to learn what works," says John Rowe, the EEOC's director in Chicago. "And even though senior management tends to be very supportive, the control arm is really the lowest level of management."

At Mitsubishi, there were "overwhelming numbers of situations in which first-line supervisors had been promoted from the ranks of the people they were now supervising," he says. "They were great friends with the harassers, and wouldn't confront them because they still wanted to be just 'one of the guys.'"

At Ford, and increasingly throughout corporate America, that won't be acceptable anymore. Salaried workers at all 23 U.S. Ford plants—with a total of about 40,000 workers—won't even be considered for a promotion for two years if they've been disciplined for not supporting the policy against sexual and racial harassment, and three years if they've been suspended for it. "Within a couple years, this will become a standard operating practice" for U.S. companies, says Michael Karpeles, head of the employment-law group at the Chicago firm of Goldberg, Kohn.

For one thing, he says, it's easy to add a box on supervisor evaluation forms covering sexual harassment—and it can save companies big money. That's because the Supreme Court has ruled that if a company actively seeks to rub out harassment, those efforts constitute an "affirmative defense," which can lessen the penalties in legal cases.

But the question is: How will supervisors be evaluated? Will it be simply their boss's impression? Or will their subordinates be polled? Will they have to be actively promoting the policy—or just not interfering with it?

The details are still to be worked out at Ford. But the few companies that have begun this practice have taken varied approaches. Some check whether supervisors attend all the required sexual-harassment seminars. Others survey employees about conduct. Some use outside consultants to interview workers and identify problems in policies.

In the end, says Mr. Zimring, managers will now have to "communicate to their employees that they agree with, personally believe in, and will enforce the harassment policy. Because as an employee, if your supervisor is making a big deal of this, then you're going to pay attention."

Abraham McLaughlin, *Christian Science Monitor*, Friday, September 10, 1999

* * *

Thanks to the following people for their helpful reviews: James Slack—University of Alabama at Birmingham; James Marshall—Michigan State University; Michael Popejoy—Palm Beach Atlantic College; and Stan Malos—San Jose University.

Notes

1. "The Changing Face of Sexual Harassment," SUSAN E. LONG & CATHERINE G. LEONARD, *HR Focus Special Supplement on Employment Law*, American Management Association, October 1999, p. S1.
2. "What You Know about Harassment Can Hurt You, Too," George A. Milite, *HR Focus*, American Management Association, December 1999, p. 9.

About the Authors

ANNE C. LEVY

Anne C. Levy, J.D., is an Associate Professor of Law, Public Policy, and Business in the Eli Broad College of Business and Graduate School of Management at Michigan State University. She teaches courses in the legal environment of business and ethics for graduate students in the MBA on-campus program, the Weekend MBA Program in Integrative Management, and the Executive MBA program. As a member of the faculty in the Executive Education program, she is also involved in presenting workshops and seminars in a variety of topic areas, including employment discrimination, sexual harassment, and wrongful discharge.

Professor Levy received her B.A. and M.A. in English from Oakland University and her J.D. *cum laude* from Wayne State Law School. Before joining the faculty at Michigan State University, Professor Levy served as Judicial Law Clerk to the Honorable Patricia J. Boyle, associate justice of the Michigan Supreme Court. Prior to attending law school, she spent many years in the field of public relations.

Professor Levy has published a variety of articles on the subject of employment discrimination in such publications as the *Albany Law Review,* the *Kansas Law Review,* and the *Wisconsin Law Review.* In addition, she has been involved in a variety of legal seminars and training sessions for employees, managers, students, faculty, and administrators on the topic of sexual harassment.

As a consultant and expert witness, Professor Levy has been involved in a number of employment discrimination cases. These have included termination proceedings, arbitrations, trials, and appeals.

MICHELE A. PALUDI

Michele A. Paludi, Ph.D., is an internationally recognized expert in academic and workplace sexual harassment. She is the editor of *Ivory Power: Sexual Harassment on Campus* (SUNY Press, 1990), coauthor of *Academic and Workplace Sexual Harassment: A Resource Manual* (SUNY Press, 1991), editor of *Sexual Harassment on College Campuses: Abusing the Ivory Power* (SUNY Press, 1996), and coauthor of *Sexual Harassment, Work, and Education: A Resource Manual for Prevention* (SUNY Press, 1998).

Dr. Paludi's book *Ivory Power* was named the 1992 recipient of the Gustavus Myers Center Award for the Outstanding Book on Human Rights in the United States.

Dr. Paludi is the author of 16 books on sexual harassment, the psychology of women, and gender. Her coedited book *Psychology of Women: Handbook of Issues and Theories* was named an outstanding academic book in the United States by the American Library Association.

Dr. Paludi is principal of Michele Paludi & Associates, Consultants in Sexual Harassment, and offers education and training in issues related to sexual harassment at schools, colleges, and organizations. In addition, she is an expert witness for academic and court proceedings involving sexual harassment.

For her research, training, and investigative work, Dr. Paludi received the 1992 Progress in Equity Award from the National and New York State Chapter of the American Association of University Women. She is also the 1988 recipient of the Emerging Leader Award from the Committee on Women of the American Psychological Association. In 1992, the YWCA awarded Dr. Paludi their Woman of Vision Award for Advocacy. Dr. Paludi was named a 1994 Woman of the Year by the New York State Business and Professional Women's Organization in 1994.

She has held faculty positions at Franklin and Marshall College, Kent State University, Hunter College, and Union College.

Dr. Paludi was a member of Governor Cuomo's Task Force on Sexual Harassment. She also chaired the U.S. Department of Education's Gender Equity Expert Panel on Sexual Harassment, Violence, and Alcohol and Other Drug Abuse in Higher Education.

ACKNOWLEDGMENTS

We would like to thank the following family members, friends, and colleagues for their encouragement and support during the research and writing of our book:

Nancy Adamson
Jaynor Johnston
Claudia Rast
—Anne Levy

Carmen Paludi Jr.
Fr. John Provost
—Michele Paludi

PART ONE

Understanding Sexual Harassment

Legal and Psychological Perspectives

CHAPTER I

The American Legal System

Case Study

Fred Farnsworth is very upset. He has just received a phone call from his lawyer, who told Fred that he is being sued by a former employee for sexual harassment. The lawyer told Fred that he faces various statutory as well as some common-law claims and that they need to talk soon. Fred is upset not only because he doesn't like the idea that he is being sued but also because he didn't understand anything that his lawyer said to him. "I'm being told that a 'girlie calendar' and 'girlie magazines' in the lounge areas may have violated the federal law, even though a recently passed state law specifically protects such displays. Also, I'm being told that the employee is claiming that one of my supervisors intentionally inflicted emotional distress. What the heck does all that mean? How do I know what type of behavior will result in emotional distress? Will I be facing several different lawsuits in several different courts?"

INTRODUCTION

To better understand the law of sexual harassment, you need to have a basic understanding of the legal process at work in the United States. Various courts and government institutions are involved in carrying out this country's laws and have a continuing effect on the development of sexual harassment law.

THE COURT SYSTEMS

There are two parallel court systems in the United States: the federal system and the state systems. The jurisdiction of each system is specified by statute or in the federal or state constitutions. Generally, federal courts hear cases involving laws that are passed by Congress, questions concerning the U.S. Constitution, and civil disputes between residents of two different states (called *diversity jurisdiction*). State courts adjudicate matters that concern laws passed by that state's legislature, the state's constitution, and civil disputes between people who are both classified as being residents of that state. Occasionally, federal courts may hear state-law claims when a case involves both federal and state matters, but the federal court must adhere to the state court's precedents in making those decisions.

Thus, Fred's concern that he may be forced into several lawsuits in several different courts is probably unfounded. A federal court could decide all of the claims, even though some may be based on state law.

In the federal system, generally speaking, the federal district court is the lowest-level court. Federal district courts are usually classified as the "trial courts," meaning that they are the first courts to hear cases, listen to the evidence, and make decisions on disputed facts about the applicable law. These decisions may be made by a judge or a jury, depending on whether a jury trial is allowed and on the preference of the parties. A jury trial must be made available when the Seventh Amendment to the Constitution requires it or when Congress specifies it in a federal law. Since 1991, federal law has allowed for a jury in employment-discrimination lawsuits, including sexual-harassment claims.

Once a decision has been given in the federal district court, the parties have an opportunity to appeal the decision to the circuit court of appeals. There are 13 circuit courts of appeals, which are responsible for hearing appeals from federal district courts in a designated region. After a decision has been reached in a circuit court of appeal, either party may apply to the United States Supreme Court for leave to appeal. If the Supreme Court decides to hear a case, it will grant *certiorari,* which means that the case will be argued before the highest court. The Supreme Court usually gets involved only in cases that present issues of vital importance or that will allow the Court to settle a disagreement in decisions between the circuits (i.e., the courts of appeals are coming to opposite conclusions about the same issue). There are currently several such situations in the area of sexual harassment, but the Supreme Court has not chosen to accept cases that would allow it to settle the issues, uniformly denying *certiorari.* When *certiorari* is denied, it does not necessarily mean that the Supreme Court agrees with the lower court's decision. It merely means, for whatever reason, that the Court does not choose to hear the issue at that time.

The state court systems operate much like the federal system. The lower courts hear the evidence and make decisions of fact and law; the appeals courts review the record and determine whether there have been any mistakes that must be corrected. Each state has different names for its various courts, but all have at least three levels, with a state-level supreme-type court having the final word if the court chooses to hear the case. The highest court in each state is the ultimate decider of issues involving state laws and state constitutions. Even the Supreme Court cannot overturn a state court in these matters, unless there is also an issue involving the Constitution. Often, however, state courts will look to the federal courts' decisions in a parallel federal law area for assistance in deciding cases under their own state laws, as is the case in the area of sexual harassment. Title VII decisions are often used by state courts in interpreting their own states' civil-rights acts.

THE TYPES OF LAWS

Both federal and state courts are involved in deciding cases in the three categories of law found in every state but Louisiana: constitutional, statutory, and common law. Constitutional cases involve interpretation and application of either the state or the federal Constitution, depending on the court system. Statutory law involves the interpretation and application of laws, often called *acts,* passed by the legislative bodies: Congress in the federal system and the state legislatures in the state system. There are both federal and state statutes dealing with employment discrimination. At the national level, the law is contained in Title VII, a section of the Civil Rights Act of 1964.

Common law is more complex than statutory law and requires more explanation. Common law is, in effect, judge-made law. Throughout the history of the English and U.S. courts, various disputes that were not covered by any statutory or constitutional dictates have arisen between parties. The judges in these cases have been called on to settle the disputes and, in doing so, make decisions about various issues in each case. For example, these issues include the duties owed by members of society to others in the community, the extent of liability of a person committing a "wrongful act," the damages that must be paid, the point at which a contract is formed, and the effect of various events on liability. As these cases were decided, a series of precedents were set, which other courts could or must (if set by a higher court) follow when deciding cases involving the same issues. As new cases presented new situations and additional issues, the law developed into a complex system called the *common law.* Thus, common law is involved in almost every legal dispute that does not involve either a specific statute or a constitution. Although there is some federal common law in areas in which the federal courts have jurisdiction, common-law cases are normally heard in state courts.

An example of a common-law claim is the one that Fred heard about in the case study—the employee is claiming that the supervisor intentionally inflicted emotional distress on her and caused her damage. This is a type of tort lawsuit—a lawsuit brought by a private party for damages sustained because of the actions of another private party.

As will be seen later with regard to the law of sexual harassment, even though a statute may allow a person to bring a statutory lawsuit against someone, there still may be common-law claims that can be brought along as well. Statutory and common-law claims may be brought together if the facts support both.

THE HIERARCHY OF LAWS

Just as there is a hierarchy in the court system, there is also a hierarchy in the types of laws. Common law is the lowest-level law, and any common-law decision that is in conflict with a statutory or constitutional rule is no longer good law. Thus, as often occurs, if a legislative body does not like a common-law precedent, it can pass a statute that will overturn the common law. No statute can overturn a constitutional mandate, however, because the constitution is the highest law, superseding all others. Whereas a state constitution is normally the ultimate law in each state, the U.S. Constitution supersedes all laws, including each state's constitution.

THE INTERPLAY OF STATE AND FEDERAL LAWS

In addition to concerns about the hierarchy of the types of law, there are also issues regarding the hierarchy between state and federal laws. When conflict arises between the state and federal laws, a decision must be made as to which law preempts or supersedes the other.

An example of this problem can be seen in the case study, where a state has attempted to change the federal law of sexual harassment by specifically protecting the use of "girlie" calendars and magazines in the workplace. In that situation, a court would have to determine whether the federal law or the state law should be enforced.

Although preemption cases can be very complex and sometimes must be decided by the Supreme Court, it is possible to state a few general rules about when federal law will preempt a conflicting state law. First, the laws that are in conflict must involve an area in which the U.S. Constitution grants power to the federal government. Second, for preemption to exist, either (1) the federal government must have shown an intent to "occupy the field," in other words, not to allow states to regulate in this area; or (2) the state law must be in conflict with the federal law.

Federal antidiscrimination laws are passed by Congress, largely under the power granted to it by Article 8 of the Constitution (often called the Commerce Clause) to regulate interstate commerce. Through a series of Supreme Court cases involving the extent of this power, Congress has been interpreted to have authority to regulate activity that has a substantial effect, directly or indirectly and individually or collectively, on interstate commerce. Although there have been challenges to laws, such as the Civil Rights Act of 1964, the Supreme Court has refused to overturn Congress's finding that discrimination with regard to employment and accommodations would have a substantial effect on interstate commerce. Thus, it has been decided that the federal government has the power to regulate various types of discrimination.

Does federal law then automatically preempt state laws dealing with discrimination? Recall that the issue requires a further analysis step. Title VII specifically states that Congress did not intend to occupy the field of employment-discrimination law, and thus states may pass laws of their own, which may in fact be even stricter than the federal law. Several states, for example, have laws that allow greater damages than Title VII does, and those laws are not preempted—a reason why many employees who have been sexually harassed choose to pursue both a federal and a state law claim when possible.

With regard to the possibility of preemption, however, a state may not enforce a law that conflicts with the federal law, and any law that legalizes behavior that the federal law prohibits would do just that. Thus, the pornographic pictures in the case study would have to go.

Another aspect of the U.S. legal system that is important in a complete understanding of the law of sexual harassment involves the "reach" of statutory laws—in other words, who must obey them. Most federal and state laws specify the individuals covered by the statute. For example, Title VII covers employers, labor organizations, and employment agencies, as well as their agents, and specifically defines those terms for purposes of the act. State laws may regulate only individuals or companies over which the state has jurisdiction. This usually means those who live or do business in the state. Federal laws may regulate not only any individual in the United States but also, in some situations, individuals who are in foreign countries. Title VII presents an interesting example of this extraterritorial jurisdiction, and the history of the application of the law presents a classic example of how legislatures can change some court decisions.

In early 1991, the Supreme Court decided the case of *EEOC v. Arabian American Oil Co.*,[1] in which an American citizen claimed that he was discriminated against by his employer, a U.S. company, while he was working for the company in a foreign country. Although the Supreme Court decided that it was within the power of Congress to regulate this activity as long as it involved a U.S. company, the Court nonetheless decided that Congress did not intend such an application.

In October 1991, Congress amended Title VII to make it clear that it did intend for U.S. nationals working in foreign offices of U.S. companies to be protected from discrimination. Thus, Title VII now regulates activity both inside and outside the United States when the employer is a U.S. company and the employee is a U.S. national.

THE ROLE OF PRECEDENT

Precedent is important in the American legal system, both in the common law and in statutory or constitutional interpretation. When a court is presented with an issue to decide, there are probably several previously decided cases that involved similar issues. Using a legal doctrine called *stare decisis,* a court will usually follow the previous decisions, unless there is some strong reason to change the course of the law. A court must follow any applicable precedents that were set by courts classified as higher courts.

Federal district courts in each region must adhere to the precedents set in their own circuit court of appeals but are not required to follow rules set in other circuits. In addition, no circuit court of appeals is bound by the decisions of another circuit court. Many of the sexual-harassment cases that will be discussed in the following chapters are decisions of the various circuit courts of appeals.

Even though a circuit court opinion does not establish precedent for another circuit's court, all courts in the federal system are required to follow the decisions of the Supreme Court, the highest court in the federal system. The Supreme Court has the final say in all matters involving interpretation of federal laws and the U.S. Constitution.

In response to Fred's question in the case study, the courts where his case will be heard will have already decided several cases with regard to how egregious behavior must be in order to fit under the "intentional infliction of emotional distress" claim. His attorney will be looking into those cases to see what the rules and facts in the previous decisions can tell Fred about the possible outcome in his case. This could help him decide whether to settle the case or go to court.

THE ROLE OF GOVERNMENT AGENCIES

The role of government agencies in the U.S. legal system must also be reviewed for a complete understanding of the law of sexual harassment. The laws that govern how agencies operate and the regulations that such agencies create are usually referred to as *administrative law.*

Although many volumes have been written about administrative law, some general principles are adequate to understand the role of the agencies involved in the discrimination arena. First, agencies are given power only when it is delegated by another branch of government. This usually means that Congress or a state legislative body delegates some of its power, in what is called an *enabling act,* to an agency that is then enabled to carry out certain specified functions. Although this power is legislative, agencies may also have some executive and judicial power. Depending on the specific provisions of its enabling act, an agency may perform a variety of functions. It may promulgate regulations that create new rights and responsibilities in its particular area of expertise. An agency may issue interpretations of specific provisions of the laws over which it has been delegated authority. These interpretations are usually called *guidelines.* An agency may hold hearings on issues of importance, make recommendations to Congress or the state legislatures, investigate possible violations of the laws, issue violation notices, hold hearings to determine liability, and assess damages.

Obviously, agencies have a great deal of influence in the development of law in the United States, but like all government entities, they are subject to limitations. Agencies may not go beyond the powers granted to them in their enabling act, and any action taken by them, including interpreting laws and promulgating regulations, is subject to challenge in the courts. For example, if the courts feel that an agency has misinterpreted the law in a guideline, they may overturn the interpretation. Usually, however, the courts give a great deal of deference to an agency determination because the agency has special expertise in the area under consideration. In addition, agency processes are controlled by the dictates of the Administrative Procedures Act, which sets out requirements for many agency actions.

The agency involved in Title VII cases is the Equal Employment Opportunity Commission (EEOC), and most states that have civil-rights laws have their own antidiscrimination agencies. The EEOC has specific powers granted to it by Congress in a variety of laws, including the Civil Rights Act of 1964, the Americans with Disabilities Act, and the Equal Pay Act. These powers include the ability to issue guidelines, investigate complaints, mediate disputes, and bring lawsuits to court. The EEOC has been involved in many cases in the area of sexual harassment and has had a strong influence on the development of law in this area. A more detailed description of the EEOC and its investigative process is found in chapter 6.

ALTERNATE DISPUTE RESOLUTION

Many employers are attempting to stop complaints of discrimination from coming to court by asking employees to enter into arbitration agreements. These agreements require that any claim, including those involving sexual harassment, be submitted to an arbitrator or arbitration panel before a court becomes involved. There is some recent evidence that the EEOC will challenge arbitration agreements if they are a precondition to getting or keeping a job. Whereas the validity of arbitration agreements in this area is not absolutely clear, it does appear that at least voluntary agreements may be enforceable if adequate measures are included to protect the rights of the complainants. This would include making sure that the employee knows exactly what she or he is signing.

Such agreements cannot circumvent the law, however, and will probably not stop lawsuits, even if arbitration is pursued first. They can be useful, though—especially with regard to the cost savings and the relative speed of the decision making—and will probably be used more frequently in the future. Anyone considering such an agreement should involve an experienced attorney in the process. Doing so will ensure that any recent court decisions have been followed and that adequate provisions are provided to uphold the agreement's validity.

SUMMARY

The U.S. system of jurisprudence involves a variety of different types of laws and two parallel court systems, each with its own jurisdiction and precedents. All of these types of laws and both the federal and state courts may be involved in a sexual-harassment case; understanding how the laws and courts operate can be helpful in understanding what to expect in such a situation.

FOR REFLECTION

1. Discuss the three types of law found in all states except Louisiana and how each type of law originates.
2. Explain the concept of preemption. Why is it so important in sexual-harassment cases?
3. Discuss the problems that may be encountered in adding an arbitration clause to an employment contract.
4. What is the EEOC? Where does it fit in the legal system? Where does it get its power? If Congress does not like a regulation that the EEOC promulgates, can Congress overturn it? If so, how?

Notes

1. *EEOC v. Arabian American Oil Co.*, 499 U.S. 244 (1991).

CHAPTER 2

Sexual Harassment from the Legal Perspective

Case Study

Victoria Janus and Marjorie Mattis are the only women who work in the maintenance department at Consolidated Dermatics. One morning, they arrive at work to find that a pin-up picture of Marjorie, which she posed for many years earlier, has been placed over the workbench of Fred Fandes, one of the other workers. Victoria wants to complain, but Marjorie urges her to forget it because it will only escalate the problem, reminding Victoria that the other workers have made life miserable for Joseph Dale because he complained about sexual harassment in the past by male workers and that Joseph had not received a salary increase since the complaint. Victoria decides to approach her boss, Mark Steel, anyway, but he tells her that one little picture won't hurt her and that if she stopped dressing in such a "sexy" manner, she might not have

this problem. When Victoria tells Marjorie about the response, Marjorie is not surprised.

"Don't forget," Marjorie reminds her, "Fred is Henrietta Fandes's brother, and she's the VP of this division."

"That's right," responds Victoria, "and Mark would never upset her because he only got his job because he's sleeping with her."

When things don't change, Victoria goes back to Mark and he tells her "You know, Vic—you're really a sexy woman. You should use that. If you'd just loosen up, I could make things a lot easier for you. In fact, there's a supervisor position open that I have to fill. It's up to you." Victoria leaves his office, packs up her personal items, and quits.

Would Victoria or Marjorie have a legal case against Consolidated Dermatics for sexual harassment? Under what circumstances might Joseph have a legal case for sexual harassment? Would the facts that Marjorie posed for the picture and that Victoria dresses in a "sexy" manner have an effect on a potential case? Has Mark been sexually harassed?

What effect, if any, would Mark's last statements have on Victoria's chances of winning a lawsuit? What about the fact that she did not report his statements to anyone in authority?

INTRODUCTION

Federal and state statutes passed by Congress or state legislatures form the foundation for the laws against sexual harassment in the workplace in the United States. As noted in the introductory material, the applicable federal statute is Title VII of the Civil Rights Act of 1964. Most states also have civil-rights laws that deal with sexual harassment that apply to businesses in those states. In addition, in many sexual-harassment cases, the plaintiffs also file traditional common-law claims against an employer or the harassers. These may include such allegations as intentional or negligent infliction of emotional distress, assault, battery, or negligent hiring or retention. These claims are often allowed to be filed along with a claim under the state and federal laws and, at times, can result in even higher damage awards than those allowed in the statutes. The outcome of such common-law claims will usually be dependent on a finding of liability for sexual harassment under the statutory law. For that reason, and because such claims are covered by traditional common-law tort standards, they will not be extensively covered in this book. A basic text on business law can help provide further understanding.

THE STATUTORY FRAMEWORK

Generally, federal law only covers people working for a business with 15 or more employees, but many state laws cover smaller businesses.[1] In Michigan, for example, any employer with one or more employees must follow the requirements of that state's civil-rights statute. Thus, most businesses in today's environment will find themselves covered by one or more of these laws. Although state laws differ in some aspects from federal law, state courts often use federal cases as precedents for interpretations of state statutes. This means that Title VII often sets the standards in the area of sexual-harassment law.

The wording of Title VII is quite simple. It states that it is illegal to "fail or refuse to hire or to discharge any individual" or to discriminate in the "compensation, terms, conditions or privileges of employment" on the basis of an employee's or prospective employee's race, color, religion, sex, or national origin. It is the courts' ever-expanding interpretation of the term *discrimination* that has made the area of discrimination more complex.

In the U.S. legal system, the role of the courts is to interpret legislative actions or statutes and decide when and how laws should apply in individual cases. Sexual-harassment lawsuits continue to present the courts with a variety of opportunities to make just such determinations.

WHO IS AN EMPLOYEE FOR PURPOSES OF THE STATUTORY LAW

Title VII requires that a person be considered an employee before the protections it provides are available. Although this may seem to be an easy determination, in fact, in a world of temporary, contract, and part-time workers, it is not always easy to decide whether a person can file a lawsuit against a company when there is an allegation of actionable harassment. In 1997, the EEOC found that the fact that the temporary help industry currently employed more than 2.3 million individuals (a 100 percent increase since 1991) required guidelines be set on the issue. Of course, dealing internally with complaints from all in the workplace that experience harassment is always in the best interests of the business, as will become clear shortly.

To determine that a business is the plaintiff's "employer" for purposes of a Title VII lawsuit, the courts have used a number of tests. The three most often used are: (1) the common-law agency test, (2) the combination common law and economic realities method, and (3) the single employer or true economic realities test.

The common-law method focuses on whether the company "controls the means and manner by which work is accomplished." The combination method looks at right to control along with additional factors relating to the degree of economic dependence of the worker on the company. The third approach uses the test put together by the National Labor Relations Board (NLRB) for determining the "employer" for purposes of union activity and affiliation. The Equal Employment Opportunity Commission (EEOC) has specified that the label used to describe the worker is not determinative. Instead, a number of criteria should be examined to determine if a business is an employer for purposes of Title VII. Although no one criterion is necessary, the more that are met, the more likely it is that the business (either the staffing firm, the business where the employee is placed, or both) will be found to be employers for purposes of the law. For example, the EEOC would find that a person is more likely to be seen as an employee of the business where they are placed when:

- The business has the right to control when, where, and how the worker performs the job
- The work does not require a high level of skill or expertise
- The business provides the tools, materials, and equipment needed to do the job
- The work is a continuing relationship between the worker and the business
- The business has the right to assign additional projects
- The company sets the hours and duration of work
- The worker is paid by the hour, week, or month rather than by a set price per job
- The worker is involved in doing the usual work of the business

These are just a few of the criteria that are listed by the EEOC, but they give an idea of what will be considered when workers are not the traditional employees that have existed in the past. In addition, it must be remembered that the agency that places the employee may also be seen as the employer and that both businesses may be liable in a lawsuit.

DEFINING SEXUAL HARASSMENT

It is not easy to state an exact, understandable, and workable definition of sexual harassment. The EEOC, the federal agency designated by Title VII to interpret the law and handle employment-discrimination complaints, has attempted to define sexual harassment using the following language:

> Unwelcome sexual advances, requests for sexual favors, and other verbal or physical conduct of a sexual nature constitute sexual harassment when (1) submission to such conduct is made either explicitly or implicitly a term or condition of an individual's employment, (2) submission to or rejection of such conduct by an individual is used as the basis for employment decisions affecting such individual, or (3) such conduct has the purpose or effect of unreasonably interfering with an individual's work performance or creating an intimidating, hostile, or offensive working environment.

As was discussed in the introduction, the EEOC definition was issued on the basis of its authority to interpret the parameters of discrimination on the basis of sex under Title VII. The EEOC has realized, however, that even that definition is incomplete. In 1997, it proposed a modification that would make the definition more consistent with the results in recent cases.

In its proposed new guidelines, the EEOC first wanted to make clear that conduct does not necessarily have to interfere with an individual's work performance in order for it to violate Title VII. This would have been accomplished by adding the words "or otherwise adversely affects an individual's employment opportunities" to part three of the above definition. Second, the agency wanted to make clear that it interpreted Title VII to prohibit any gender-based harassment, even though it may not be sexual in nature. Thus, behavior that has no overtly sexual overtones but that "denigrates or shows hostility or aversion toward a person because of their gender" would be illegal. Unfortunately, because of a controversy that erupted about another part of the guidelines that interpreted religious harassment, the agency withdrew the guidelines, intending to reissue them at a later date. Even though the new guidelines were withdrawn, current EEOC practices and court decisions make it clear that the proposed sexual harassment wording merely reflected current interpretations and will continue to be part of the law.

The EEOC definition, though often quoted, is not of great help in understanding exactly what behavior is covered or how a responsible employer should deal with potential problems. Nonetheless, many businesses feel that merely quoting the EEOC definition in a policy is adequate to avoid liability, even though most employees and even managers don't have a clue as to what it means. Unfortunately, understanding is the key to dealing with sexual harassment in the workplace, and this is why it is important to go beyond the EEOC definition and look more closely at the entire issue of sexual harassment.

THE TWO TYPES OF SEXUAL HARASSMENT

There are two types of sexual harassment situations described by the EEOC definition: *quid pro quo* and hostile or discriminatory work environment. In two 1998 cases, *Faragher v. City of Boca Raton* and *Burlington Industries v. Ellerth,*[2] the Supreme Court blurred the difference between these types of harassment, though it is still useful to look at each individually as the behavior and potential liability continue to be different for each.

Quid Pro Quo Harassment

The first sexual harassment cases involved what has been termed a *quid pro quo* situation. *Quid pro quo* is a legal term, most often used in contract cases, that roughly translates to "something for something." In a contract case this means that each party must receive some benefit in order for there to be a binding agreement. Under the EEOC definition, *quid pro quo* cases involve behavior in which "submission to such conduct is made either explicitly or implicitly a term or condition of an individual's employment [or] submission to or

Burlington Industries v. Ellerth
U.S. Supreme Court
1998

Issue: What standard for employer liability should be applied to a case where an employee refuses the unwelcome and threatening sexual advances of a supervisor, yet suffers no adverse, tangible job consequences?

Facts: Kimberly Ellerth was a salesperson in one of Burlington's divisions in Chicago from March 1993 until May 1994. During her employment, she alleged that her supervisor, Ted Slowik, subjected her to constant sexual harassment. Slowik was a vice president in one of Burlington's business units, and although he was not Ellerth's direct supervisor, Ellerth's supervisor reported to him.

Ellerth argued that among the alleged constant remarks and gestures from Slowik, three were particularly egregious. In the summer of 1993, while on a business trip, Slowik invited Ellerth to the hotel lounge. When Ellerth gave no encouragement to remarks he made about her breasts, he told her to "loosen up" and stated, "[y]ou know, Kim, I could make your life very hard or very easy at Burlington." In March 1994, when Ellerth was being considered for a promotion, Slowik expressed reservations during the promotion interview because she was not "loose enough" and reached over and touched her knee. Although she did receive the promotion, Slowik told her that "you're gonna be out there with men who work in factories, and they certainly like women with pretty butts/legs." Lastly, in May 1994 Ellerth called Slowik, asking permission to insert a customer's logo into a fabric sample, he told her "I don't have time for you right now Kim—unless you want to tell me what you're wearing." When she asked again a few days later, he denied her request, but added a comment about the fact that wearing shorter skirts would make her job a lot easier. Ellerth never informed anyone in authority about Slowik's behavior and, after being told by her supervisor that she needed to return telephone calls to customers in a prompt manner, Ellerth quit.

Decision: An employer is subject to vicarious liability for sexual harassment by a supervisor, whether or not tangible job injury results. When there is a tangible job injury that results from a refusal to submit to a supervisor's sexual demands, he or she establishes that the employment decision itself constitutes a change in the terms and conditions of employment and Title VII is violated. In addition, when there is a tangible job injury, there is no defense available to the employer. If a tangible job injury does not occur, it must be shown that the conduct meets the test of being "severe or pervasive." If this is shown, an affirmative defense is available to the employer. The affirmative defense requires the employer to prove that (a) the employer exercised reasonable care to prevent and correct promptly any sexually harassing behavior and (b) the plaintiff employee unreasonably failed to take advantage of any preventive or corrective opportunities provided by the employer or to avoid harm otherwise.

The "bottom line" for the plaintiff: The District Court had granted summary judgment for Burlington Industries, finding that, although a "hostile environment" and *quid pro quo* had been proven by Ellerth, the employer was not liable because she had not complained about Slowik's behavior. The Supreme Court sent the case back to the District Court to re-look at the case and allow further evidence on whether the employer could prove the affirmative defense.

rejection of such conduct by an individual is used as the basis for employment decisions affecting such individual."

Basically, in a *quid pro quo* case the employee is claiming that a supervisor or someone with authority to confer workplace benefits is offering those benefits in exchange for sexual favors or is threatening to take away economic benefits if the employee doesn't accept the "offer." As the law is defined, this places a discriminatory condition on the employee; terms of employment are being changed because of her or his gender. In short, in *quid pro quo* situations, because of their sex, employees are being forced to comply with conditions that other workers do not face.

To be illegal, the "offer" in a *quid pro quo* case must be "unwelcomed" by the employee. This requirement basically means that the employee did not want to be subjected to this "choice." Although this is rarely an issue in *quid pro quo* cases, it does become more relevant in hostile environment situations and will be discussed later in this chapter in that context.

Quid pro quo cases were being filed as early as the 1970s. One of the most influential was *Barnes v. Costle,*[3] a lawsuit that alleged that a supervisor was instrumental in abolishing an employee's position because she spurned his sexual advances. The court found that the employee was presented with an offer—continued employment for sexual favors—and suffered a loss of her job because she did not accept. In *Barnes,* the court agreed with the EEOC's interpretation that this behavior violated Title VII and set down guidelines for deciding such cases. Although most harassment cases are brought by women, when men do claim sexual harassment, it usually involves *quid pro quo* harassment, rather than the "hostile environment" claim discussed shortly.

Since *Barnes,* the courts have been unanimous in allowing these types of lawsuits. Because they involve blatantly illegal behavior, *quid pro quo* cases have proven relatively simple for the courts to decide. The biggest issue becomes a determination of fact, that is, whether this illegal bargain was in fact proposed and, usually, whether it was the basis of the detriment suffered by the plaintiff.

Although most *quid pro quo* cases have involved an employee who suffered a workplace detriment because she or he did not go along with the illegal behavior, an interesting new situation is beginning to appear in court cases. This involves instances where an "offer" is made, yet the subordinate employee did not suffer adverse circumstances. This could be because (1) the plaintiff gave in to the advances, (2) the person with the power advantage was still "negotiating," or (3) the perpetrator did not carry through with the expected response.

In 1998, the U.S. Supreme Court decided a case that sought to clarify the difference between a *quid pro quo* case from one in which hostile environment (discussed in detail later) is alleged. The case, *Burlington Industries v. Ellerth,* involved a situation in which Kimberly Ellerth alleged that she was subjected to "boorish and offensive remarks and gestures" by a mid-level manager, Ted Slowik. These remarks included, according to Ellerth's account, statements such as: "You know Kim, I could make your life very hard or very easy at Burlington" after a comment about her breasts; "Are you wearing shorter skirts now, Kim, because it would make your job a whole heck of a lot easier?"; and an expression of reservation during a promotion interview that she was not "loose enough" for the advancement although she did receive the promotion. Slowik was not Ellerth's immediate supervisor, although Ellerth's supervisor did report to Slowik, who had power to make hiring and promotion decisions, subject to the approval of his supervisor, who signed the paperwork.

After about a year, Ellerth left Burlington Industries without having informed anyone in authority about Slowik's conduct, despite knowing that Burlington had a policy against sexual harassment. She complained to the EEOC and filed a lawsuit alleging sexual harassment in violation of Title VII. A question arose at trial as to whether Ellerth had the elements for a *quid pro quo* case because there were three comments that could be construed as threats to deny her tangible job benefits. However, she had suffered no tangible job detriment. It was unclear, at that time, whether a *quid pro quo* case could be alleged based on the threat itself, or whether the threat needed to be carried out. As you will shortly see, a case involving a *quid pro quo* claim involves a greater chance of liability for an employer, as even a policy that is not used by the plaintiff is no defense.

Eventually, this case was heard by the Supreme Court, which was expected to decide clearly whether in Ellerth's case, an unfulfilled threat of tangible workplace injury allowed a claim of *quid pro quo* sexual harassment situation. The Court noted, however, that the real issue at the heart of the *quid pro quo* question was the level of Burlington's liability.

The Court assumed the premise that a judge or jury could find "in Slowik's remarks numerous threats to retaliate against Ellerth if she denied some sexual liberties" but went on to state that the demarcation between *quid pro quo* and hostile environment cases was "of limited utility."

The Supreme Court went on to explain that a tangible employment action that results from a refusal to submit to a supervisor's sexual demands, by itself, met the requirement of Title VII that a "term or condition of employment" be affected before the employer could be liable. As will be seen later, when there is no such action (i.e., in a hostile environment case), this requirement becomes more of an issue.

Thus, in the Ellerth case, the Supreme Court stated that the allegations constituted a hostile environment case but accepted the district court's findings that the conduct was severe and pervasive and, thus, violated Title VII. The Court did note, however, that Ellerth involved numerous alleged threats and specifically stated that it "expressed no opinion as to whether a single unfulfilled threat is sufficient to constitute discrimination in the terms or conditions of employment."

In conclusion, the Supreme Court stated what is now the rule with regard to any sexual harassment by management, blurring the distinction between *quid pro quo* and hostile environment cases:

> An employer is subject to vicarious liability to a victimized employee for an actionable hostile environment created by a supervisor with immediate (or successively higher) authority over the employee. When no tangible employment action is taken, a defending employer may raise an affirmative defense to liability or damages, subject to proof by a preponderance of the evidence.

This affirmative defense will be discussed further in the next section, but even though the Supreme Court may be seen to have made some change in the law, it has not made any change in the fact that *quid pro quo* harassment remains extremely dangerous and expensive for employers. As before, there will be no defense, even if an excellent anti-harassment policy and procedure is in place and the employee who suffers the tangible employment injury never complained about the behavior. In addition, the parameters of a "tangible job injury" remain unclear. Managerial employees often have great power to affect a number of detrimental workplace decisions on employees who do not allow sexual liberties. These can range from the obvious ones, such as firing and denial of promotion, to the less obvious ones, such as assignment of undesirable workplace space, increased "observation" of daily work, or denial of leave time.

In the case study, it is alleged that Mark Steel received his job as the benefit in a quid pro quo offer. This may involve a situation as discussed in Ellerth. Mark does not appear to have suffered any detriment here, and a quid pro quo claim is not possible unless one has occurred. If the offer was "unwelcomed" by him, however, it is possible that he may be able to bring a hostile environment claim (see below), but the employer would have "the affirmative defense," as will be discussed shortly.

Employer Liability for *Quid Pro Quo* Harassment

As *Ellerth* made clear, an employer is vicariously liable in a case involving harassing behavior and a tangible employment injury. "Vicarious liability" means that the employer is liable for the actions of the employee, despite the fact that it did not condone or in any way participate in the behavior. It is because it has placed the person in a position where this can occur that the courts apply this standard, which has been in place for a very long time and is now part of Title VII law. Sometimes, when an employee injures a person outside of the workplace, this same liability is called *respondeat superior,* or "let the master answer."

In addition, though, when a tangible employment injury is involved in a harassment case, there is no defense. The law calls this situation "strict liability," and it is not applied based on fault or intentional or negligent behavior but because someone has to pay for the damages, and it should be those who hired and retained this person.

It becomes very clear that it is vital that the authority supervisors have over subordinates be carefully considered by business. Employers are finding that it is necessary to put into place a number of important initiatives to protect themselves from the possibility of abuse of managerial power. These include careful procedures for setting and carrying out promotion criteria, establishing zero tolerance for relationships between management and subordinate employees, and removal of managers from an situation where such a relationship exists (the legal difficulties inherent in removing or transferring the subordinate employee will be discussed at length later). In addition, as is currently the case in many workplaces, behavior such as relationships with or dating of subordinates are becoming part of the evaluation of a manager's performance. Such conduct by managers, when they are educated on the problem, displays poor managerial judgment and unsatisfactory management skills and should be dealt with appropriately in the evaluation process.

"HOSTILE" OR WORK ENVIRONMENT HARASSMENT

The Supreme Court, while deciding that Karen Ellerth was not able to make out a *quid pro quo* claim, specifically noted that she had a valid claim for the second type of sexual harassment, one involving conduct that creates what has been termed a "hostile work environment." These cases can involve behavior by a supervisor, coworker, or a third party (such as a customer) if the behavior "has the purpose or effect of unreasonably interfering with an individual's work performance or creating an intimidating, hostile, or offensive working environment." These types of cases are most often involved when the term "sexual harassment" is used now and are the basis of most of the confusion with regard to what is appropriate and legal in workplaces today.

Work environment sexual harassment cases are far more complex than *quid pro quo* lawsuits, causing a variety of problems for courts, government agencies, and employers. Though it is a continually evolving area of the law, there are a variety of elements and criteria that remain constant. What is confusing for businesses is that there is an ever-increasing understanding by judges and juries that a variety of what used to be seen as "natural" and "normal" workplace interaction between the sexes can create an environment that makes it more difficult for one gender to succeed. This is really the essence of whether conduct is "benign" or whether it affects a term or condition of employment, the basis for a violation of Title VII.

Trade journals and business publications often report on new cases that expand what was once thought to be the limits of liability in this area. Every day, courts are being presented with cases involving behavior that some had once viewed as appropriate and assigning liability that may not have been expected. The number of lawsuits that continue to be filed and the size of the companies involved continue to show that, even those with large human resource and legal staffs, firms need to be even more vigilant in following the law's changes, requiring continuing training and awareness, and finding ways to discover and deal with harassment out in the open before it becomes a headline in the national media.

Though the "official term" for this type of case is "hostile or intimidating work environment," this legal term is neither particularly useful nor especially clear. It appears to be describing a workplace where vigilantes are roaming about with guns looking for workers to harass. However, much more subtle behavior, which many might not regard as what is usually viewed as "hostile or intimidating," can also be the basis of a work environment sexual harassment claim. A clearer and more descriptive term is "discriminatory work environment," because the basis of these claims is that some behavior, conduct, work rule, or a combination thereof has created an environment that makes it more difficult for workers of one gender to succeed.

Pivotal "Hostile" Environment Cases

At first, because of the complex psychological issues involved in determining what creates an environment that is less conducive to the success of one gender than the other, courts were reticent to become involved in work environment sexual harassment cases.

Although many lower federal courts had agreed with the EEOC definition and the use of Title VII for such cases in the 1970s and 1980s, it was not until 1986 that the Supreme Court agreed that a sexually discriminatory work environment, in fact, fit within Title VII's prohibition of discrimination on the basis of sex. In the famous case of *Vinson v. Meritor Savings Bank*,[4] the Supreme Court decided that the EEOC was correct in its interpretation that Title VII was intended to cover discriminatory work environment situations. *Vinson* involved outrageous behavior by Sidney Taylor, a bank supervisor, who forced intercourse on the plaintiff, as well as exposing himself to her and other employees. Taylor had not explicitly or implicitly made an offer of workplace benefits, however. The lower court had decided that this conduct still violated Title VII because it created a hostile work environment for women.

The Supreme Court in *Vinson* stated that it agreed that certain conduct, directed toward women, whether or not it is directly linked to the grant or denial of an economic benefit, could constitute a violation of Title VII if the conduct "has the purpose or effect of unreasonably interfering with an individual's work performance or creating an intimidating, hostile, or offensive working environment."

Since the *Vinson* case, courts have grappled with the problem of when workplace behavior crosses over the boundaries of Title VII. Though *Vinson* may have sent shock waves through the business community, it merely signaled the beginning of a complex and continuing determination as to the line between appropriate and hostile or intimidating behavior. In the years since *Vinson*, that line has been continually changing to recognize that what was once "normal workplace" behavior is, in reality, illegal sexual harassment.

In the early cases, it appeared that only overtly abusive behavior would result in a finding that there was a discriminatory or hostile work environment. For example, as the Supreme Court noted in a later decision, the *Vinson* case involved "appalling conduct" and some "especially egregious examples of harassment." Mechelle Vinson was

---

Meritor Savings Bank v. Vinson
U.S. Supreme Court
1986

Issue: Do unwelcome sexual advances that create an offensive or hostile working environment violate Title VII? If so, is an employer absolutely liable for the discriminatory acts of a supervisor toward a subordinate?

Facts: In 1974, Mechelle Vinson brought this case against her supervisor Sidney Taylor and her employer, Meritor Savings Bank, claiming that during her four years at the bank she had been subjected to continuing sexually harassing behavior. She testified that early in her employment, Taylor suggested that they go to a motel to have sexual relations. She refused this request, but out of what she described as fear of losing her job, she eventually agreed. After this, Vinson claimed that Taylor made repeated demands upon her for sexual favors, usually at the bank branch, both during and after business hours. She estimated that over the next several years she had intercourse with him 40 or 50 times. In addition, she testified that Taylor fondled her in front of other employees, followed her into the women's restroom when she went there alone, exposed himself to her, forcibly raped her on several occasions, touched and fondled other women employees.

Decision: A claim of "hostile environment" sex discrimination can be brought under Title VII when behavior is sufficiently severe or pervasive to alter the conditions of employment and create an abusive working environment. When this standard is met, the employer's liability for supervisory acts of discrimination is not absolute but must be decided using traditional principle/agent rules.

Ultimate conclusion for the plaintiff: Because the District Court had found that Michelle Vinson's allegations about the behavior of Taylor, even if true, would not constitute a violation of Title VII, the case was sent back to the District Court to determine whether Mechelle Vinson had indeed been subjected to a "hostile environment" during her employment at the bank.

subjected to intense abuse by her supervisor; it was clear, under any standard, that the environment in which Ms. Vinson worked was "abusive and hostile."

Courts began to find, however, that conduct that was not so overtly abusive could also create a problem environment. In 1991, for example, the Ninth Circuit Court of Appeals found discrimination in a situation that presented what could be viewed as a much less abusive environment. The case, *Ellison v. Brady*,[5] involved a coworker's continuing "romantic" overtures to Kerry Ellison, an employee of the Internal Revenue Service. There were no threats or physical contact between the two workers. The man involved had expressed his interest in a relationship in writing on two or three occasions, and in conversations he "pestered her with unnecessary questions."

Even though the behavior of the coworker in *Ellison* may have seemed to the managers in charge to be merely annoying and not of the type that would cause legal liability, they found that they were wrong. The district court had deemed the behavior "trivial and isolated" and, in essence, had determined that this was part of the "dating ritual," but the appeals court specifically decided, when it viewed the situation from the perspective of women in the society, that a hostile environment had been created for Ms. Ellison. (This "reasonable woman" perspective will be discussed later in this chapter.)

In this case, the employer's negligent handling of the situation, perhaps because it was relying on the fact that previous cases had required a more intense level of harassment for liability, resulted in extensive liability. Ms. Ellison's employer should not have been surprised. What is clear is that any "list" of conduct that could lead to problems is inexhaustive. As the *Ellison* court specifically stated when discussing the type of behavior that creates a discriminatory work environment, "Our examples are illustrative and not exclusive because we realize that sexual harassment is a rapidly expanding area of the law."

In 1991, the U.S. Supreme Court took another look at hostile environment cases and agreed that behavior that was not nearly as abusive as that of the supervisor in *Vinson* could still violate Title VII. In *Harris v. Forklift Systems, Inc.*,[6] the court had to decide "how serious" behavior must be to have the effect of violating Title VII. Some lower courts had been applying a standard that appeared to require that conduct be intense enough to "seriously affect the psychological well-being" of the plaintiff. This amounted, in some cases, to a requirement that the employee have suffered a serious psychological injury.

With *Harris*, the Supreme Court rejected such a requirement and made it clear that there cannot be a "mathematically precise test" for determining how intense harassment had to be for a hostile environment to be created. Because of the wide range of potential behaviors

Harris v. Forklift Systems, Inc.
U.S. Supreme Court
1993

Issue: Whether conduct, to be actionable as "hostile work environment" harassment must seriously affect an employee's psychological well being or lead the plaintiff to suffer injury.

Facts: Teresa Harris worked as a manager at Forklift Systems, Inc., an equipment rental company, from April 1985 until October 1987. Charles Hardy, Forklift's president, often insulted her because of her gender and often made her the target of unwanted sexual innuendoes. These included telling her, in the presence of other employees: "You're a woman, what do you know?" and "We need a man as a rental manager." He also called her a "dumb-ass woman" and suggested that the two of them "go to the Holiday Inn" to negotiate Harris' raise. Hardy occasionally asked Harris and other female employees to get coins from his front pants pocket, threw objects on the ground and asked women to pick them up, and made sexual innuendoes about the women's clothing. In mid-August, Harris complained to Hardy about his conduct and was told by Hardy that he was surprised that she was offended, claimed he was only joking, and apologized. Early in September, the conduct began again and, when Harris was in discussion with a customer, Hardy asked her, in front of other employees, "What did you do, promise the guy . . . some [sex] Saturday night." On October 1, Harris quit.

Decision: As long as the work environment would reasonably be perceived, and is perceived, as hostile or abusive, there is no need for it also to be psychologically injurious. Whether an environment is "hostile" or "abusive" can be determined only by looking at all of the circumstances. These may include the frequency of the discriminatory conduct; its severity; whether it is physically threatening or humiliating, or a mere offensive utterance; and whether it unreasonably interferes with an employee's work performance. Psychological harm, like any other relevant factor, may be taken into account, but is not required.

The "bottom line" for the plaintiff: The District Court had granted summary judgment for Forklift Systems, Inc., in essence, throwing out Harris's case. The Supreme Court sent the case back to the District Court with instructions to apply the proper standard in determining whether Hardy had created a hostile environment for Harris.

and the infinite variations of harassment, it stated that it could not formulate an exact statement as to what conduct does or does not result in illegal sexual harassment. The Court did note, however, that "Title VII comes into play before the harassment leads to a nervous breakdown."

Although it was not especially clear regarding the exact *types* or *amount* of behavior that would create a hostile environment, the Supreme Court did state that certain *effects* might be expected when behavior had "crossed the line."

> "A discriminatorily abusive work environment, even one
> that does not seriously affect employees' psychological well-
> being, can and often will detract from employees' job per-
> formance, discourage employees from remaining on the job,
> or keep them from advancing in their careers."[7]

As is the case with all lists in this area of the law, however, this list of effects is not exhaustive. As the Supreme Court itself knew, it would be foolish to think that these are the only effects that might be expected. Looking at any single "benchmark," such as whether there is a measurable decrease in an employee's job performance, may not be helpful. As Justice Ginsberg noted in her concurrence in *Harris,* a decrease in tangible work productivity is not necessary for the environment to be discriminatory. The best course, as the Supreme Court directed, is to look at the totality of the circumstances with regard to each case.

In 1998, the Supreme Court decided three more cases that examined two issues in the area of work environment harassment cases: the *Ellerth* case previously discussed, *Faragher v. City of Boca Raton,*[8] and *Oncale v. Sundowner Offshore Services.*[9] The cases, though clarifying some previously unclear questions, did not substantially change the parameters of these types of cases.

Faragher, decided in conjunction with *Ellerth,* finally made clear the limits of employer liability when a supervisor was involved in creating a hostile work environment based on gender. As noted in the discussion of *Ellerth,* an employer was found to be vicariously liable for the conduct of a supervisory employee, subject to the opportunity to prove the "affirmative defense." This affirmative defense will be more carefully examined in the employer liability section of the chapter.

Oncale involved a hostile environment case brought by a male who alleged that other males in the workplace had engaged in conduct that was pervasive and severe and altered the "terms and conditions of employment" on the basis of his gender. The issue that the Supreme Court had to decide was whether members of the same gender as the complaining employee could be seen as creating a discriminatory work environment. The Court determined that "same-sex"

IN BRIEF

Joseph Oncale v. Sundowner Offshore Services
U.S. Supreme Court
1998

Issue: Whether workplace harassment can violate Title VII's prohibition against discrimination because of sex when the harasser and the harassed employee are of the same sex.

Facts: Joseph Oncale began working for Sundowner Offshore Services on a Chevron, Inc. oil platform in the Gulf of Mexico. He was employed as a roustabout on an eight-man crew that included co-worker, Brandon Johnson, and supervisors, Danny Pippen, the driller, and John Lyons, the crane operator. On several occasions, the three men, in front of the rest of the crew, forcibly subjected Oncale to sex-related humiliating actions against him. Pippen and Lyons also physically assaulted Oncale in a sexual manner and Lyons threatened him with rape. Oncale complained to supervisory personnel but no action was taken. Valent Hohen, the company's Safety Compliance Clerk, told Oncale that he had also been picked on by the men and called Oncale a name that suggested homosexuality.

Decision: "Same-sex" sex discrimination, including sexual harassment, is actionable under Title VII, as long as it meets the criteria for such cases. Common sense, and an appropriate sensitivity to social context, will enable courts and juries to distinguish between simple teasing or roughhousing among members of the same sex, and conduct which a reasonable person in the plaintiff's position would find severely hostile or abusive.

The "bottom line" for the plaintiff: The District Court had granted summary judgment for Sundowner Offshore Services, in essence, throwing out Oncale's case. The Supreme Court sent the case back to the District Court with instructions to allow the case to go to trial where Oncale would have to prove all of the elements of a "hostile" environment sexual harassment case had been met and the employer was liable under the standards for employer liability.

sexual harassment would be covered by Title VII as long as all the necessary elements had been proven.

Recall the situation with Joseph Dale in the case study at the beginning of this chapter. Other male workers were harassing him. Oncale would allow him to bring a lawsuit for harassment.

The Elements of a "Hostile" Environment Claim

Clearly, there are no easy answers in this area of the law. Even the Supreme Court appears to know more about what effect illegal behavior will have than about the type or severity of behavior needed to create a discriminatory work environment. In the end, a court or jury will have to decide, based on the unique circumstances in each case, whether Title VII has been violated in any particular situation.

There are some guidelines, however, which are helpful in making a determination as to whether there is, legally speaking, a hostile environment in a workplace. These guidelines have been developed through precedents in a variety of cases, as a set of standards has begun to emerge. In general, these require that the harassing behavior or conduct be proven to be gender-based, affect a term or condition of employment, and be "unwelcomed."

Is the Harassing Conduct Based on Gender?

As has been stated, "sexual harassment," in its legal use, means conduct that *discriminates* in some way against a worker on the basis of her or his gender. Because the harassment must be *discriminatory* to violate Title VII or any state law that designates gender as a protected category, the behavior or the environment created by the behavior must have the purpose or effect of making success on the job more difficult for one gender than the other.

The conduct that creates an unequal opportunity for success does not need to be sexual in nature, although often it is of this type. Physical or verbal conduct that is gender-based and that belittles or demeans an employee is sexual harassment, whether or not it has a sexual connotation. As the Supreme Court noted in *Oncale,* "[H]arassing conduct need not be motivated by sexual desire to support an inference of discrimination on the basis of sex. A trier of fact might reasonably find such discrimination, for example, if a female victim is harassed in such sex-specific and derogatory terms by another woman as to make it clear that the harasser is motivated by general hostility to the presence of women in the workplace."

It is perhaps not too difficult to see that overtly belittling behavior or demeaning comments directed at those of one gender, rather than the other, would be viewed as gender-based. The statements are made because of the person's gender. Thus, when someone of one gender is adversely treated or is subject to epithets or comments that are not directed at workers of the other gender, this criterion is satis-fied.

What is more difficult to understand, however, is the situation in which all workers are subjected to the same behavior but the "effect" is different because of a person's gender. Though it could be stated, on one hand, that these sorts of behavior and displays are not discrimina-tory because both men and women must see and hear them, many courts have determined that the effect is quite different for men and women. We will discuss this issue later in this chapter and more fully in the next chapter, as it involves the complex interplay of psychology and socialization. Legally speaking, however, it will suffice to say that this element is also satisfied when the court or jury finds that the envi-ronment, because of differences in male and female perceptions, is "uniquely hostile to one gender," changing the terms or conditions of employment for the employee because of his or her gender. "The crit-ical issue, Title VII's text indicates, is whether members of one sex are exposed to disadvantageous terms or conditions of employment to which members of the other sex are not exposed" (*Oncale*).

The requirement of difference in treatment for one gender is also the basis for the EEOC's refusal to allow a Title VII lawsuit for a type of conduct that one might assume could be the basis of a lawsuit: favoritism. This involves a situation where the employer is sued because a supervisor bestowed favorable treatment on a person with whom she or he had a sexual relationship and a third party claims either that she or he would have received the benefits had it not been for the relationship or that the relationship created a hostile environ-ment.

The EEOC has stated that Title VII does not prohibit preferential treatment based on consensual romantic relationships. Though it may be unfair, the agency claims that it is not illegal because it does not discriminate—both men and women are disadvantaged for reasons other than their gender. This shows that, while often that which is unfair is also illegal, there are times when unfairness can occur with-out any legal remedy available.

Are Conditions of Employment Affected?

To violate Title VII, the harassment must be more than "trivial." It must be severe enough to alter the conditions of employment. In this area the real difference is found between conduct that could be the basis of a lawsuit and that which, if dealt with appropriately by the employer (discussed in later chapters), would not result in legal liabil-ity. Thus, an isolated incident of harassment, though obviously behav-ior that harasses, may not be considered severe enough to form the basis of a lawsuit, unless it is ignored and the conduct continues or increases.

As the Supreme Court noted in *Vinson,* "not all workplace conduct that may be described as 'harassment' affects 'a term, condition, or privilege' of employment within the meaning of Title VII."[10] Thus, to meet the legal standard, the harassment must be seen as "sufficiently severe or pervasive to alter the conditions of the [the victim's] employment and create an abusive working environment." In *Harris,* the Supreme Court discussed this requirement, stating that certain evidence should be examined, even though it made clear that no one individual circumstance was key.

> We can say that whether an environment is "hostile" or "abusive" can be determined only by looking at all the circumstances. These may include the frequency of the discriminatory conduct; its severity; whether it is physically threatening or humiliating, or a mere offensive utterance; and whether it unreasonably interferes with an employee's work performance."[11]

The objective severity of harassment often depends, according to a further clarification by the Supreme Court in *Oncale,* "on a constellation of surrounding circumstances, expectations, and relationships which are not fully captured by a simple recitation of the words used or the physical acts performed."

Behavior or conduct that might, by itself, not be deemed sufficient to meet this legal level of liability, if combined with other conduct or the wrong response by the company can be elevated into a situation where employment terms or conditions are altered. As one court noted:

> [A] holistic perspective is necessary, keeping in mind that each successive episode has its predecessors, that the impact of the separate incidents may accumulate, and that the work environment created thereby may exceed the sum of the individual episodes.[12]

The case study presents an interesting situation with regard to this element of a hostile environment case. Is the one instance of harassing behavior—the picture of Marjorie—severe enough to be said to alter the conditions of employment? Would the company's lack of adequate response and the supervisor's comments raise it to the level of a hostile or discriminatory work environment? It is possible that this might be the case.

The determination of when behavior reaches a level of severity or seriousness as to alter the conditions of employment is often complex and involves many of the same explorations used in deciding whether behavior is gender-based. Because of uniqueness between the sexes, some workplace conduct may not have the same effect on men as it would on women. An understanding of complex psychological issues is often needed to make a correct determination as to whether the "abusiveness" of an environment has reached the level of being called legally discriminatory.

Because human nature and psychology is involved, courts often rely heavily on sociological and psychological testimony about the effects of certain behavior to help them make a decision as to whether the terms or conditions of employment have been affected in a workplace situation. Studies done by psychologists and sociologists and their testimony as expert witnesses have been instrumental in moving courts to recognize that when the effect of behavior is understood, conduct that might appear at first glance to be "trivial" may, in fact, reach the level of creating a discriminatory work environment. This is why what was deemed workplace "fun" in the past may be considered illegal harassment today.

Effect vs. Intent

The EEOC has always interpreted the law to require that the effect and not the intent of harassing behavior be the important consideration in determining whether a term or condition of employment is affected. Lower courts and the Supreme Court agree with this interpretation. A discriminatory environment is created not by what is in the mind of the person who is involved in carrying out the behavior but by what effect it has on the person viewing the behavior.

This effect versus intent focus is difficult for many people in the workplace to understand and accept. Although some workers who harass may be well aware that they are using certain behavior to cause problems or to victimize those with whom they are not comfortable in the workplace, others may actually be acting on subconscious feelings of anxiety or anger. Workers, for example, may display sexual posters for a variety of reasons and will resist any suggestion that they are harassing others, even if their underlying motive is, in fact, to make another feel uncomfortable and out of place. Still others may not believe that certain behavior is a problem because it is how the workplace has always been structured. They may be totally unaware of the effect that their behavior has on others, not understanding differing perspectives.

It is vital that everyone in the workplace be made to recognize that it is not the intent of the behavior that is important nor the fact that some may not view the environment as hostile, abusive, or offensive. What is important is the effect of the conduct on other workers.

To determine whether a term or condition of employment has been affected, the courts will not be concerned with whether anyone had a discriminatory motive. They will be looking to see whether this behavior would have a detrimental effect on a reasonable person *and* whether it had an effect on the plaintiff. These are called the "objective" and "subjective" tests.

The Objective Test

A determination of when an environment reaches the discriminatory level requires that the courts use an objective test with regard to the effect of conduct or behavior. Although some people may find even the most "trivial" behavior offensive, it is clear that the decision as to whether terms or conditions of employment have been changed must be made using an objective perspective: that of an average or reasonable person and not a hypersensitive individual. Would a *reasonable* person be affected? As courts are finding out, this decision is often dependent on whose perspective is used: a reasonable woman or a reasonable man.

Often, a court will find that the first decision it must make in a sexual harassment case is what perspective must be used to determine whether behavior has had the effect of affecting a term or condition of employment. Because psychologists report that men and women experience, view, react to, and deal with behaviors differently, the same conduct, if viewed from the perspective of a reasonable woman may have quite a different effect than if judged from the perspective of a reasonable man. There are a variety of reasons put forward for this differing perspective, many involving differing socialization, some of which will be dealt with more extensively in the chapter on psychology.

A determination as to whether a situation is viewed through the eyes of a man or a woman will make a great deal of difference to the outcome of a case. The next chapter will explain this phenomenon in more psychological terms, which are being heard more and more in court proceedings and which are having a great influence on the shape of the law of sexual harassment. While the Supreme Court has stated that it is important that an objective view of the environment be used to judge whether it is discriminatory, it has not specifically decided this issue but has indicated that it accepts the view that gender is an important consideration in deciding whether "terms or conditions of employment" are affected. In *Oncale*, the Court noted "[w]e have emphasized, moreover, that the objective severity of harassment should be judged from the perspective of a reasonable person in the plaintiff's condition."

Although this issue seems to have been debated a great deal in the past, it is beginning to appear that the Supreme Court's recent rulings are resulting in more courts accepting some form of the "reasonable victim" standard. As we previously discussed, the *Ellison* court specifically stated that it was viewing the conduct directed at Ms. Ellison through the eyes of a reasonable woman and determined that this resulted in a verdict for the plaintiff. It further stated that this was the only correct way to decide these cases and directed the courts in the 9th Circuit to use the "reasonable woman" standard in sexual harassment lawsuits involving a female plaintiff and a claim of "hostile environment." Many other courts have also taken this step, including the courts in *Lipsett v. University of Puerto Rico*,[13] *Andrews v. City of Philadelphia*,[14] and *Burns v. McGregor Elec. Indus., Inc.*[15]

Although the term "reasonable person" may seem gender-neutral, claims have been made that the traditional "reasonable person" is in fact male-oriented. Some, including the number of courts that have adopted the differing perspective standard, claim that any other approach would disregard the law's intent. One judge noted that not viewing the behavior from the perspective of the gender being subjected to the harassment would permit employers to "sustain ingrained notions of reasonable behavior fashioned by the offenders."[16]

Because the trend is definitely toward a gender-specific standard and because the key to a finding of liability in these cases is proof that it creates an environment that disadvantages one gender compared with the other, an employer would be well advised to view reported behavior through the perspective of a reasonable person of the same gender as the employee making the complaint. In addition, the EEOC continues to use the "reasonable victim" standard when it investigates charges of harassment. Thus, for example, a male manager who sees nothing wrong with certain conduct in the workplace should, to protect himself and his employer, look at and deal with the behavior through the perspective of the women in the workplace, if that would result in a different understanding and response.

Is the supervisor in the case study looking at this situation through the eyes of the person who is being made uncomfortable? It is possible that Victoria looks at the displaying of the picture differently than Mark and that it has quite a different effect on her than on him. He should be dealing with this situation from her perspective, in order not to cause more problems for his company.

The Subjective Test

The determination of whether a term or condition of employment is changed is not just an objective one. The Supreme Court in the *Harris* case added a further requirement, noting that plaintiffs must also satisfy a subjective test: whether this particular plaintiff perceived that the conditions were altered. This means that the plaintiff, her- or himself, must have been adversely affected by the behavior.

Though this may seem to add to the plaintiff's burden, in fact, courts have always had to determine that damage has occurred, and, without some subjective perception, it is unlikely that a person could prove damage. Leaving an employer because of a hostile environment is unlikely if an individual does not perceive that environment to be abusive. In addition, pain and suffering damages would be difficult (if not impossible) to prove when there is no perception that this is the type of environment that would cause emotional damages. Thus, although the courts will continue to be required to find a subjective element, it is unlikely that this will have much impact on cases in this area.

In fact, in one case, an appeals court disagreed with the district court's determination that the plaintiff had not perceived her environment to be discriminatory because she did not consult a physician for any psychological problems, quit, avoid the office, or react angrily and was not hindered from performing her assigned tasks. The appeals court noted that the employee had stated that the conduct upset and embarrassed her and made her feel uncomfortable and surmised that a desire to keep her job may have been the reason for the lack of response. The employee had also complained when it was explained to her that she had some recourse and the "absence of a noticeable decline in job productivity should therefore not be unduly emphasized."[17]

The "Terms or Conditions of Employment" Element and Workplace Complaints

It must be noted that judging whether behavior meets the legal level of severity or "alters a term or condition of employment," though important in the courtroom, is not particularly useful in a managerial setting. All behavior that can be seen as harassment on the basis of gender, no matter how "trivial," should be dealt with in an appropriate manner. It is good business practice to take any potentially demeaning or sexual behavior in the workplace seriously and assume that, if not dealt with appropriately, it at least contributes or may contribute to changing the terms or conditions of employment and, thus, later legal liability.

Is the Behavior "Unwelcomed"?

For an employer, a more helpful determination than whether an incident is "serious" enough to alter the condition of employment is finding out whether the behavior (if found to have occurred) was "welcomed" by the employee or employees. This, in fact is the "gravamen" or the crux of a sexual-harassment case, according to the Supreme Court in *Vinson*. Any *unwelcome* behavior is potentially problematic for managers and employers. Thus, the "welcome/unwelcome" element is key in deciding on an appropriate response to the situation.

The Supreme Court in the *Vinson* case stated that conduct could be "unwelcome" even though it may seem to be voluntarily accepted.

An employee may "go along with" the behavior (in fact, Vinson had intercourse with her supervisor 40 or 50 times) without protest, yet, if she felt she had no choice, it could still be unwelcome. This is much like the situation of a rape committed with a threat of violence. Even though the victim does not fight the rape, it cannot be said that she wanted it to occur or that, given a choice, she would have let it happen. In reality, Mechelle Vinson had no meaningful choice.

The burden of determining whether the conduct is unwelcomed is not very cumbersome when the behavior is of the overt belittling or demeaning variety. Most courts recognize that, absent some overwhelming evidence, it is appropriate to presume that a harassed employee did not want to be treated in such a manner. A determination of whether the behavior is "welcome" appears to be more complex in the situation in which the harassment takes the form of more covert behavior, including sexual propositions or other sexual behavior in the workplace. This is where "asking someone for a date" and sexual harassment can be differentiated. If the person "welcomed" the overtures, it is appropriate behavior. If not, then it will cross the line into potentially costly conduct.

Admittedly, it is not inappropriate for employees to be considering a personal relationship with coworkers. When two employees are at about the same level in the organizational hierarchy, a polite and socially acceptable overture for a date or lunch would not be considered legal sexual harassment. Once the invitee has indicated no interest, however, further conduct, having been shown to be "unwelcome," would then become harassment and could create, in itself or in cumulative (depending on the severity, intensity, etc.), a discriminatory work environment.

There are times when an employee is in fact having a consensual relationship with another employee and may welcome sexual behavior from that person. As should be obvious, this does not mean that he or she can be said to welcome sexual behavior from others in the workplace. In addition, there may be times when a consensual relationship is ended by one of two, and further overtures would not be welcome. While employees maintain the right to claim that behavior that was once welcome is no longer so, EEOC policies require in this situation that the employee make clear to the other partner that the relationship has concluded and further exchanges of a personal nature are not wanted.

Manifestations of "unwelcomeness" are not always required, however. This is especially true when a supervisor is involved in behavior with a subordinate. Because of the power differential, an employee is often not required by the courts to express disinterest before claiming that any conduct was not "welcomed" by her or him, when the person involved in the harassment is a superior. The power differential may mean that, even though there may have been the appearance of "voluntary" acceptance of the behavior, it was not "welcome."

Supervisors hold a tacit threat of possible retribution over employees, and even though most people would like to believe that others are interested in us for our personality and good looks, there is no way to know whether it is the "threat" or the natural charisma that is the reason for this situation. Some workers feel trapped into a relationship, even if the company has a mechanism in place for filing sexual harassment complaints. As one court noted, even if a channel exists for reporting such behavior, an employee may feel, in some workplaces, that registering a complaint against a supervisor will result in more trouble than keeping quiet.

As can easily be seen, it is not often easy to determine from circumstantial evidence, such as the worker's immediate response, whether conduct is welcome or unwelcome. Silence, for example, in the face of an incident, like nonreporting, may not be a good indicator of "welcomeness." In fact, lack of response, as one court noted, may, itself, evidence "*un*welcomeness." The coping mechanisms employed by some people include keeping silent and hoping that the behavior will stop. Thus, just because there is no outward sign by an employee that conduct is unwanted or that, given a choice, she or he would want this to occur, one cannot always presume otherwise.

In addition, an employee's response or behavior with regard to sexual conduct in other environments may not be a good indicator of whether conduct is "welcomed." The EEOC has stated that evidence of a party's general character and past behavior toward others has limited if any value in determining whether behavior is "welcomed." One court, in adopting the EEOC's interpretation, rejected an employer's contention that the plaintiff's own past conduct and use of foul language showed that "she was the kind of person who could not be offended by such comments and therefore welcomed them generally." The Court stated that the key was whether the *particular* conduct in question was "welcome" and that "use of foul language or sexual innuendo in a consensual setting does not waive . . . legal protections against unwelcome harassment."[18]

This same case shows the folly of making a presumption about a particular worker, no matter what her or his background. In *Burns v. MacGregor Electric,* the plaintiff had claimed that a discriminatory work environment existed because nude magazine pictures of her had been posted in the workplace. The employer tried to use the fact that she had posed for such pictures as proof that she "welcomed" sexual behavior by her coworkers; at the district court level, the company won on this argument. The appeals court did not agree, however, and reversed the lower court, noting that sexuality in one context was quite different than in another. Thus, someone who wishes to maintain a professional standing in the workplace might act quite differently in that environment than in an outside setting.

In the case study, Marjorie is the one who posed for the picture. Is that relevant to a determination of whether she "welcomed" the conduct? How about the fact that she did not want to complain? Many courts would not allow an employer to presume that the conduct was "welcome," and a separate determination should be made.

An employer should also be careful not to assume that "unlady-like" behavior means that the employee welcomes offensive or sexual conduct. As one court noted, in responding to a claim that the plaintiff's own demeanor precipitated the worker's behavior:

> Even if we ignore the question why "unladylike" behavior should provoke not a vulgar response but a hostile, harassing response, and even if [the employee's] testimony that she talked and acted as she did in an effort to be "one of the boys" is (despite its plausibility) discounted, her words and conduct cannot be compared to those of the men and used to justify their conduct and exonerate their employer. The asymmetry of positions must be considered. She was one woman; they were many men . . . Her use of terms . . . could not be deeply threatening, or her placing a hand on the thigh of one of her macho coworkers intimidating . . . We have trouble *imagining* a situation in which male factory workers sexually harass a lone woman *in self defense* as it were; yet that at root is General Motors' characterization of what happened here. It is incredible on the admitted facts.[19]

When a complaint is filed, an employer may logically presume that the behavior, if substantiated, was "unwelcome," unless there is credible evidence that it was not. What kind of evidence could be deemed useful in overcoming this presumption? This is a very tricky issue. The Supreme Court has stated that evidence of the plaintiff's dress, speech, or participation in the conduct is not irrelevant, but many courts are somewhat reticent to allow its use. For example, should the fact that a woman wears sexy clothes to work mean that she wants to be demeaned? Logically, that may be difficult to substantiate, and such "defenses" appear akin to the now discredited "she was raped because she dressed like she was asking for it" rationale. If sexy dress is occurring in a workplace, it may, in fact, signal that there is some belief on the part of some people that they are judged and evaluated better in that workplace when they dress and act in a sexual manner. Such a situation may raise a danger flag because it could mean that a discriminatory work environment has already been created, and a new program of workforce education may be vitally needed.

Victoria's mode of dressing in the case study appears to signal to Mark that she is "asking for" the behavior that occurs. Though the Supreme Court has stated that it would not be irrelevant in a lawsuit, few courts allow such evidence. Relying on this in any future legal action to defend against a hostile or discriminatory work environment claim would probably be foolish. Mark should focus instead on whether it was, indeed, "welcomed" by Victoria; most of the more relevant evidence would indicate otherwise.

There are other problems with the determination of welcomeness of conduct in the workplace. First, though it may be true that the conduct was "welcomed" by the person to whom the behavior is directed, it may not be legally advisable to allow it to continue. This is because it is now clear that discriminatory work environment lawsuits are possible and will be upheld from persons who are not themselves the focus of harassing behavior or conduct but who are forced to work in a place where this occurs. Thus, courts are saying that those who work in an environment where demeaning, belittling, or sexual behavior is directed at other workers may also work in a hostile or intimidating work environment and are potential plaintiffs. Allowing reports of behavior by anyone who witnesses it makes good sense: managerially and legally. The person making the third-party report may be saying that this type of behavior is "unwelcomed" by her or him, even if the employee on whom the conduct was focused claims otherwise. This should be taken seriously and dealt with appropriately.

In the case study, Marjorie could be seen as the focus of the behavior, but Victoria is obviously bothered by it. Even if Marjorie was determined to "welcome" the display, it may be contributing to a hostile or discriminatory work environment for Victoria.

Another problem for a manager can be determining whether behavior is unwelcome in a situation where a relationship has existed between the parties involved, but a complaint is filed by one of the two alleging conduct in the workplace is "harassment." The EEOC makes it clear that, between coworkers, when a consenting relationship or welcomed conduct has occurred in the past, it is the responsibility of the party who "changes" the rules to make clear to the other person that any further advances or conduct will not be welcomed. Thus, when such a situation exists it should not be viewed as harassment if it is determined that no indication has been given to the employee against whom a complaint has been made that conduct that was once welcomed is no longer appropriate. The complaining employee should make this clear; any further conduct, after that notice, should be dealt with as strictly as the employer would deal with any other act of harassment.

Conduct that Does Not Elicit Complaints—Welcomed?

Workers who are in the minority or who feel lack of organizational power, may find it especially difficult to respond to harassment in a manner that might overtly manifest unwelcomeness. This is especially true with regard to reporting harassing behavior. Many companies make the mistake of claiming that they have no harassment because none has been reported when, in fact, the environment is so bad that harassed employees fear coming forward as much as enduring the problem.

There are many reasons why people hesitate to report incidents of sexual harassment, including their concerns about not being believed and the fear of publicity or being branded a troublemaker or worse. In many workplaces, these fears are well grounded, as the situation does become worse if harassment is reported. These environments are usually ones in which the subject of harassment is not taken seriously, the policies and procedures are not adequate, and, consequently, the potential for legal liability is high. Encouraging reporting is vital, but even if no reports are forthcoming, an employer should not just assume all is well or that the conduct that may be occurring is welcomed.

Examples of Harassing Behavior

A closer look at exactly what types of behavior may have the effect of creating a hostile or discriminatory work environment will help in more completely understanding this somewhat complex area. The problem with any such exploration, however, is that these types of cases are all different and very fact-specific, so any discussion of behavior that does create a discriminatory environment must begin from the presumption that just because a behavior does not fit in with previous lists does not mean that it is appropriate or legally defensible.

The EEOC definition of sexual harassment is intentionally vague, and the commission has made it clear that its determination of whether certain conduct creates a discriminatory environment will only be made by looking at the totality of the circumstances. Such factors as the nature of the behavior and its context can often be critical.

The EEOC specifically lists "sexual advances, requests for sexual favors, and other verbal or physical conduct of a sexual nature" as possibly harassing behavior in the workplace, if they are "unwelcomed" by the person to whom this behavior is directed. The EEOC also views any gender-based verbal or physical conduct, even if not sexual in nature, as problematic. Inflammatory and patently offensive epithets and slurs or comments demeaning another because of his or her gender and any physical touching of intimate areas of the body can be the basis of a legal claim. In fact, the EEOC has stated that it will "presume that the unwelcome, intentional touching of a charging party's (the person making the claim of discrimination) intimate body areas is sufficiently offensive to alter the conditions of her working environment and constitute a violation of Title VII." The EEOC has also specifically noted that sexual slurs and displays of "girlie" pictures will be viewed as offensive.

Thus, the picture in the workplace in the case study has specifically been listed by the EEOC as behavior that could create a hostile environment. The company should react quickly to remove it.

As will be discussed further in the next chapter, harassing behavior has been said to run on a continuum from staring at or commenting on a woman's body all the way to conduct that can best be described as rape. This continuum can encompass a variety of conduct that may not appear to be problematic at first glance. In one case, for example, a female manager claimed that her employer had contributed to the discriminatory or hostile work environment by requiring her to sit with the other women during a meeting, even though the other women all held subordinate positions in the company, and the male managers were placed together behind the females.

In this rapidly expanding area, there appear to be some trends with regard to new problem areas for employers. For example, plaintiffs are alleging that a variety of work rules, especially those involving certain dress codes, are creating discriminatory environments. In one such case, an employer ordered its female lobby attendants to wear suggestive uniforms. This resulted in whistling and rude comments by customers that, the court found, demeaned the women and their roles as professional workers. The court found that the dress code created a hostile work environment and awarded damages for the plaintiffs. This trend appears to be expanding, as even restaurants that have traditionally used sexual attraction in their marketing strategies are now finding themselves facing lawsuits.

With the expansion of what behavior could be seen as contributing to a discriminatory work environment, employers should be concerned when imposing requirements of dress on workers. Any work rules that require women to dress or act in a way that makes them sexually attractive to customers or other workers may not be advisable from a legal perspective and should be carefully examined. Of course, cleanliness and grooming standards are appropriate, but managers imposing or enforcing such standards should analyze whether they are indeed "benign" standards or merely ones that reinforce a view that women should dress in a sexy, attractive, or "attracting" manner.

Technology is also contributing to the ways in which sexual harassment may occur. Cases are beginning to include claims that a discriminatory environment is being created by such behavior as sexually suggestive or demeaning electronic mail messages or pornographic images on company computers. This can be especially problematic because of the possibility for anonymity in such situations, and companies may need to explore ways to pinpoint the source and handle such offensive behavior.

In addition, any work "norms" that may be viewed as demeaning should also be analyzed. Recently, courts have taken a new look at the "women are expected to fetch the coffee" situations and references to workers as "my girl," finding them to potentially contribute to the creation of an environment that violates equal opportunity dictates. When examining such practices, businesspeople are being advised not to look at them from the perspective of "this is the way we have always done things." They should ask about the purpose of the rule or norm. Does it demean or lower the regard for one gender? Is it intended to increase business by using sexuality? The courts have not been kind to such rationales for discriminatory behavior and are requiring that businesses start to examine whether the old ways are not illegal ways.

Another example of situations that may result in legal liability is that which occurred in an early sexual harassment case. In *Broderick v. Ruder,*[20] the court noted that conduct, which included romantic involvements between male supervisors and female subordinates, frequent parties, and afternoon-long lunch "hours," was harassment of the other women in the workplace who did not participate in the behavior and thus did not receive the preferential treatment.

Employers should be more concerned with whether behavior is a problem for an employee than with whether it reaches the level of legal liability. An appropriate response to any complaint makes good business sense.

The need to respond adequately is important for a variety of reasons. What is very clear is that a business's inadequate response to behavior—whether or not the behavior itself was adequate to meet the legal severity standard—could be used as further evidence of a hostile environment. Thus, although a crude joke told by coworkers might not reach the level of Title VII liability, a response to a complaint about such behavior that demeans, intimidates, or ridicules the person making the complaint may, when added to the joke, contribute to the behavior, reaching a level that the law would recognize as altering the conditions of employment. The necessity for appropriate responses by managers to each and every unwelcome harassing behavior becomes very clear. What is said and done during the course of an investigation may make the difference between a resolved problem and a time- and resource-consuming legal battle. Clearly, it is vital that managers deal with problems appropriately; correct handling of complaints will be dealt with more specifically in chapter 4. This is not only because of its potential for escalating the previous behavior to a level of legal harassment but also because some responses may be illegal in themselves. When potential sexual harassment is reported, managers should be very careful not to do anything that could be viewed as retaliation against an employee for making a complaint about sexual harassment. Retaliation is specifically listed as conduct that violates Title VII in the law itself; thus, an unthinking response on the part of a manager, such as moving a complaining employee, can become extraordinarily burdensome for both the manager and the business. In addition, the law states that anyone exercising rights under Title VII is protected from retaliation, and this means that others, such as those who are witnesses or who speak up for other employees, have legal rights. Employers must be careful when making an adverse employment decision with regard to anyone involved in a sexual harassment complaint if there is any chance that the decision may be viewed as retaliation for complaining, aiding a complainant, or being involved in another way. Further information about lawsuits involving complaints of retaliation will be discussed at the end of this chapter.

Employer "Excuses"

Employers in a variety of cases have tried to use affirmative defenses when they find that they have maintained a "hostile" or discriminatory work environment. The defenses fall into three basic categories, none of which has worked to any great degree in the courts. A business that attempts to use them should be aware of the problems.

"Equal Opportunity Harassers"

There are circumstances when an employer may believe it can claim that there is no violation of Title VII, even though the workplace is not conducive to success. This would be a situation, for example, where a supervisor is abrasive, annoying, and downright difficult to work with, no matter what the employee's gender. Although "equal opportunity harassers" do exist, a company that wishes to use this as a defense obviously does not comprehend fundamental and rudimentary human relations concepts, an obvious problem of its own. In addition, it must always be remembered that just the fact that behavior is "universal" may not be a defense if the "effect" is seen as different on one gender than on the other. This was the result in a 1994 case involving harassment by a person the employer claimed "consistently abused men and women alike." In *Steiner v. Showboat Operating Co.,*[21] the Ninth Circuit Court of Appeals did not agree that this meant there was no discrimination for two reasons:

> The numerous depositions of Showboat employees reveal that Trenkle was indeed abusive to men, but that his abuse of women was different. It relied on sexual epithets, offensive, explicit references to women's bodies and sexual conduct. . . .

[W]hile his abuse of men in no way related to their gender, his abuse of female employees, especially Steiner, centered on the fact that they were females. It is one thing to call a woman "worthless" and another to call her a "worthless broad."

Furthermore, even if Trenkle used sexual epithets equal in intensity and in an equally degrading manner against male employees, he cannot thereby "cure" his conduct toward women.[22]

Thus, it may well be that the "equal opportunity harasser" defense may not be adequate to remove liability.

"Social Context"

Claims have been made by some employers that workers could not claim to feel threatened or demeaned by pornographic material or belittling sexual behavior because it is so prevalent in the society and because many women view pornography themselves. As previously noted in the context of a plaintiff's social and work demeanor, the courts differentiate between what occurs in the workplace and in the outside world. When the effect of pornography on a work environment is understood, the context is important. Most courts reject this defense and note that Title VII is designed to change the workplace, not the whole society. This distinction is clearly explained by the following passage from a law review article often quoted by judges:

[W]hile publicly disseminated pornography may influence all viewers, it remains the expression of the editors of *Penthouse* or *Hustler* or the directors of *Deep Throat*. On the wall of an office, it becomes the expression of a coworker or supervisor as well.

In this context the effect of pornography on workplace equality is obvious. Pornography on an employer's wall or desk communicates a message about the way he views women, a view strikingly at odds with the way women wish to be viewed in the workplace. Depending upon the material in question it may communicate that women should be the objects of sexual aggression, that they are submissive slaves to male desires, or that their most salient and desirable attributes are sexual. Any of these images may communicate to male coworkers that it is acceptable to view women in a predominately sexual way. All of the views to some extent detract from the image most women in the workplace would like to project: that of professional, credible coworker.[23]

Title VII guarantees equal opportunity in employment, not on the street corners, and the attempted use of such a "defense" is not sound.

Workers need to understand that behavior that is acceptable in their own social setting or circles may not be acceptable or allowed in the workplace.

"Status Quo"

Some employers have tried to show that, because plaintiffs knew the environment was discriminatory when they applied for positions, they should be required to accept situations into which they voluntarily thrust themselves. This is an "assumption of the risk" defense that makes the incorrect assumption that equal employment opportunity merely means equal access to employment. Title VII, as courts have concluded, requires true equal opportunity. Sometimes, this requires that the old way of doing things, which is detrimental to others' best efforts, must be changed so that both genders have an even chance for success. Courts have little use for this type of claim because Title VII was designed to change discriminatory behavior and most believe that it is the employer's duty to make sure that this happens:

> No reasonable person could imagine that General Motors was genuinely helpless, that it did all it reasonably could have done. The evidence is plain that it (or at least its gas turbine division) was unprepared to deal with problems of sexual harassment even when those problems were rubbed in its face, and also incapable of improvising a solution. Its efforts at investigation were lackluster, its disciplinary efforts nonexistent, its remedial efforts perfunctory. The U.S. Navy has been able to integrate women into the crews of warships; General Motors should have been able to integrate one woman into a tinsmith shop.[24]

The Limits of Liability for "Hostile" Environments

Businesses' liability for sexual harassment is very far-reaching in every jurisdiction. As employers, companies are liable under Title VII and most state laws for the actions of supervisors and coemployees and could face both statutory and common-law claims. With regard to *quid pro quo* harassment, as discussed earlier, the standard is strict liability. If it happens, the employer is liable. Hostile environment liability is somewhat different. There are two different standards, depending on whether the discriminatory acts were perpetrated by a coworker or an "agent" or supervisor.

According to most courts, when only coworkers, clients, or customers are involved in perpetrating the conduct, liability attaches when the employer knew or should have known and did not adequately remedy the situation. An employer is deemed to "know" when any of its agents, usually a manager, knows about the behavior, either because of a complaint or because he or she witnessed or was told of the incident. An employer "should have known," legally speaking, when it is so pervasive that a reasonable employer, through its agents, should not have been able to ignore its existence. A good manager will make it his or her job to find out what is going on in the workplace and how subordinate managers are conducting themselves. If there is no earlier "notice," the employer certainly is deemed to have "notice" when it is notified that a complaint has been filed by a government agency.

What is obvious about the direction of the courts is that anyone may potentially be seen as contributing to or creating a discriminatory work environment for employees and, thus, businesspeople need to deal with behavior no matter who is involved. It is not just the conduct of coworkers or supervisors with which the law requires businesses to deal. In addition, customers or clients who are harassing the employees of a company with whom they do business can also create legal liability for the employer of the person being harassed. The usual cases that deal with this type of harassment involve customers harassing waitresses, but recent cases seem to be moving toward other customer or client situations. Sales staff increasingly are reporting harassing behavior by employees at client companies. Although these cases present challenges with regard to the appropriate manner for handling the problem, it is clear that the fact that a company needs the goodwill of the client will not act as a defense to a sexual harassment claim. An appropriate response in such situations might involve talking to a high-level person at the client company in a spirit of cooperative effort to solve the problem. It would not hurt to remind clients that an adequate solution would also help reduce their potential for liability. As we will discuss later, harassers rarely target only one person and may be causing legal problems within their own company.

Liability of an employer for a supervisor's sexual harassment is even more extensive than for coworkers'. There is no "notice" requirement, and in *Vinson* the Supreme Court told the courts to "look to agency principles" to determine the extent of liability. Although agency principles can be rather confusing and complex, it is reasonably clear that an employer is liable for the conduct when the supervisor is acting as its agent or in an agency capacity. A short discussion of the law of agency is helpful.

A principal, defined by *Black's Law Dictionary* as "one who has permitted or directed another to act for his benefit and subject to his direction and control," is liable for the acts of her or his agents in various circumstances. The *Restatement of Agency,* a series of volumes that discuss common-law rules, is usually relied on by courts to help in determining the parameters of a principal's liability for an agent's behavior.

The *Restatement* states, first, that any wrongdoing of the agent while the agent is operating under the actual authority of the principal is imputed back to the principal. An agent is operating under actual authority either when he or she is carrying out the express authority given to him or her by the principal or is acting under the implied authority, actions which are necessary in order to carry out the express authority. When a supervisor is involved in sexual harassment, it can easily be found that this wrongdoing, which is like a common-law tort or civil wrong, is occurring while the supervisor is involved in the actual authority granted to him or her by the employer; that is, managing and controlling the workplace and the work environment.

There are courts, however, that will not impute liability if the agent is involved in intentional wrongful acts while carrying out the principal's actual authority. In that situation, there are alternate bases provided in the *Restatement* for imputing liability to the principal. These include situations in which it is decided that the agent is acting under the apparent authority of the principal when the wrongdoing occurs or when the agent is aided in carrying out the wrongful act by the authority granted to him or her. Thus, a finding that the employer misled the employees into believing that the supervisor had the authority to manage the workplace in any manner and by his or her own standards would create apparent authority to harass. An employer can create this impression when there is no adequate policy and procedure in effect that allows alternate reporting outside of the chain of command. Second, if the court finds that the authority granted by the employer to control and manage the workplace has aided the supervisor in harassing the employee(s), this also would result in imputed liability.

With these many alternate bases for liability, most courts have been very consistent in making the employer liable when the supervisor is involved in the harassment. What this means, then, is that it is most likely that whenever and wherever the supervisor is involved with subordinate employees, any discriminatory behavior that is perpetrated by the supervisor is the legal responsibility of the employer. This responsibility for the acts of someone in a supervisory capacity is imposed because the supervisor is in a position of disparate power over the employees, and the employer is required by law to be very careful with regard to choosing those in whom it will vest such authority.

An important qualifier of this authority occurs, however, when the employer makes very clear to the employees that sexual harassment is not condoned, approved, or authorized in that workplace. A serious pronouncement and responsive action by the employer can be said to remove the apparent authority to control the work environment in a negative manner and would take away the "aid" to the harassment, which might be afforded by unlimited power and authority. The employees must know that no one at any level has the right or author-ity to harass or create a discriminatory environment and that actions will be immediately taken upon any violation of this rule. This is done with a policy and procedure that meets the standards set out by the courts and the EEOC. Once this is in place, employer liability is greatly reduced and most situations should be quickly resolved by the internal procedures put in place.

An important point to note in the area of legal liability for sex-ual harassment is that there may be many possible defendants in a Title VII lawsuit. Although the Act specifies that an employer, a labor organization, or an employment agency is liable, the definition given includes any agent of those listed. The courts are divided on the indi-vidual liability of the agents, that is, supervisors and managers who either perpetrated, condoned, or did not handle correctly discrimina-tory behavior.

The liability of the agents themselves is a new and developing area of the law. Some courts adhere to the rule that only the employer can be liable for creating a hostile environment. This means that even if a supervisor helped create the hostile environment, he or she could not be sued individually under Title VII. There does appear to be some liability, however, for highly placed corporate managers. In the *Robinson* case, for example, the court declared that the principles of employer liability could be broadened to include certain individual corporate officers. Noting that it is inconceivable that Congress intended to exclude from liability the very persons who have engaged in the employment practices that are the subject of the lawsuits, the court went on to declare that Title VII "works to hold responsible those who control the aspects of employment accorded protection by that law."[25]

Who are these people who could be said to exercise effective con-trol in the workplace and make or contribute meaningfully to employ-ment decisions? While this trend toward more extensive liability is new and developing, a look at the two individuals found liable along with the employer in the *Robinson v. Jacksonville Shipyards* case is helpful in determining who may be personally liable under Title VII. The vice president for operations at Jacksonville Shipyards, Inc. (JSI), was found liable for the hostile work environment because "his responsibility extended to the creation and implementation of JSI's sexual harassment policies. Their failure is his failure. Additionally, he personally intervened in Robinson's complaint and directed that no remedial action be taken." The industrial relations manager of JSI was liable because "he held responsibility for the day-to-day administra-tion of the sexual harassment complaint machinery. Its failure is his failure." Additionally, he had also personally intervened and directed that no remedial action be taken.

IN BRIEF

Ford: The High Cost of Harassment
Business Week
November 15, 1999

In early September, Ford Motor Co. reached a $17.5 million deal with the feds to settle ugly sexual harassment allegations at two Chicago-area factories. Civil rights leaders hailed the accord as a model for Corporate America. The car maker agreed to set aside $7.5 million to compensate victims of harassment and $10 million more to train managers and male workers to stop what women alleged to be a years-long pattern of groping, name-calling, and parties with strippers and prostitutes.

Ford also agreed to triple the number of female supervisors in the plants, where women comprise just 14% of the workforce. And Ford will withhold raises and promotions from managers at any Ford plant who fail to stop harassment from occurring. Such terms are unprecedented, say officials at the U.S. Equal Employment Opportunity Commission, the nation's top civil rights agency. Better yet, says EEOC chief Ida L. Castro, Ford agreed to resolve the case without engaging the agency in a costly legal battle.

But Ford's eagerness to quietly settle the charges has blown up in its face. On Oct. 15, U.S. District Judge Elaine E. Bucklo cleared the way for a class action against the auto maker, which could leave the company open to millions more in damages. Her decision is a major setback for Ford, which had hoped the EEOC-brokered deal would persuade Bucklo to deny an attempt by 14 women to convert their federal lawsuits into a single class action.

Instead, Bucklo sharply criticized the settlement, saying it let Ford off the hook without admitting liability and lacked the teeth to ensure its compliance. Ford will still carry out the deal, which allows the 850 female employees at the two plants to make monetary claims. Or they can seek damages by joining the class action Bucklo okayed. The suit also asks for a permanent injunction to force Ford to clean up its act.

Bad Publicity
The case could deal a sharp blow to the public image of a company that has long cultivated friendly relations with employees and unions. By negotiating a voluntary settlement, Ford hoped to avoid the kind of negative publicity that engulfed Mitsubishi Motor Manufacturing of America Inc. in 1996, after the EEOC sued the Japanese automaker

maker on behalf of 300 women after some complained of similar behavior. Mitsubishi vigorously fought the allegations at first but eventually agreed to a $34 million settlement in 1998.

Ford now may suffer a similar black eye. The women's lawyers include a firm that extracted a record $176 million payout from Texaco Inc. in 1996 to settle racial discrimination charges. Ford has appealed Bucklo's ruling and insists the deal was the most expedient way to handle the women's grievances and resolve any outstanding behavioral issues in the plants. "We want to make it very clear to everybody that what was formerly passable with a wink is now intolerable," says Jim Padilla, Ford's top manufacturing executive. The EEOC also defends the deal, which it says would provide more immediate relief to female factory workers than a drawn-out class action. Says John P. Rowe, director of the EEOC's Chicago office: "We believe those women will all have an infinitely better working environment because we acted now."

But the plaintiffs aren't convinced. "They're cockier than ever," says 31-year-old Victoria Williams, who returned to her assembly job on Sept. 5 after a two-month medical leave to deal with the stress she says was caused by sexual harassment at work. She returned two days before the conciliation agreement and says, if anything, the environment is worse. "The way they prance around, and the looks they give you, it's as if they're saying, 'We can do what we want,'" she says. Some women who brought charges of harassment say they have been disciplined for speaking out, says Williams. And while the pornography that had been prevalent in the plant is now out of sight, Williams says, inappropriate sexual behavior continues. Padilla says Ford has received no complaints of retaliation since the EEOC deal was announced, and if there are any, "we will terminate" the managers responsible.

Allegations of tawdry behavior at the two Chicago-area factories have generated at least 30 formal complaints to the EEOC since 1994. The first wave started that year, when some female workers at Ford's parts-stamping plant in Chicago Heights came forward with tales of crude language and sexually explicit name-calling, plus unwanted groping, grabbing, and massaging by male co-workers and supervisors. An EEOC investigation concluded in early 1996 that women at the plant, as a class, were indeed subjected to a sexually hostile work environment. Ford reached a private settlement with the 11 women in February, 1998, for nearly $2 million, says the EEOC's Rowe.

The following month, another group of women, this time from a Chicago plant that builds Taurus and Sable sedans, made similar allegations. Ford responded by dispatching Padilla's predecessor to Chicago to lecture workers on appropriate behavior and to announce new steps to enforce its "zero tolerance" harassment policy. Since January, 1998, Ford has fired 10 male employees and disciplined 29 others.

But the crackdown changed little, plaintiffs claim. In August, 1998, a second group of women at the stamping plant filed a lawsuit. Again, the EEOC investigated and concluded, in September, 1998, that female employees at both plants had been subjected to sexual harassment. Among the EEOC's findings: that women had been called "bitches, whores, and offensive references to female genitalia" and that women had been "grabbed, groped, and . . . massaged without their consent." The agency also found that sexually explicit graffiti and pornographic materials inside the plant had contributed to a sexually offensive environment.

Meanwhile, in August, 1998, Chicago police broke up a late-night party in the assembly plant parking lot that allegedly featured strippers and prostitutes. Female workers say male co-workers routinely pass around photos of lewd behavior at employee parties on and off Ford premises. A spokesperson says such displays are "unacceptable."

Mockery

Ford managers and union officials have done little to stop the harassment, the women charge. "The men made a mockery of" prevention efforts, says Williams. The problem won't go away, she says, until Ford faces more than "a slap on the wrist" and insists on a commitment all the way down to the lowest levels of management. Ford insists that it is taking the problem seriously. It has a 1-800-number hotline for reporting harassment, and the $10 million for training will reach every employee at the two plants. After the EEOC deal, Padilla addressed all employees at the plants and mailed letters to their homes.

Nevertheless, Judge Bucklo said at an Oct. 8 hearing that she was "disappointed in the way this has worked out." The EEOC deal calls for three independent monitors to oversee implementation and distribute damages to women. The judge agreed with the plaintiffs that the three-year deal falls short because it doesn't include a permanent injunction, backed by the threat of contempt of court, to prevent future harassment. It also lets Ford off without admitting liability. "In short," Bucklo later wrote, "the agreement lacks bite."

The EEOC's Rowe insists that his agency has the weapons to ensure Ford's compliance. "The agency doesn't go away after monetary relief has been paid out," he says. Still, the women who say they have been harassed are looking for a bigger bite out of Ford.

Interestingly, Title VII does not provide for personally suing a coworker for a violation of the Act. The various common-law suits mentioned earlier are available for personally holding coworkers liable, however, and are often joined with a Title VII case. The same situation exists with regard to supervisors or managers who in some way contributed to the plaintiff's damages, even if the court does not allow a direct Title VII case against them. Thus, for example, a manager or coworker may be sued for intentional infliction of emotional distress at the same time that the employer is sued for a violation of the federal law. Interestingly, the damages assessed with regard to these claims may even be higher because state common-law lawsuits, even in states with damage "caps," usually allow for larger sums than does the federal statute.

Anyone in the workplace could potentially find her- or himself facing some form of sexual harassment. Women and men are both protected by Title VII. If a man is subjected to sexual harassment, he has a claim, just as does a woman.

Mark Steel in the case study may file a claim under Title VII if he believes that his supervisor has subjected him to sexual harassment. Men and women have the right to equal employment opportunity.

An employee may file a harassment claim when she or he has been harassed by someone in authority or by those who are equal in organizational power. Interestingly, there are also some new lawsuits in the area of sexual harassment that involve lawsuits by supervisors who have been harassed by subordinates. Though it is hard to imagine that this is possible, with the power that supervisors hold over subordinates, psychologists have identified the fact that there are many sources of power in the workplace. One of these is gender power, which may allow some workers to feel more comfortable and safe being involved in behavior or conduct that demeans a woman who is higher in the organizational chain of command. If this is coupled with a lack of support in the company for tough disciplinary measures by the female supervisor, a hostile environment might be legally sustainable. Although it is not clear what the limits of this would be, it is advisable for companies to make it clear, by word and action, that they stand strongly behind their female managers in trying to control these types of problems. This requires helping enforce training and disciplinary decisions at all levels of the organization and making sure that others in the managerial ranks are not doing or saying anything that might undermine the authority of the supervisor involved in the problematic situation. Any behavior or conduct directed at a supervisor that would fit under the usual "hostile environment" parameters should be viewed as seriously as the company views other insubordination.

Who Is an Employee for Purposes of Title VII?

Although it is sometimes easy to determine who are the employees for whom the employer is responsible under Title VII, today's workplace, with temporary workers, contract workers, and independent contractors, sometimes makes it a more difficult determination than in the past. What is clear is that an employer cannot escape Title VII liability just because the employees technically work for another company but are leased, assigned, or otherwise placed in the employer's workplace. The EEOC has discussed this situation quite extensively in an Enforcement Guidance, which is easy to find on the Internet.[26] Basically, however, most courts look to see who really is in control of the day-to-day work done by the employee. Some courts call this the "right of control" test. In making a determination as to who has Title VII responsibilities for a worker, the courts often look at such factors as who has control over the worker's hours of work; who has the right to hire and fire the worker from a position; who supervises the worker; what the worker's opportunities are for earnings or profits; and what rights the worker has to work for others. In addition, a person filing a complaint under Title VII need not only name one party as the employer, so all parties deemed to be an employer of the workers may find themselves as defendants in the lawsuit.

DAMAGES AVAILABLE IN SEXUAL HARASSMENT LAWSUITS

When employees are able to prove that sexual harassment has occurred, there are a variety of damages that they can receive. Some of these can add up to hundreds of thousands and even millions of dollars.

Equitable Damages

Title VII allows a judge or jury to award what are termed "equitable" damages. These include back pay for a period not to exceed 2 years; attorney's fees; reinstatement to the position that the employee would have been in and seniority to which the employee would have been entitled had the discrimination not occurred; orders to "cease and desist" the harassing conduct; injunctions against further harassment or that require the employer to create a comprehensive sexual harassment policy and procedures; and occasionally "front pay," which is granted for a period of time to allow the employee to recover from the emotional effects of harassment and begin new employment.

Back pay is usually available to an employee who is discharged from a company for a discriminatory reason. When an employee quits the company of his or her own volition and files a lawsuit, employers have challenged an award of back pay on the basis that this remedy is not available to those who leave employment voluntarily. Though this has traditionally been true, the courts have usually tempered this by applying the doctrine of "constructive discharge." In most jurisdictions, an employee can be found to have been constructively discharged if the court or jury determines (1) that the environment was so abusive that a reasonable employee would have felt compelled to resign and (2) that the resignation was actually caused by the harassment. In a few circuits, there is also a requirement that the employer "intended" to cause the resignation of the harassed employee. While this could be a difficult thing for plaintiffs to prove, some courts that require this element have modified it somewhat, often allowing a conclusion of "intent" based on the fact that a person is held to intend the foreseeable consequences of his or her conduct. Thus, if the conduct is unreasonably abusive, the resignation of the victim could be a foreseeable consequence.

As stated previously, back pay is awarded where an employee has been removed from the job for a discriminatory reason. Sometimes, however, even though a nondiscriminatory reason is the basis of the discharge, back pay may also be available if that reason can be tied to the harassment.

Employers often contend, for example, that they discharged a worker for excessive absences, and thus, back pay should not be available. In some cases, however, courts have found that the abusive environment caused the absences themselves and still will award back pay. This has also been found to be the situation in cases where the employee was discharged for poor work attitude or deteriorating job performance, when it was decided that these rationales were merely the effect of a discriminatory work environment. As one court noted:

> [A]n expert of sexual harassment on the job . . . testified that
> women subject to sexual harassment will have increases in
> work performance problems, including increases in on the
> job errors, as a direct result of harassment on the job.[27]

This correlation between deteriorated job performance and other work quality problems and harassment is an important one for businesses to keep in mind. Although it may seem that there is a perfectly acceptable reason to fire an employee who is not doing an adequate job, it is often necessary to do a more complete investigation of the situation. This may mean discussing the situation in a nonthreatening environment with the employee to make sure that there is no discriminatory situation looming in the background. If so, taking care of the problem with regard to the environment should also take care of the problem of the inadequate performance without the potential future liability.

Other Damages

Though it originally only allowed equitable damages, Title VII was amended in 1991 to allow pain and suffering damages and, in the case of intentional discrimination, punitive damages. The pain and suffering damages are "capped," however on a sliding scale, depending on the size of the company. This sliding scale allows up to: $50,000 for businesses with 15–100 employees; up to $100,000 for 101–200 employees; up to $200,000 for 201–500 employees; and up to $300,000 for more than 500 employees. Under common law and many state civil rights acts, these damages are also available, but there is often no cap on the pain and suffering damages. This can result in the very high jury awards that are now beginning to be seen.

Retaliation

Recently, employers have been realizing that there is an ancillary matter that is extremely important when a sexual harassment (or any antidiscrimination) complaint is made. This is because there is a provision for a second claim when the employer takes actions that appear to be "punishment" for the employee's original complaint of a violation of any law protecting them against discrimination.[28] For example, when an employee complains about harassing conduct and shortly thereafter is denied a promotion, it is possible that a retaliation complaint may be filed with the EEOC.

According to the EEOC's *Compliance Manual,* there are three essential elements in order for a retaliation claim to be upheld: (1) there was some sort of activity by the employee that is protected by Title VII; (2) there was an adverse action taken by the employer; and (3) there is a causal connection between the protected activity and the adverse action. What is vital to understand is that, if these are proven, the employer will be liable for a retaliation violation, even if the original complaint by the employee was found to be without merit!

Was There Protected Activity?

To prove that retaliation has occurred, the employee must first prove that he or she was involved in activity that is protected by Title VII. In a sexual harassment situation, this may mean that the employee either made a complaint to the employer or filed a complaint with the EEOC. In addition, protected activity includes testifying, assisting, or participating in any manner in an investigation, proceeding, hearing, or lawsuit under Title VII or being "closely associated" with someone who has done so.

A formal complaint is not required, however. The EEOC states that the communication could be explicit or implicit. If the complaint is made to anyone, including coworkers, union officials, an attorney, newspaper reporter, Congressperson, or anyone else, it will constitute opposition. Picketing or involvement in a work slow-down may also be viewed as opposition, as would a complaint on behalf of another. As long as the communication of the employee's opposition to a situation or conduct could reasonably be viewed as a complaint about a possible Title VII violation, the first requirement would be satisfied. The EEOC notes that "because individuals often may not know the specific requirements of the anti-discrimination laws" a "broad or ambiguous complaint of unfair treatment" can be viewed as opposition.

The first element is also met even though the employee was mistaken about the unlawfulness of the challenged practices. As long as the person had a reasonable and good-faith belief that the opposed practice violated Title VII, the employer may not do anything that may be seen as retaliation.

Some specific examples given by the EEOC will help in understanding the parameters of "protected activity." Protected activity has included: an employee calling the president to protest discrimination; a complaint to a foreman about anti-female graffiti, even though the employee making the complaint did not see it as a sexual harassment matter; and refusal to obey an order to discriminate illegally. Also, it must be remembered that those not directly involved in the protected activity can be seen as possible retaliation victims. Persons who have been allowed to claim retaliation have included the parent, spouse, or child of a complaining employee and a new employee who opposed her *previous* employer's allegedly discriminatory practices.

Was There Adverse Action by the Employer?

The second requirement for a retaliation claim is the employer subjected the employee to some kind of adverse treatment. This adverse action does not have to satisfy the requirement for a sexual harassment complaint that terms, conditions, or privileges of employment are affected, although trivial annoyances will not be seen as adverse actions.

Examples of adverse actions have been denials of promotions, refusals to hire, denial of job benefits, demotion, suspension, and discharge. In addition, threats, reprimands, negative evaluations, or harassment may be seen as retaliation. In one situation, the EEOC found an adverse action constituted retaliation when a supervisor excluded an employee from a regular weekly lunch after she filed a sex discrimination charge.

What many employers do not know is that adverse actions can be alleged after the employment relationship has ended. The Supreme Court unanimously held in *Robinson v. Shell Oil Co.*[29] that Title VII prohibits retaliation against former employees as well as current employees. In *Robinson,* the plaintiff had claimed that his former employer had given negative job references in retaliation for protected activity. The Court also stated that a retaliation complaint could be filed against the former employer, even if the negative reference had not caused the prospective employer to refrain from hiring the individual.

Is There a Causal Connection?

For a retaliation claim to be upheld, there must be a causal connection between the protected activity and the adverse action. Direct evidence, of course, will always create problems for the employer. In one case, an individual sued her former employer alleging that her supervisor sexually harassed her. The case was settled, and the individual applied for a job with a second employer. She received a conditional offer subject to a reference check. When the new employer called the previous employer, the supervisor stated that the employee was a "troublemaker," started a sex harassment lawsuit, and was not anyone that the new employer "would want to get mixed up with." The individual was not hired. Notes were found that documented the phone conversation, and the EEOC found retaliation by both the former and the prospective employer.

Because explicit statements by employers that they are undertaking the adverse action in response to protected activity are rare, however, there are other ways that this may be proven. In fact, according to the EEOC, the most common way of proving a causal connection is through circumstantial evidence.

An inference of causation may be raised if the adverse action took place shortly after the protected activity and the decision maker was aware of the employee's participation in the protected activity. An inference of retaliation may occur even if the time between protected activity and adverse action is not immediate. In one case, a 14-month interval was found adequate when the manager mentioned the employee's consent several times during the time period.

Circumstantial evidence of a causal connection is also found where there is no legitimate nondiscriminatory reason for the adverse action taken against the employee. This legitimate reason would need to be proven by credible evidence, usually well-documented reasons, including specific problems, events, and so on. Also, any situation in which there is evidence that the employee had not been treated the same as other employees or was subjected to heightened scrutiny after engaging in protected activity is especially problematic.

Thus, it becomes clear that any adverse employment action taken against employees involved in any way with a sexual harassment complaint must be carefully considered and documented. Questions must be carefully contemplated at this time. Is there evidence that anyone in the workplace is undertaking this action in retaliation for the affected employee's participation in protected activity? Are there adequate, legitimate, and well-documented reasons for the action? Has this person suddenly been subjected to more careful scrutiny— perhaps an increase in the usual number of performance evaluations or a sudden downturn in evaluation scores? These must be carefully considered if the employer is to avoid a retaliation claim in addition to or even without another discrimination claim. This could result not just in more investigations or lawsuits but also in a heightened risk of punitive damages, which was discussed earlier in this chapter.

Recall in the case study that Marjorie claims that Joseph Dale has been further harassed and has not received any salary increases since he filed a complaint. If this is true, Joseph may have a cause of action for retaliation under Title VII.

SUMMARY

The law with regard to sexual harassment, especially that which creates a "hostile" or discriminatory environment, continues to evolve and develop as new cases are heard. It is not easy to predict how far liability might extend in the future or to come up with a comprehensive list of behaviors that will be seen as contributing to a hostile environment. All that is clear is that the best course for an employer or manager to take to avoid liability is to better understand the entire concept of sexual harassment, including its basis and its effects, and then adopt and carry out stringent sexual-harassment policies and procedures. Taking the matter seriously from the beginning may remove the necessity to take it even more seriously in the courtroom in the future. It has been estimated that each day in court can cost an employer over $100,000—that is serious business for anyone.

Clearly, there is no need for any business to find itself charged in a sexual harassment lawsuit. Liability can be avoided, but, unfortunately, there may always be those who do not take the prudent path. Until everyone understands and responds appropriately, the law will continue to provide a remedy for employees with no other recourse, remedies that can be very costly for their employers.

FOR REFLECTION

1. Discuss why it is so difficult to exactly define the term "sexual harassment."
2. Differentiate between *quid pro quo* and hostile-environment lawsuits.
3. Explain why a lack of reporting does not necessarily indicate that there is no problem in the workplace.

4. Discuss the reasonable woman standard. To what does it apply? Why do courts use it?
5. Explain why courts and the EEOC differentiate between a person's social and workplace behavior.
6. Discuss the concept of agency as it relates to employer liability for sexual harassment.
7. Why must harassing behavior affect a term or condition of employment in order to be the basis of a lawsuit?
8. When does harassing behavior affect a term or condition of employment? What definitive test can be used to make that determination?
9. Discuss why employers need to be concerned with the conduct of clients or customers.
10. Why was the *Vinson* case so important? What did *Oncale* add to the *Vinson* decision?
11. Why is *quid pro quo* so serious for employers?
12. List five actions that an employer can take to help avoid liability for sexual harassment.
13. What are EEOC guidelines?
14. What is a constructive discharge? What is its relevance in a sexual harassment lawsuit?
15. Explain why an employer may have difficulty using the "equal opportunity harasser," "status quo," or "social context" defenses.
16. What does "continuing violation" mean for businesses?
17. Explain the concept of a retaliation lawsuit.

Notes

1. Title VII also covers labor organizations and employment agencies. Sexual harassment standards also apply to these groups, but this book will specifically use the term *employer*, in keeping with its intent to clarify the law with regard to workplace harassment.
2. 524 U.S. 742 (1998).
3. 561 F.2d 983 (1977).
4. 477 U.S. 57 (1986).
5. 924 F.2d 892.
6. 510 U.S. 17 (1993).
7. *Harris* at 371.
8. 524 U.S. 775 (1998).
9. 523 U.S. 75 (1998).
10. *Vinson* at 67.
11. *Harris* at 371.
12. *Robinson v. Jacksonville Shipyards*, 760 F.Supp 1486, 1524 (M.D. Fla. 1991).
13. 864 F.2d 881 (1st Cir 1988).
14. 895 F.2d 1469 (3d Cir. 1990).

15. 989 F.2d 959 (8th Cir. 1993).
16. First stated by Judge Damon Keith in his dissent in *Rabidue et al. v. Osceola Refining*, 805 F.2d 611, 626 (6th Cir. 1986).
17. *Dey v. Colt Const. & Development Co.*, 28 F.3d 1446 (7th Cir. 1994).
18. *Burns v. McGregor Electronic Industries*, 989 F.2d 959, 963 (8th Cir. 1993).
19. *Carr v. Allison Gas Turbine Div. Gen Motors*, 32 F.3d 1007, 1011 (7th Cir. 1994).
20. 685 F.Supp. 1269 (D.D.C. 1988).
21. 25 F.3d 1459 (9th Cir. 1994).
22. 25 F.3d at 1464.
23. Kathryn Abrams, *Gender Discrimination and the Transformation of Workplace Norms*, 42 *Vanderbilt Law Review* 1183, 1212 n.118 (1989).
24. *Carr v. Allison Gas Turbine Div. Gen Motors*, 32 F.3d 1007, 1012 (7th Cir. 1994).
25. 760 F.Supp. 1486 (M.D. Fla 1991).
26. Document available at http://www.eeoc.gov/docs/conting.txt.
27. *Moffett v. Gene B. Glick Co.*, 621 F.Supp. 244, 262 (N.D. Ind. 1985), *rev'd on other grounds*, 644 F.Supp. 983 (N.D. Ind. 1986).
28. The federal law protects against retaliation for complaints of violations of any federal discrimination law, including Title VII, the Age Discrimination in Employment Act, the Equal Pay Act, and the Americans with Disabilities Act. Because of the scope of this book, the term Title VII will be used.
29. 519 U.S. 337, 117 S. Ct. 843 (1997).

CHAPTER 3

Sexual Harassment from the Psychological Perspective

Case Study

Mary has just arrived at her first job. Upon her arrival she is met by a supervisor who shows considerable interest in her work and experience in college. Mary is flattered by his interest and agrees to discuss her work-related ideas over lunch in a restaurant downtown. After a few lunches where the conversation is general and social rather than focused on professional issues, Mary finds that the supervisor is touching her—rubbing his knees against hers, placing his hand on her back and arms, and once patting her on the bottom. He asks Mary to meet him outside of work for early dinners. She declines,

offering various excuses, and tries to maintain a polite but distant tone in her conversations with him. One day the supervisor asks Mary to come into his office to discuss a project. Once she is inside the office, he closes the door, moves toward her, and puts his arms around her. Mary tries to push him away, but he holds her tighter and tries to kiss her. There is a knock on the door, he releases Mary, and she opens the door and hurries out of the office.

Is this sexual harassment? Why or why not? If you believe this is sexual harassment, when did the harassment begin?

INTRODUCTION

How did you answer the questions related to the case study? Do you believe sexual harassment occurred between the supervisor and the new employee? Most individuals to whom this scenario is shown agree that sexual harassment occurred. However, answers to the second question (When did the harassment begin?) are typically quite different. For example, most women report the harassment began when the supervisor started to ask Mary out for lunch; most men, on the other hand, believe the sexual harassment began when the supervisor cornered Mary in his office. When do you believe the sexual harassment began?

The responses to this scenario, adapted from Paludi and Barickman,[1] illustrate how much confusion still exists because of a lack of a clear, concise, widely accepted definition of sexual harassment. Such definitions are important because they educate individuals in the workplace and promote discussion and conscientious evaluation of experiences.

There are two major types of definitions of sexual harassment. The first type includes legal and regulatory constructions. We addressed the first type of definition in chapter 2. The second type of definition is developed empirically by investigating what various groups of individuals perceive as sexual harassment under different circumstances. This chapter focuses on the second type of definition, based on *actual behaviors* that constitute sexual harassment. Following an overview of the definitions, we will discuss the differential interpretations that women and men in the workplace give to these behaviors. We will also address the relationship between the way individuals define sexual harassment and how they cope with this form of victimization.

EMPIRICAL DEFINITION OF SEXUAL HARASSMENT

Empirical definitions of sexual harassment are based on data and usually developed by researchers in the field of human-resource management and psychology. Empirical definitions are derived from women's and men's descriptions of their experiences of harassment. These descriptions are categorized, and the categories are then used as the elements of the definition. For example, Frank Till[2] classified the responses to an open-ended sexual harassment survey of college women and derived the following five categories of generally increasing severity:

> gender harassment
> seductive behavior
> sexual bribery
> sexual coercion
> sexual imposition or assault

According to Till's research, *gender harassment* consists of generalized sexist remarks and behavior not designed to elicit sexual cooperation but to convey insulting, degrading, or sexist attitudes about women. *Seductive behavior* is unwanted, inappropriate, and offensive sexual advances. *Sexual bribery* is the solicitation of sexual activity or other sex-linked behavior by promise of a reward (e.g., salary increase or promotion). *Sexual coercion* is the solicitation of sexual activity by threat of punishment (e.g., failure to give a promotion or being fired), and *sexual imposition or assault* includes gross sexual imposition, assault, and rape.

In the case study, Mary experienced seductive behavior on the part of her supervisor when he touched her, rubbed his knees against hers, and invited her to dinners. She experienced sexual imposition in her supervisor's office when he held her tightly and attempted to kiss her.

The legal definition identifies the conditions under which a behavior may constitute sexual harassment, but generally does not give specific examples. Empirical definitions rely on the responses of individuals asked to describe their experiences. These definitions are limited to the data provided by a particular sample. Several researchers have attempted to bridge the benefits of both types of definitions.[3] For example, Louise Fitzgerald and Alayne Ormerod suggested that a definition of sexual harassment should identify that sexual harassment: (1) is the sexualization of a professional relationship; (2) frequently occurs in the context of an organizational power differential (e.g., supervisor-employee); (3) can occur in the absence of a formal power differential (e.g., hostile environment); (4) consists of unwanted and unwelcome behaviors—both verbal and nonverbal in nature; and (5) can be viewed along a continuum, from sexist remarks to nonverbal seductive gestures to sexual assault.[4]

Empirical definitions include both the legal description of the nature and elements of sexual harassment and an enumeration of types of harassment based on an empirically derived classification scheme. These definitions also address contextual issues by assuming that all sexist or sexual behaviors constitute harassment when they occur within the framework of a formal power differential. When the participants are of equal formal power, it is the recipient's reactions that constitute the defining factor.

A summary of the legal and psychological interpretations of sexual harassment is presented below.

1. Sexual harassment does not fall within the range of personal private relationships. Harassment happens when a person with power (organizational and/or sociocultural) abuses that power to intimidate, coerce, or humiliate someone because of her or his sex.
2. Verbal harassment may include unwelcome sexual innuendos, comments, and sexual remarks
   suggestive, obscene, or insulting sounds
   implied or overt threats
   pressure for sex

3. Physical harassment may include unwelcome
   patting, pinching, or brushing up against the body
   coerced sexual intercourse
   assault
   leering or ogling
   obscene gestures
4. Sexual harassment is a breach of the trust that normally exists among employees.
5. Sexual harassment does create confusion because the boundary between professional roles and personal relationships is blurred. The harasser introduces a sexual element into what should be a professional situation.
6. Sexual harassment can be an action that occurs only once, or it may be repeated.
7. In voluntary sexual relationships, individuals can exercise freedom of choice in deciding whether to establish a close, intimate relationship. This freedom of choice is absent in sexual harassment.

These answers to the question "What is sexual harassment?" are crucial to the process of helping those who have been sexually harassed because most victims do not know the definition. Consequently, they do not identify what has happened to them as sexual harassment. The incidence of sexual harassment thus reflects an underreporting of this abuse.[5]

In exhibit 3.1 we list some additional case studies for you to review.

INCIDENCE OF SEXUAL HARASSMENT IN THE WORKPLACE

Sexual harassment is similar to other forms of sexual victimization, such as rape, incest, and domestic violence, in which various factors combine to produce underreporting and underestimates.[6] Several major studies (as well as smaller-scale ones) do suggest that sexual harassment in the workplace is widespread.[7] For men, as we will discuss, the incidence is substantially less.[8] The U.S. Merit Systems Protection Board addressed sexual harassment in the federal workplace and reported that 42 percent of all women employees reported being sexually harassed.[9] Merit Systems reported that many incidents occurred repeatedly, were of long duration, and had a sizable practical impact, costing the government an estimated minimum of $189 million over the 2-year period covered by the research project.

Results also indicated that 33 percent of the women reported receiving unwanted sexual remarks, 28 percent reported suggestive looks, and 26 percent reported being deliberately touched. These

EXHIBIT 3.1

Sample Case Studies on Sexual Harassment

Do you think sexual harassment occurred in each of the following scenarios? Why or why not?

Jamie's boss insists that the waitresses wear short black skirts and low-cut white blouses to work at the cafe. Jamie asks her boss if this dress code has to be put into effect because she feels very uncomfortable in this outfit: customers ogle her and comment about her breast size and buttocks. Jamie's boss reminds her that he can find someone to replace her very quickly.

Danielle's coworkers have been using their electronic-mail system to rate Danielle and other women employees in terms of their sexual attractiveness. Lately Danielle hears her coworkers snicker as she goes by their desks. She has decided to take some of her vacation days in hopes that this behavior will cease by the time she returns to work.

Pat's supervisor has asked Pat out for drinks and dinner for the last few weeks. Pat has refused the supervisor's requests. Pat called a meeting to discuss receiving a fairly negative three-month performance appraisal. In this meeting, the supervisor says, "You had your chance."

Don has been visiting Antoinette at her desk in the front office, and both have started to engage in sexual banter. They also touch each other and engage in "cat calls" right in front of the other secretaries. Dru, a secretary whose desk is right next to Antoinette's, feels uneasy about the banter and touching. She doesn't find the jokes funny—in fact, she thinks they're sexist. She wishes she could have her desk moved because she can't seem to concentrate on her work whenever Don and Antoinette are together.

behaviors were classified in the study as "less severe" types of sexual harassment. When "more severe" forms of sexual harassment were addressed, 15 percent of the women reported experiencing pressure for dates, 9 percent reported being directly pressured for sexual favors, and 9 percent had received unwanted letters and telephone calls. One percent of the sample had experienced actual or attempted rape or assault. Merit Systems repeated their study of workplace sexual harassment in 1987 and reported identical results to their 1981 findings.[10]

Research by Barbara Gutek on women in the civilian workplace reports similar findings as well: Approximately half the female workforce experiences sexual harassment.[11] Based on telephone interviews generated through random-digit dialing procedures, Gutek's results suggested that 53 percent of women had reported one incident they believed was sexual harassment during their working lives, including degrading, insulting comments (15 percent); sexual touching (24 percent); socializing expected as part of the job requirement (11 percent); and expected sexual activity (8 percent).

Occupational Group Differences

Some studies reported in the literature suggest that group differences in sexual harassment are common. For example, Fitzgerald and colleagues found that women who were employed in a university setting (e.g., faculty, staff, and administrators) were more likely to experience sexual harassment than were women students in the same institution.[12] Gold reported that her sample of blue-collar tradeswomen experienced significantly higher levels of all forms of sexual harassment (e.g., gender harassment, seductive behavior, sexual bribery, sexual coercion, and sexual assault) than did either white-collar professional women or pink-collar clerical women.[13] LaFontaine and Tredeau also reported similar findings in their sample of 160 women, all college graduates employed in male-dominated occupations (e.g., engineering and management).[14]

Nancy Baker studied a sample of 100 women employed in either traditional or nontraditional occupations, where "traditionality" was defined by the sex distribution in the work group.[15] Baker also divided the traditional group into pink- and blue-collar workers. The pink-collar group comprised women who were secretaries and clerical workers. The blue-collar group was made up of women who were industrial workers. Baker reported that high levels of sexual harassment are associated with having low numbers of women in the work group. For example, machinists reported significantly high frequencies of all levels of sexual harassment. Clerical women reported experiences that were more similar to those of the traditional blue-collar workers than the nontraditional blue-collar workers. Baker also reported that women in the pink-collar and traditional blue-collar groups encountered just as many men as the machinists during the workday, but were treated differently. Thus, these results suggest that as women approach numerical parity in various segments of the workforce, sexual harassment may decline.

This perspective has also been raised by Gutek, who argued that sexual harassment is more likely to occur in occupations in which "sex-role spillover" has occurred.[16] Gutek's model suggests that when occupations are dominated by one gender or the other, the sex role of the dominant sex influences (e.g., spills over) the work-role expectations for that job. Thus, sexual harassment can be viewed as a side effect of organizing society around gender stereotypes, an issue to which we now turn.

GENDER STEREOTYPING:
RELATIONSHIP TO SEXUAL HARASSMENT

Gender stereotypes are the structured set of beliefs people hold about personal attributes of men and women, as well as their physical characteristics and behaviors.[17] Gender stereotypes are not based on factual information; they are the thoughts or beliefs we all hold about the supposed nature of women and men. For example, women are typically perceived as helpful, loyal, patient, submissive, dependent, nurturing, and sexual. Men are typically perceived as independent, dominant, and aggressive. These gender stereotypes are not left behind when women and men go to work each day. Some occupations that individuals perceive as most suitable for women are congruent with beliefs about women being nurturing, loyal, helpful, and so on (e.g., teacher, nurse).[18] Moreover, some occupations deemed suitable for women emphasize women's status as a sex object (e.g., cocktail waitress, flight attendant).[19]

Gender stereotypes imply that men should be sexually aggressive and women should be ready and willing to be sex objects. Sexual harassment may occur when these gender stereotypes spill over into the workplace. Thus, when individuals act on their thoughts about women and men, they may engage in behavior that is discriminatory. For example, research suggests that women are evaluated less favorably than men for identical performance on a job.[20] In addition, men tend to turn their focus away from women and also to move away from them, in contrast to their behavior toward other men.[21] Furthermore, men have higher expectations for other men's abilities than for women's abilities; thus, they attribute women's successful performance on the job to luck, cheating, sexuality, or the fact that someone likes them. The causal attribution of lack of ability, however, is used by men to describe anything not perfect about women's job performance.[22] In exhibit 3.2 we present a list of some myths and realities related to women and men in the workplace.

Thus, to categorize individuals according to criteria means their suitability will be evaluated by these terms as well. In the workplace, this process produces discriminatory behavior when it leads an individual to judge or evaluate a coworker or subordinate based on some quality unrelated to job performance. Women employees may be evaluated by their coworkers and supervisors in terms of their sexuality and their performance as sex objects instead of their merit as workers.[23] Gender stereotypes are related to the amount of perceived power one has in the workplace. It is to this issue—the interrelationships between gender and power—that we now turn in our discussion of the psychological perspective to understanding sexual harassment.

EXHIBIT 3.2

Myths and Realities of Gender Comparisons

Myth: Women have lower self-esteem than men.

Fact: Overall, women and men are similar in their personal views of self-confidence and self-esteem. They do, however, differ in the areas in which they feel self-confident. Women are more likely to rate themselves as higher in social competence, whereas men see themselves as powerful and dominant.

Myth: Women lack the motivation to achieve.

Fact: Women and men can be equally motivated to achieve, but both are influenced by different factors that push their achievement levels. Women are motivated to achieve in situations where there is less competition or social comparison.

Myth: Women are more suggestible than men.

Fact: Women are just as likely as men to imitate others' behavior spontaneously. When there is pressure to conform to an ambiguous situation, women and men are equally susceptible to persuasive face-to-face communication.

Myth: Men are more analytical than women.

Fact: To analyze, one must disregard unimportant aspects of a situation in favor of the important features of a task. Both women and men are just as apt to pay attention to unimportant details as to the important ones.

Myth: Men are more affected by environment; women, by heredity.

Fact: Both men and women are affected by both heredity and environment—parents, teachers, peers, media.

From James A. Doyle and Michele A. Paludi, *Sex and Gender: The Human Experience,* 3rd edition. Copyright © 1995 Times Mirror Higher Education Group, Inc., Dubuque, Iowa. All Rights Reserved. Reprinted by permission.

A PSYCHOLOGICAL ANALYSIS OF WHY SEXUAL HARASSMENT OCCURS

Men's Relationships with Men

Kathryn Quina related common forms of sexual harassment in the workplace to characters in the comic strip *Beetle Bailey:*[24]

> General Halftrack is the archetypic older gentleman whose dowdy wife starves him for affection. His secretary, Miss Buxley—who can't type—drives him wild with her sexy fig-

ure and short skirts. "Killer" (short for "lady killer"—a curiously violent name) is always whistling at "chicks" (who love it), accompanied by Beetle, who is equally aggressive but not as successful. Zero just stares at women's bodies.

Quina reminds us that although we may laugh when reading the comic strip, these behaviors are not humorous when expressed in the workplace. Paludi has focused not on men's attitudes toward women but on men's attitudes toward other men, competition, and power.[25] Many of the men with whom Paludi has discussed sexual harassment often act out of extreme competitiveness and concern with ego, or out of fear of losing their positions of power. They don't want to appear weak or less masculine in the eyes of other men, so they will engage in rating women's bodies, pinching women, making implied or overt threats, or spying on women. Women are the game to impress other men. When men are being encouraged to be obsessively competitive and concerned with dominance, it is likely that they will eventually use violent means to achieve dominance. Men are also likely to be abusive verbally and intimidating in their body language.[26] Deindividuation is quite common among male office workers who, during their lunch break, rate women coworkers numerically as they walk by in the cafeteria. These men discontinue self-evaluation and adopt group norms and attitudes. Under these circumstances, group members behave more aggressively than they would as individuals.[27]

Aggression and Sexual Harassment

The element of aggression that is so deeply embedded in the masculine gender role is present in sexual harassment. For many men, aggression is one of the major ways to "prove" their masculinity, especially among those men who feel some sense of powerlessness in their lives.[28] The theme of male-as-dominant or male-as-aggressor is so central to many men's self-concepts that it literally carries over into their interpersonal communications, especially with women coworkers. Sexualizing a professional relationship may be the one way that such a man can still prove his masculinity when he can find few other ways to prove himself in control or to be the dominant person in a relationship.[29]

Who Harasses?

Men who sexually harass have not been distinguishable from their colleagues who don't harass with respect to age, marital status, faculty rank, occupation, or academic discipline.[30] Men who harass have a tendency to do so repeatedly to many women, and men who harass hold attitudes toward women that are traditional, not egalitarian.[31]

For example, John Pryor noted that sexual harassment bears a conceptual similarity to rape.[32] He developed a series of hypothetical scenarios that provided opportunities for sexual harassment if the man so chose. Men participating in this study were instructed to imagine themselves in the roles of the men in the scenarios and consider what they would do in each situation. They were further instructed to imagine that, whatever their chosen course of action, no negative consequences would result from their choices. Men's scores on the survey, measuring their likelihood to engage in sexual harassment, were related to gender-role stereotyping and negatively related to feminist attitudes and the component of empathy having to do with the ability to take the standpoint of the other.

Thus, this research suggests that the man who is likely to initiate severe sexually harassing behavior appears to be one who emphasizes male social and sexual dominance and who demonstrates insensitivity to other individuals' perspectives. Furthermore, men are less likely than women to define sexual harassment as including jokes, teasing remarks of a sexual nature, and unwanted suggestive looks or gestures. Men are also significantly more likely than women to agree with the following statements, taken from Paludi's "attitudes toward victim blame and victim responsibility" survey:

> Women often claim sexual harassment to protect their reputations.
> Many women claim sexual harassment if they have consented to sexual relations but have changed their minds afterward.
> Sexually experienced women are not really damaged by sexual harassment.
> It would do some women good to be sexually harassed.
> Women put themselves in situations in which they are likely to be sexually harassed because they have an unconscious wish to be harassed.
> In most cases when a woman is sexually harassed, she deserves it.

Sexual harassment, similar to rape, incest, and battering, may be understood as an extreme acting out of qualities that are regarded as supermasculine in this culture: aggression, power, dominance, and force.[33] Thus, men who harass are not pathological but rather exhibit behaviors characteristic of the masculine gender role in American culture.

Can and Do Women Harass Men?

A review of the empirical research in this area suggests the following:

1. Women are highly unlikely to date or initiate sexual relationships with their coworkers or supervisors.[34]

2. A small number of men in the workplace believe they have been sexually harassed by women. The behaviors many of these men label as sexual harassment, however, do not fit the legal definition of either *quid pro quo* or hostile environment sexual harassment.[35]

3. Men are more likely than women to interpret a particular behavior as sexual. For example, in research by Barbara Gutek, men were likely to label a business lunch as a "date" if it was with a female manager.[36]

4. The great majority of men report that they are flattered by women's advances, whereas women report feeling annoyed, insulted, and threatened.[37]

5. It is rare for a woman to hold the organizational and sociocultural power that would allow her to reward a man for sexual cooperation or punish him for withholding it, even if gender-role prescriptions did not ensure that she was extremely unlikely to demand sexual favors in the first place.[38]

Research suggests that many of men's experiences with sexual harassment are with other men. Consequently, men may be reluctant to disclose this information due to homophobic concerns.[39]

Sexual Harassment: Women, Men, Sex, Power, and Aggression

Sandra Tangri and her colleagues have labeled three theoretical models that incorporate this gender/power/aggression analysis.[40] The *natural/biological model* interprets sexual harassment as a consequence of sexual interactions between people, either attributing a stronger sex drive to men than to women (i.e., men "need" to engage in aggressive sexual behavior) or describing sexual harassment as part of the "game" between sexual equals. This model does not account for the extreme stress reactions suffered by victims of sexual harassment.

The *sociocultural model* posits sexual harassment as only one manifestation of the much larger patriarchal system in which men are the dominant group. Therefore, harassment is an example of men asserting their personal power based on sex. According to this model, sex would be a better predictor of both recipient and initiator status than would organizational position. Thus, women should be much more likely to be victims of sexual harassment, especially when they are in male-populated occupations. This model gives a much more accurate account of sexual harassment because the overwhelming majority of victims are women and the overwhelming majority of harassers are men.

The *organizational model* asserts that sexual harassment results from opportunities presented by relations of power and authority that derive from the hierarchical structure of organizations. Thus, sexual harassment is an issue of organizational power. Because workplaces are defined by vertical stratification and asymmetrical relations among supervisors and subordinates, individuals can use the power of their positions to extort sexual gratification from their subordinates.

Related to this are the research findings that suggest that individuals who harass typically do not label their behavior as sexual harassment despite the fact they report they frequently engage in behaviors that fit the legal definition of sexual harassment.[41] Such individuals deny the inherent power differential between themselves and their employees, as well as the psychological power.

The behavior that legally constitutes harassment is just that, despite what the supervisor's or coworker's intentions may be. The impact on the individual—her or his reaction to the behavior—is the critical variable.[42]

INTERPRETATION OF SEXUAL HARASSMENT: IMPACT ON RECIPIENTS

Several reports have documented the high cost of sexual harassment to women. Louise Fitzgerald and Alayne Ormerod noted that the outcomes of the harassment/victimization process can be examined from three main perspectives: work-related, psychological or emotional, and physiological or health-related.[43]

Work-Related Outcomes   Research has documented the following responses to career development as a consequence of being sexually harassed: changes in work habits, drop in performance because of stress, absenteeism, withdrawal from work, and changes in career goals.[44]

Psychological Outcomes   The consequences to women students and employees of being harassed have been devastating to their emotional health. Psychological outcomes of harassment include depression, helplessness, strong fear reactions, loss of control, disruption of victims' lives, and decreased motivation.[45] Research has indicated that, depending on the severity of the harassment, between 21 percent and 82 percent of women report that their emotional condition deteriorated as a result of the sexual harassment. Furthermore, like victims of rape who go to court, sexual harassment victims experience a second victimization when they attempt to deal with the situation through legal or institutional means.[46] Stereotypes about sexual harassment and women's victimization tend to blame women for the harassment.[47] These stereotypes center around the myths that sexual harassment is a form of seduction, that women secretly want to be sexually harassed, and that women do not tell the truth.[48]

Physiological outcomes   The following physical symptoms have been reported in the literature concerning academic and workplace sexual harassment: headaches, sleep disturbances, disordered eating, gastrointestinal disorders, nausea, weight loss or gain, and crying spells.[49] Researchers and clinicians have argued that victims of sexual harassment can exhibit a post-abuse syndrome characterized by shock, emotional numbing, constriction of affect, flashbacks, and other signs of anxiety and depression.[50]

The label *sexual harassment trauma syndrome* has been applied to the effects of sexual harassment on physical, emotional, interpersonal, and career aspects of employees' lives.[51] Components of this syndrome are presented in Exhibit 3.3. These responses are influenced by disappointment in the way others react and the stress of harassment-induced life changes, such as moves, loss of income, and disrupted work history.[52]

Fitzgerald, Gold, and Brock constructed an empirically based system for classifying individuals' responses to sexually harassing behaviors.[53] They classified individuals' responses into two categories: *internally focused strategies* and *externally focused strategies.* Internal strategies represent attempts to manage the emotions and cognitions associated with the behaviors victims have experienced. Fitzgerald et al. identified the following classification system for internally focused strategies:

Detachment
   Individual minimizes situation; treats it as a joke
Denial
   Individual denies behaviors; attempts to forget about situation
Relabeling
   Individual reappraises situation as less threatening; offers
   excuses for harasser's behaviors
Illusory control
   Individual attempts to take responsibility for harassment
Endurance
   Individual puts up with behavior because of not believing
   help is available or fearing retaliation

Externally focused strategies focus on the harassing situation itself, including reporting the behavior to the individual charged with investigating complaints of sexual harassment. Fitzgerald, Gold, and Brock classified externally focused strategies into the following categories:

Avoidance
   Individual attempts to avoid situation by staying away from
   the harasser

EXHIBIT 3.3

Sexual Harassment Trauma Syndrome

Not all symptoms will be expressed by every individual. Common symptoms include:

Career Effects
Changes in work habits
Drop in work performance because of stress
Absenteeism
Withdrawal from work
Changes in career goals

Emotional Reactions
Shock, denial
Anger, frustration
Insecurity, embarrassment
Confusion, self-consciousness
Shame, powerlessness
Guilt, isolation

Physical Reactions
Headaches
Inability to concentrate
Sleep disturbances
Lethargy
Gastrointestinal distress
Respiratory problems
Phobias, panic reactions
Nightmares
Eating disorders
Dermatological reactions

Changes in Self-Perception
Poor self-concept or self-esteem
Lack of competency
Powerlessness
Isolation

Social, Interpersonal Relatedness, and Sexual Effects
Withdrawal
Fear of new people
Lack of trust
Change in physical appearance
Change in social network patterns
Negative attitudes about sexual relationships

Adapted from M. A. Paludi and R. B. Barickman, *Academic and Workplace Sexual Harassment: A Resource Manual* (Albany: State University of New York Press, 1991). By permission of the State University of New York Press. © 1991.

Assertion or confrontation
   Individual refuses sexual or social offers or verbally con-
   fronts the harasser
Seeking institutional or organizational relief
   Individual reports the incident and files a complaint
Social support
   Individual seeks support of others to validate perceptions of
   the behaviors
Appeasement
   Individual attempts to evade the harasser without confronta-
   tion; attempts to placate the harasser

Ormerod and Gold, using this classification system, noted that internal strategies represented by far the most common response overall.[54] Most victims do not tell the harasser to stop. Their initial attempts to manage the initiator are rarely direct.[55] Typically, harassers are more powerful physically and organizationally than the victims, and sometimes the harasser's intentions are unclear. The first or first several harassing events are often ignored by victims—especially when they are experiencing hostile environment sexual harassment where the behavior may be more subtle.[56] Victims may interpret or reinterpret the situation so that the incident is not defined as sexual harassment. Many times victims ignore the perpetrator.

Victims of sexual harassment (especially women of color) may fear retaliation should they confront the harasser.[57] The economic reality for most women is that they can't simply leave a workplace where they are being sexually harassed.[58]

SEXUAL HARASSMENT: ISSUES ACROSS THE LIFE CYCLE

So far in our discussion, we have summarized research and theories dealing with sexual harassment of women and men in the workplace. As most human-resource managers and therapists know, sexual harassment that happens to employees is very similar to what occurred to these same individuals as students. Consequently, a great deal of research has been exploring the incidence and psychological dimensions of sexual harassment in schools, colleges, and universities.[59] We now present an overview of the issues we discussed in this chapter specifically with respect to students. It is important to consider individuals' prior experiences with sexual harassment. They can help us understand whether individuals use an internally or externally focused strategy in dealing with sexual harassment in the workplace.

Incidence of Sexual Harassment of Students

Research has suggested that, similar to employees, most elementary school students[60] and secondary school students[61] do not label experiences as sexual harassment despite the fact the behavior they have experienced meets the legal definition of either *quid pro quo* or hostile environment harassment. The American Association of University Women studied 1,632 students in grades 8 through 11 from 79 schools across the United States.[62] Students were asked, "During your whole school life, how often, if at all, has anyone (this includes students, teachers, other school employees, or anyone else) done the following things to you *when you did not want them to?*"

Made sexual comments, jokes, gestures, or looks
Showed, gave, or left you sexual pictures, photographs, illustrations, messages, or notes
Wrote sexual messages or graffiti about you on bathroom walls, in locker rooms, etc.
Spread sexual rumors about you
Said you were gay or lesbian
Spied on you as you dressed or showered at school
Flashed or "mooned" you
Touched, grabbed, or pinched you in a sexual way
Pulled at your clothing in a sexual way
Intentionally brushed against you in a sexual way
Pulled your clothing off or down
Blocked your way or cornered you in a sexual way
Forced you to kiss him or her
Forced you to do something sexual other than kissing

Results suggested that four out of five students (81 percent) reported that they had been the target of some form of sexual harassment during their school lives. With respect to gender comparisons, 85 percent of girls and 76 percent of boys surveyed reported that they had experienced unwelcome sexual behavior that interfered with their ability to concentrate at school and with their personal lives. The AAUW study also analyzed the data for race comparisons. African-American boys (81 percent) were more likely to have experienced sexual harassment than white boys (75 percent) and Latinos (69 percent). For girls, 87 percent of whites reported having experienced behaviors that constitute sexual harassment, compared with 84 percent of African-American girls and 82 percent of Latinas.

The AAUW study also suggested that adolescents' experiences with sexual harassment were most likely to occur in the middle school or junior high school years of sixth to ninth grade. The behaviors reported by students, in order from most often experienced to least often experienced, include the following:

Sexual comments, jokes, gestures, or looks
Touched, grabbed, or pinched in a sexual way
Intentionally brushed against in a sexual way
Flashed or "mooned"
Had sexual rumors spread about them
Had clothing pulled at in a sexual way
Shown, given, or left sexual pictures, photographs, illustrations,
    messages, or notes
Had their way blocked or were cornered in a sexual way
Had sexual messages or graffiti written about them on bath-
    room walls, in locker rooms, etc.
Forced to kiss someone
Called gay or lesbian
Had clothing pulled off or down
Forced to do something sexual other than kissing
Spied on as they dressed or showered at school

Students reported that they experience these behaviors while in the classroom or in the hallways as they are going to class. Although the majority of harassment in schools is student-to-student, 25 percent of harassed girls and 10 percent of boys reported they were harassed by teachers or other school employees.[63]

With respect to the incidence of sexual harassment of college and university students, Dziech and Weiner reported that 30 percent of undergraduate women suffered sexual harassment from at least one of their instructors during the women's four years of college.[64] When definitions of sexual harassment include sexist remarks and other forms of gender harassment, the incidence in undergraduate popula-tions nears 70 percent.[65]

Bailey and Richards reported that of 246 women graduate stu-dents in their sample, 13 percent indicated they had been sexually harassed, 21 percent had not enrolled in a course to avoid such behav-ior, and 16 percent indicated they had been directly assaulted.[66] Bond (1988) reported that 75 percent of the 229 women who responded to her survey experienced jokes with sexual themes during their gradu-ate training, 69 percent were subjected to sexist comments demeaning to women, and 58 percent reported experiencing sexist remarks about their clothing, body, or sexual activities.[67]

Fitzgerald, Shullman, Bailey, Richards, Swecker, Gold, Ormerod, and Weitzman investigated approximately 2,000 women at two major state universities.[68] Half of the women respondents reported experi-encing some form of sexually harassing behavior. The majority of these women reported experiencing sexist comments by faculty. The next largest category of sexually harassing behavior was seductive behavior, including being invited for drinks and a backrub by faculty members, being brushed up against by their professors, and having their professors show up uninvited at their hotel rooms during out-of-town academic conferences or conventions.

Research on the interface of race and sexual harassment[69] suggests that the incidence of academic sexual harassment of ethnic-minority women students is even greater than that reported by white women. Research has suggested that ethnic-minority women are more vulnerable to receiving sexual attention from professors.[70] Ethnic-minority women are subject to stereotypes about sex, are viewed as mysterious, and are less sure of themselves in their careers.[71] Thus, although all students are vulnerable to some degree, male teachers and faculty tend to select those who are most vulnerable and needy. For certain student groups, the incidence of sexual harassment appears to be higher than others.[72] For example:

Girls and women of color, especially those with "token" status

Graduate students, whose future careers are often determined by their association with a particular faculty member

Students in small colleges or small academic departments, where the number of faculty available to students is quite small

Girl and women students in male-dominated fields (e.g., engineering)

Students who are economically disadvantaged and work part-time or full-time while attending classes

Lesbian women, who may be harassed as part of homophobia

Physically or emotionally disabled students

Women students who work in dormitories as resident assistants

Girls and women who have been sexually abused

Inexperienced, unassertive, socially isolated girls and women, who may appear more vulnerable and appealing to those who would intimidate or entice them into an exploitative relationship

Schools most likely to have a high incidence of sexual harassment are ones, according to research,[73] that

Have no policy prohibiting sexual-harassment

Do not disseminate the policy or report information regarding sexual harassment

Have no training programs for teachers, staff, and students

Do not intervene officially when sexual harassment occurs

Do not support sexual-harassment victims

Do not quickly remove sexual graffiti

Do not sanction individuals who engage in sexual harassment

Do not inform the school community about the sanctions for offenders

Have been previously all-male or have a majority of male students

Sexual harassment is thus a major form of victimization of students in our system of higher education.[74]

FROM THE PSYCHOLOGY LABORATORY TO THE WORKPLACE: USING PSYCHOLOGICAL RESEARCH AND THEORIES TO DEAL WITH SEXUAL HARASSMENT

The psychological research and theories summarized thus far have tremendous implications for dealing with sexual harassment in the workplace.

For example, the research on women's and men's differential perceptions of identical behavior suggests the need for training programs to include units on attributions and attitudes about women's and men's verbal and nonverbal communication styles.[75] Because women tend to view sexual harassment as an abuse of power and men tend to view it as flirtation and flattery, both sexes should be present together in training sessions. In training sessions, many women are pleased that the issue will finally be addressed; many men are worried that they can't joke or have fun with women anymore. It is helpful to include women and men in the same training sessions so that these differential perceptions can be identified and discussed. We will return to this issue in appendix 1.

Separate sessions for women and men may perpetuate stereotypes that all men are guilty of sexual harassment and all women are victims. This latter type of training is also divisive and contributes to further harassment of women by men. Both women and men have the same rights and responsibilities with respect to sexual harassment and must be provided the same information concerning these rights and responsibilities.[76]

In addition to integrating psychological research and theories into training programs for employees, this information must be taken into account in policy statements and investigatory procedures. In part II of this book we discuss effective policy statements and investigatory procedures on sexual harassment, viewing the issue from the perspectives of both the recipient and the initiator.

SUMMARY

In this chapter we reviewed the current research and theories from the field of psychology on workplace sexual harassment. In our discussion, we reviewed the literature on women's and men's perceptions of identical behavior, their attributions and attitudes about sexual harassment, and how they cope with this form of victimization—either internally or externally. We also addressed the need to view sexual harassment along a life-cycle perspective and addressed the incidence and dimensions of sexual harassment during junior high school, high school, and college.

To summarize:

Sexual harassment can be viewed as an abuse of power and the reflection of the low status of individuals in the workplace.

Many individuals cling to the myth that sexual harassment includes only physical assault. In fact, sexual harassment is far more pervasive than sexual assault.

Sexual harassment is unwelcome sexual advances or requests for sexual favors.

Sexual harassment also includes other verbal or physical conduct of a sexual nature.

Although generalizations are difficult given the nature of the available data, it does appear reasonable to estimate that one out of every two women will be harassed at some point in her work history.

Research suggests that as women approach numerical parity in various segments of the workforce, sexual harassment may decline.

Men may experience sexual harassment as well, but the incidence for women is much greater than that for men.

Most victims do not use an externally focused strategy for dealing with sexual harassment.

Victims of sexual harassment often fear retaliation should they confront the harasser.

Women may not label their experiences as sexual harassment, despite the fact that the experiences meet the legal definition of this form of victimization. Consequently, they may not label their stress-related responses as being caused or exacerbated by the sexual harassment.

Sexual harassment has a radiating impact and can thus affect the working experiences of all women and men in an organization.

FOR REFLECTION

1. Discuss the difference between legal and empirically derived definitions of sexual harassment.
2. Define the following empirically derived categories of sexual harassment:
   Gender harassment
   Seductive behavior
   Sexual bribery
   Sexual coercion
   Sexual imposition

3. Discuss what is meant in the psychological literature by the term *formal power differential.*
4. Provide examples of verbal forms of sexual harassment.
5. Provide examples of physical forms of sexual harassment.
6. Discuss the results of the 1981 study conducted by the U.S. Merit Systems Protection Board.
7. Identify occupational group differences in sexual harassment.
8. What is a gender stereotype? Give an example of a gender stereotype related to a woman and to a man.
9. Cite examples of the operation of gender stereotypes in the workplace.
10. Discuss the relationship between masculine aggression and sexual harassment.
11. What explanatory model offered do you believe best explains sexual harassment in the workplace? Cite evidence for your position.
12. Outline some of the symptoms common to the sexual harassment trauma syndrome.
13. Discuss the difference between internally and externally focused strategies for dealing with sexual harassment.
14. Discuss the results of the 1993 American Association of University Women study with adolescents.
15. Discuss the incidence and psychological dimensions of sexual harassment among college and university students.
16. What is the relationship between gender stereotyping and hostile work environments?
17. Discuss the interface between sexual harassment and race.
18. Cite ways the research cited in this chapter can be useful for developing and implementing training programs in sexual-harassment awareness.

Notes

1. Adapted from M. PALUDI & R. BARICKMAN, ACADEMIC AND WORKPLACE SEXUAL HARASSMENT: A MANUAL OF RESOURCES (1991).
2. F. TILL, SEXUAL HARASSMENT: A REPORT ON THE SEXUAL HARASSMENT OF STUDENTS (1980).
3. See L. FITZGERALD & A. ORMEROD, *Sexual Harassment in Academia and the Workplace,* in PSYCHOLOGY OF WOMEN: A HANDBOOK OF ISSUES AND THEORIES (F. Denmark & M. Paludi, eds., 1993).
4. L. FITZGERALD & A. ORMEROD, *Sexual Harassment in Academia and the Workplace,* in PSYCHOLOGY OF WOMEN: A HANDBOOK OF ISSUES AND THEORIES (F. Denmark & M. Paludi, eds., 1993).
5. L. FITZGERALD, S. SWAN, & V. MAGLEY, *But Was It Really Sexual Harassment? Legal, Behavioral, and Psychological Definitions of the Workplace Victimization of Women,* in SEXUAL HARASSMENT: THEORY, RESEARCH AND TREATMENT

(W. O'Donohue, ed., 1997). V. MAGLEY, C. HULIN, L. FITZGERALD, & M. DeNARDO, *Outcomes of Self-Labeling Sexual Harassment,* JOURNAL OF APPLIED PSYCHOLOGY 84, at 390–402.

6. See M. PALUDI (ed.), PSYCHOLOGY OF SEXUAL VICTIMIZATION: A HANDBOOK (1999).

7. J. PRYOR & N. WHALEN, *A Typology of Sexual Harassment: Characteristics of Harassers and the Social Circumstances under Which Sexual Harassment Occurs,* in SEXUAL HARASSMENT: THEORY, RESEARCH AND TREATMENT (W. O'Donohue, ed., 1997).

8. L. FITZGERALD, S. SWAN, & V. MAGLEY, *But Was It Really Sexual Harassment? Legal, Behavioral, and Psychological Definitions of the Workplace Victimization of Women,* in SEXUAL HARASSMENT: THEORY, RESEARCH AND TREATMENT (W. O'Donohue, ed., 1997). M. DONOVON & F. DRASGOW, *Do Men's and Women's Experiences of Sexual Harassment Differ? An Examination of the Differential Test Functioning of the Sexual Experiences Questionnaire,* MILITARY PSYCHOLOGY 11, at 265–282.

9. U.S. MERIT SYSTEMS PROTECTION BOARD, SEXUAL HARASSMENT OF FEDERAL WORKERS: IS IT A PROBLEM? (1981).

10. U.S. MERIT SYSTEMS PROTECTION BOARD, SEXUAL HARASSMENT OF FEDERAL WORKERS: AN UPDATE (1987).

11. B. GUTEK, SEX AND THE WORKPLACE (1985).

12. L. FITZGERALD, et al., *The Incidence and Dimensions of Sexual Harassment in Academia and the Workplace,* JOURNAL OF VOCATIONAL BEHAVIOR 32, at 152–175.

13. Y. GOLD, *The Sexualization of the Workplace: Sexual Harassment of Pink-, White-, and Blue-Collar Workers,* Paper presented to the Annual Conference of the American Psychological Association (August, 1987).

14. E. LAFONTAINE & L. TREDEAU, *The Frequency, Sources, and Correlates of Sexual Harassment among Women in Traditional Male Occupations,* SEX ROLES 15, at 423–432.

15. N. BAKER, Sexual Harassment and Job Satisfaction in Traditional and Nontraditional Industrial Occupations (1989) (unpublished Ph.D. dissertation, California School of Professional Psychology, Los Angeles).

16. B. GUTEK, SEX AND THE WORKPLACE (1985).

17. S. FISKE & L. STEVENS, *What's So Special about Sex? Gender Stereotyping and Discrimination,* in GENDER ISSUES IN CONTEMPORARY SOCIETY (S. Oskamp & M. Costanzo, eds., 1993). J. DOYLE & M. PALUDI, SEX AND GENDER: THE HUMAN EXPERIENCE (1997). K. DEAUX & M. KITE, *Gender Stereotypes,* in PSYCHOLOGY OF WOMEN: A HANDBOOK OF ISSUES AND THEORIES (F. Denmark & M. Paludi, eds., 1993).

18. J. DOYLE & M. PALUDI, SEX AND GENDER: THE HUMAN EXPERIENCE (1997). N. BETZ, *Women's Career Development,* in PSYCHOLOGY OF WOMEN: A HANDBOOK OF ISSUES AND THEORIES (F. Denmark & M. Paludi, eds., 1993).

19. R. ASHMORE, *Sex, Gender, and the Individual,* in HANDBOOK OF PERSONALITY: THEORY AND RESEARCH (L. Pervin, ed., 1990).

20. J. DOYLE & M. PALUDI, SEX AND GENDER: THE HUMAN EXPERIENCE (1997).

21. B. LOTT, *The Perils and Promise of Studying Sexist Discrimination in Face-to-Face Situations,* in IVORY POWER: SEXUAL HARASSMENT ON CAMPUS (M. Paludi, ed., 1990).

22. K. DEAUX & M. KITE, *Gender Stereotypes,* in PSYCHOLOGY OF WOMEN: A HANDBOOK OF ISSUES AND THEORIES (F. Denmark & M. Paludi, eds., 1993).

23. J. DOYLE & M. PALUDI, SEX AND GENDER: THE HUMAN EXPERIENCE (1997).

24. Reprinted from K. QUINA, *The Victimization of Women,* in IVORY POWER: SEXUAL HARASSMENT ON CAMPUS (M. Paludi, ed., 1990).

25. M. PALUDI (ed.), SEXUAL HARASSMENT ON COLLEGE CAMPUSES: ABUSING THE IVORY POWER (1996).

26. J. DOYLE & M. PALUDI, SEX AND GENDER: THE HUMAN EXPERIENCE (1997).

27. M. PALUDI, ed. SEXUAL HARASSMENT ON COLLEGE CAMPUSES: ABUSING THE IVORY POWER (1996). M. Paludi, *Sexual Harassment in Schools,* in SEXUAL HARASSMENT: THEORY, RESEARCH AND TREATMENT (W. O'Donohue, ed., 1997).

28. S. ZALK, *Men in the Academy: A Psychological Profile of Harassers,* in SEXUAL HARASSMENT ON COLLEGE CAMPUSES: ABUSING THE IVORY POWER (M. Paludi, ed., 1996).

29. L. BOWES-SPERRY & J. TATA, *A Multiperspective Framework of Sexual Harassment: Reviewing Two Decades of Research,* in HANDBOOK OF GENDER AND WORK (G. Powell, et al., eds., 1999).

30. L. FITZGERALD & L. WEITZMAN, *Men Who Harass: Speculation and Data,* in IVORY POWER: SEXUAL HARASSMENT ON CAMPUS (M. Paludi, ed., 1990). M. STITES, *What's Wrong with Faculty-Student Consensual Relationships?* in SEXUAL HARASSMENT ON COLLEGE CAMPUSES: ABUSING THE IVORY POWER (M. Paludi, ed., 1996).

31. J. PRYOR, *Sexual Harassment Proclivities in Men,* SEX ROLES 17, at 269–290.

32. J. PRYOR, *Sexual Harassment Proclivities in Men,* SEX ROLES 17, at 269–290. K. QUINA, *The Victimization of Women,* in IVORY POWER: SEXUAL HARASSMENT ON CAMPUS (M. Paludi, ed., 1990).

33. L. FITZGERALD, *Sexual Harassment: Violence against Women in the Workplace,* AMERICAN PSYCHOLOGIST 48, at 1070–1076. K. QUINA, *The Victimization of Women,* in IVORY POWER: SEXUAL HARASSMENT ON CAMPUS (M. Paludi, ed., 1990). M. PALUDI (ed.), PSYCHOLOGY OF SEXUAL VICTIMIZATION: A HANDBOOK (1999).

34. L. FITZGERALD & A. ORMEROD, *Sexual Harassment in Academia and the Workplace,* in PSYCHOLOGY OF WOMEN: A HANDBOOK OF ISSUES AND THEORIES (F. Denmark & M. Paludi, eds., 1993).

35. B. GUTEK, SEX AND THE WORKPLACE (1985).

36. B. GUTEK, SEX AND THE WORKPLACE (1985).

37. B. GUTEK, SEX AND THE WORKPLACE (1985).

38. L. FITZGERALD, S. SWAN, & V. MAGLEY, *But Was It Really Sexual Harassment? Legal, Behavioral, and Psychological Definitions of the Workplace Victimization of Women,* in SEXUAL HARASSMENT: THEORY, RESEARCH AND TREATMENT (W. O'Donohue, ed., 1997). S. KURTH, B. SPILLER, & C. BROWN TRAVIS, *Consent, Power, and Sexual Scripts: Deconstructing Sexual Harassment,* in SEXUALITY, SOCIETY, AND FEMINISM (C. Brown Travis, et al., eds., 2000).

39. M. STOCKDALE, *The Direct and Moderating Influences of Sexual Harassment Pervasiveness, Coping Strategies, and Gender on Work-Related Outcomes,* PSYCHOLOGY OF WOMEN QUARTERLY 22, at 521–535. L. FITZGERALD, S. SWAN, & V. MAGLEY, *But Was It Really Sexual Harassment? Legal, Behavioral, and Psychological Definitions of the Workplace Victimization of Women,* in SEXUAL HARASSMENT: THEORY, RESEARCH AND TREATMENT (W. O'Donohue, ed., 1997).

40. S. TANGRI, et al., *Sexual Harassment at Work: Three Explanatory Models,* JOURNAL OF SOCIAL ISSUES 38, at 33–54.
41. L. FITZGERALD & L. WEITZMAN, *Men Who Harass: Speculation and Data,* in IVORY POWER: SEXUAL HARASSMENT ON CAMPUS (M. Paludi, ed., 1990).
42. A. LEVY, *The Law and Workplace Sexual Harassment,* in PSYCHOLOGY OF SEXUAL VICTIMIZATION: A HANDBOOK (M. Paludi, ed., 1999).
43. B. DANSKY & D. KILPATRICK, *Effects of Sexual Harassment,* in SEXUAL HARASSMENT: THEORY, RESEARCH AND TREATMENT (W. O'Donohue, ed., 1997). L. MUNSON, C. HULIN, & F. DRASGOW, *Longitudinal Analysis of Dispositional Influences and Sexual Harassment: Effects on Job and Psychological Outcomes,* PERSONNEL PSYCHOLOGY 53, at 21–46.
44. B. DANSKY & D. KILPATRICK, *Effects of Sexual Harassment,* in SEXUAL HARASSMENT: THEORY, RESEARCH AND TREATMENT (W. O'Donohue, ed., 1997). B. GUTEK & M. KOSS, *Changed Women and Changed Organizations: Consequences of and Coping with Sexual Harassment,* JOURNAL OF VOCATIONAL BEHAVIOR, 42, at 28–48.
45. R. THACKER & S. GOHMANN, *Emotional and Psychological Consequences of Sexual Harassment: A Descriptive Study,* JOURNAL OF PSYCHOLOGY 130, at 429–446. L. FITZGERALD, *Sexual Harassment: Violence against Women in The Workplace,* AMERICAN PSYCHOLOGIST 48, at 1070–1076. B. DANSKY & D. KILPATRICK, *Effects of Sexual Harassment,* in SEXUAL HARASSMENT: THEORY, RESEARCH AND TREATMENT (W. O'Donohue, ed., 1997).
46. B. GUTEK & M. KOSS, *Changed Women and Changed Organizations: Consequences of and Coping with Sexual Harassment,* JOURNAL OF VOCATIONAL BEHAVIOR 42, at 28–48. J. HAMILTON, S. ALAGNA, L. KING, & C. LLOYD, *The Emotional Consequences of Gender-Based Abuse in the Workplace: New Counseling Programs for Sex Discrimination,* WOMEN AND THERAPY 6, at 155–182.
47. L. FITZGERALD, *Sexual Harassment: Violence against Women In the Workplace,* AMERICAN PSYCHOLOGIST 48, at 1070–1076.
48. J. GRUBER & L. BJORN, *Women's Responses to Sexual Harassment: An Analysis of Sociocultural, Organizational, and Personal Resource Models,* SOCIAL SCIENCE QUARTERLY 67, at 814–826.
49. K. SCHNEIDER & S. SWAN, *Job-Related, Psychological, and Related Outcomes of Sexual Harassment,* paper presented to the annual conference of the Society of Industrial and Organizational Psychology (1994). B. DANSKY & D. KILPATRICK, *Effects of Sexual Harassment,* in SEXUAL HARASSMENT: THEORY, RESEARCH AND TREATMENT (W. O'Donohue, ed., 1997).
50. J. HAMILTON, S. ALAGNA, L. KING, & C. LLOYD, *The Emotional Consequences of Gender-Based Abuse in the Workplace: New Counseling Programs for Sex Discrimination,* WOMEN AND THERAPY 6, at 155–182.
51. P. CRULL, *Stress Effects of Sexual Harassment on the Job: Implications for Counseling,* AMERICAN JOURNAL OF ORTHOPSYCHIATRY 52, at 539–544.
52. K. QUINA, *The Victmization of Women,* in SEXUAL HARASSMENT ON COLLEGE CAMPUSES: ABUSING THE IVORY POWER (M. Paludi, ed., 1996).
53. L. FITZGERALD, et al., *Responses to Victimization: Validation of an Objective Policy,* JOURNAL OF COLLEGE STUDENT PERSONNEL 27, at 34–39.
54. A. ORMEROD & Y. GOLD, *Coping with Sexual Harassment: Internal and External Strategies for Coping with Stress,* paper presented to the annual conference of the Association for Women in Psychology (March, 1988).

55. M. PALUDI & R. BARICKMAN, SEXUAL HARASSMENT, WORK, AND EDUCATION: A RESOURCE MANUAL FOR PREVENTION (1998).
56. L. FITZGERALD, *Sexual Harassment: Violence against Women In the Workplace,* AMERICAN PSYCHOLOGIST 48, at 1070–1076.
57. I. MCQUEEN, *Investigating Sexual Harassment Allegations: The Employer's Challenge,* in SEXUAL HARASSMENT: THEORY, RESEARCH AND TREATMENT (W. O'Donohue, ed., 1997).
58. B. DANSKY & D. KILPATRICK, *Effects of Sexual Harassment,* in SEXUAL HARASSMENT: THEORY, RESEARCH AND TREATMENT (W. O'Donohue, ed., 1997). NEW YORK DIVISION OF HUMAN RIGHTS, *Survey of the Costs of Sexual Harassment,* in SEXUAL HARASSMENT, BUILDING A CONSENSUS FOR CHANGE (J. Avner, Chairperson, 1993).
59. S. FINERAN & L. BENNETT, *Gender and Power Issues of Peer Sexual Harassment among Teenagers,* JOURNAL OF INTERPERSONAL VIOLENCE 14, at 626–641. N. STEIN, N. MARSHALL, & L. TROPP, SECRETS IN PUBLIC: SEXUAL HARASSMENT IN OUR SCHOOLS (1993).
60. N. STEIN, *Sexual Harassment in School: The Public Performance of Gendered Violence,* HARVARD EDUCATIONAL REVIEW 65, at 145–162.
61. J. STROUSE, M. GOODWIN, & B. ROSCOE, *Correlates of Attitudes toward Sexual Harassment among Early Adolescents,* SEX ROLES 31, at 559–577. S. FINERAN & L. BENNETT, *Gender and Power Issues of Peer Sexual Harassment among Teenagers,* JOURNAL OF INTERPERSONAL VIOLENCE 14, at 626–641.
62. AMERICAN ASSOCIATION OF UNIVERSITY WOMEN, HOSTILE HALLWAYS (1993).
63. AMERICAN ASSOCIATION OF UNIVERSITY WOMEN, HOSTILE HALLWAYS (1993).
64. B. DZIECH & L. WEINER, THE LECHEROUS PROFESSOR (1984).
65. M. PALUDI, ed. SEXUAL HARASSMENT ON COLLEGE CAMPUSES: ABUSING THE IVORY POWER (1996).
66. N. BAILEY & M. RICHARDS, *Tarnishing the Ivory Tower: Sexual Harassment in Graduate Training Programs in Psychology,* paper presented at the annual meeting of the American Psychological Association (August 1985).
67. M. BOND, *Division 27 Sexual Harassment Survey: Definition, Impact, and Environmental Context,* COMMUNITY PSYCHOLOGIST 21, at 7–10.
68. L. FITZGERALD, et al., *The Incidence and Dimensions of Sexual Harassment in Academia and the Workplace,* JOURNAL OF VOCATIONAL BEHAVIOR 32, at 152–175.
69. See J. SHELTON & T. CHAVOUS, *Black and White College Women's Perceptions of Sexual Harassment,* SEX ROLES 40, at 593–615. A. BARAK, *Cross-Cultural Perspectives on Sexual Harassment,* in SEXUAL HARASSMENT: THEORY, RESEARCH AND TREATMENT (W. O'Donohue, ed., 1997). B. PIOTRKOWSKI, *Gender Harassment, Job Satisfaction, and Distress Among White and Minority Women,* JOURNAL OF OCCUPATIONAL HEALTH PSYCHOLOGY 3, at 33–43.
70. B. DZIECH & L. WEINER, THE LECHEROUS PROFESSOR (1984).
71. D. DEFOUR, *The Interface of Racism and Sexism,* in SEXUAL HARASSMENT ON COLLEGE CAMPUSES: ABUSING THE IVORY POWER (M. Paludi, ed., 1996).
72. R. BARICKMAN, et al., *Sexual Harassment of Students: Victims of the College Experience,* in VICTIMOLOGY: AN INTERNATIONAL PERSPECTIVE (E. Viano, ed., 1992).
73. B. SANDLER & M. PALUDI, EDUCATOR'S GUIDE TO CONTROLLING SEXUAL HARASSMENT (1993).

74. S. FINERAN & L. BENNETT, *Gender and Power Issues of Peer Sexual Harassment among Teenagers,* JOURNAL OF INTERPERSONAL VIOLENCE 14, at 626–641. M. Paludi (ed.), SEXUAL HARASSMENT ON COLLEGE CAMPUSES: ABUSING THE IVORY POWER (1996).

75. M. PALUDI & R. BARICKMAN, SEXUAL HARASSMENT, WORK, AND EDUCATION: A RESOURCE MANUAL FOR PREVENTION (1998). R. MOYER & A. NATH, *Some Effects of Brief Training Interventions of Sexual Harassment,* JOURNAL OF APPLIED SOCIAL PSYCHOLOGY 28, at 333–356.

76. M. PALUDI & R. BARICKMAN, SEXUAL HARASSMENT, WORK, AND EDUCATION: A RESOURCE MANUAL FOR PREVENTION (1998).

PART TWO

Preventing Sexual Harassment in the Workplace

CHAPTER 4

Avoiding Liability through an Effective Policy

Case Study

The following policy was just issued at a large manufacturing company:

It is the policy of Consolidated Dermatics that all employees be able to enjoy a work environment free from all forms of discrimination, including sexual harassment. No employee, either male or female, should be subjected to discrimination.

Sexual harassment does not refer to occasional compliments of a socially acceptable nature. It refers to: (1) unwelcome sexual advances or requests for sexual favors or other verbal or physical conduct when submission to such conduct is made either explicitly or implicitly a term or condition of an individual's employment, (2) submission to or rejection of such conduct by an individual is used as the basis for employment decisions affecting such individual, or (3) such

conduct has the purpose or effect of unreasonably interfering with an individual's work performance or creating an intimidating or hostile work environment.

Each supervisor has a responsibility to maintain the workplace free from discrimination. This includes discussing this policy with employees and assuring them that they are not to endure insulting, degrading, or exploitive sexual treatment

Procedure
Any employee who believes he or she has been the subject of discrimination, including sexual harassment, should report the alleged incident immediately to his or her supervisor and also to the Director of Personnel. An investigation will be undertaken immediately, and any employee who has been found by

the company to have discriminated against another employee will be subject to appropriate sanctions.

Any questions about this policy or the procedure should directed to your supervisor or to Marvin Donner, Director of Personnel.

INTRODUCTION

As has been seen in earlier chapters, sexual harassment is a particularly troublesome type of job discrimination. Some people contend that it involves the "normal" social interaction between the sexes and are resistant to change behavior that has been ingrained through the years. Because such reticence is not a defense to a charge of sexual harassment, a company must find ways to deal with it effectively and efficiently. Usually this means putting together a policy and procedure that works—a task that is not easy because of the unique nature of the phenomenon. It is not impossible, though, and companies that are serious about the problem are reporting great success in rooting it out through effective, comprehensive programs. The matter must be approached seriously and with a firm resolve or any undertaking will be doomed to failure. Success requires action to prevent *and* remedy sexual harassment, as well as to train the entire workforce on the various aspects of the issue.

POLICIES AND *QUID PRO QUO* HARASSMENT

As was discussed in chapter 2, when a person with authority abuses that authority by making unwelcomed threats or promises of benefits in exchange for sexual favors, the employer is in a very difficult situation. There is little, if anything, that can be done to avoid liability. Despite any policy and procedures the company may have against this type of behavior, if it happens, the employer is liable. A business should try to prevent it with appropriate training and sanctions, but if an investigation shows that quid pro quo harassment occurred, the company should do whatever it can to remedy the problem for the affected employee. Then, it is probably time to remove the offending manager from the workplace before more trouble occurs!

POLICIES AND HOSTILE ENVIRONMENT HARASSMENT

Hostile environment situations operate somewhat differently with regard to employer liability. Because businesses are not strictly liable in those situations, there is an opportunity to take affirmative actions that will limit the potential for lawsuits and legal liability. The courts and the EEOC have put great emphasis on the need for effective, workable, fail-safe policies and procedures for the elimination of sexual harassment, and cases are now being dismissed in which employers have these in place. The *Ellerth* "affirmative defense" reiterated the Supreme Court's focus on the requirement that employers be involved in comprehensive programs to rid the workplace of harassment in order to avoid liability.

An Overview of an Effective Policy

A good policy requires more than a statement of compliance with the law. It must be designed to both prevent harassment and remedy any which might occur. Many courts have noted that the cases before them would never have come before them if the employer had taken care of the problem by instituting such a policy and carrying it out in an appropriate manner. The Supreme Court itself, in *Meritor Savings Bank v. Vinson,* made it clear that effective policies and procedures need to be carefully thought out. As the justices stated, the Court did not accept the argument that "the mere existence of a grievance procedure and a policy against discrimination, coupled with respondent's failure to invoke that procedure" protected an employer from liability.

What, then, must a policy and procedure include? As a starting point, it is helpful to look at the EEOC's guidelines, which lay down the framework for the goals of an effective program.

> Prevention is the best tool for the elimination of sexual harassment. An employer should take all steps necessary to prevent sexual harassment from occurring, such as affirmatively raising the subject, expressing strong disapproval, developing appropriate sanctions, informing employees of their right to raise and how to raise the issue of harassment under Title VII, and developing methods to sensitize all concerned.

Obviously, however, this is just a framework. Cases in which courts have made comments about the adequacy or, more usually, the inadequacy of the policies in the cases before them, help fill out this structure. In at least one case, *Robinson v. Jacksonville Shipyards,*[1] the court supervised the design of a policy and procedure, giving employers an excellent example to use as a guide. A copy of that policy is included in the Appendix.

Although many businesses may believe that their current policies are adequate, many are still deficient in important areas. No particular form is necessary, but there are certain aspects that courts continually look for and that will help a business eliminate problems long before a court or government agency has to even look at the policy. A paragraph expressing disapproval is clearly inadequate in today's legal climate; the policy approved by the court in *Robinson* required the company to put together a veritable manual, many pages in length. Though this is not required, it is an indication that a sentence or two will not be adequate.

Key Elements in an Effective Policy

There are several important elements that must be in an effective policy. A company that pays attention to each of these will be doing what is necessary to put together a program that will meet the needs of employees and managers and that will stand the ultimate test in court, if that should ever become necessary. Interestingly, a court test of a policy probably will never happen if the policy is designed to do what it would be tested for: its ability to prevent and handle problems before they get out of control and before the level of legal liability is reached.

Setting an Appropriate Tone   An overriding consideration for any sexual harassment policy is whether it sets a tone of appropriate seriousness and concern for the employees' rights. There are many ways that this is accomplished, including making sure that *everyone,* from the lowest-level workers to the highest-level managers, knows of the seriousness of the matter and of their responsibility in carrying out this policy.

Creating a Separate Sexual Harassment Policy   The courts have made it clear that a general policy against discrimination is inadequate with regard to sexual harassment liability. Because sexual harassment presents unique problems with regard to identifying problem behavior and reporting requirements, the EEOC has supported the view that a separate policy needs to be adopted. Thus, a sexual harassment policy must be clearly identified with procedures that may differ, if necessary, from the normal complaint procedures in effect at the company.

In the case study, the company has a general-purpose policy, rather than a specific policy designed for eradicating sexual harassment. This may be deemed inadequate if it is challenged in a complaint or lawsuit.

Expressing Strong Disapproval   It is not enough to state that sexual harassment is forbidden. The policy must communicate the company's serious and strong disapproval of any such behavior or conduct. The seriousness of the company's commitment should be made clear in the choice of language used and in the comprehensiveness of the program. Giving a high-level person with strong authority ultimate responsibility for carrying out this policy and communicating that fact to the employees is also a good way to show the seriousness with which the company views this matter. Employees are very perceptive. They will only take seriously that which the management takes seriously, and they can see through perfunctory attempts at compliance with the law. If the workforce believes that this is a very important matter to the company and that it will be dealt with it in an appropriate manner, many potential harassers will fall into line.

In the case study, the person identified with the policy appears to be Marvin Donner, the director of personnel. It is important that Donner be someone of authority who is known to be respected by the employees and the company "higher ups." Workers know that "big jobs" go to "big people" and will draw inferences about the employer's commitment from the people named in the policy. Perhaps the CEO should be listed or write a letter that is appended to the policy.

Encouraging Reports   It is not enough that the policy *allows* for a reporting of behavior or conduct. According to the U.S. Supreme Court and the EEOC, it must *encourage* victims to come forward. This can be specifically stated, but the tone of the policy will really make the difference between allowing and encouraging.

It is a good idea to preface the policy with a statement that the company is not just dealing with this because it presents the potential for legal problems. By stating that harassment has no place in the company and serves no business purpose and that the well-being of the employees is important to management, the employer is telling the employees that this is a place where people care about more than just their productivity. This creates an atmosphere in which people perceive their own problems as important to their managers and an environment in which they will feel comfortable resisting or reporting inappropriate and unwelcome behavior.

Clarifying Prohibited Conduct   Employees and managers must know what it is that they are expected to do or not do. As chapters 2 and 3 make clear, it is not easy to define the exact parameters of sexual harassment and the law continues to expand the definition. It is possible to give an understanding, however, by a general description of the various types and some examples.

Specifics   The big question with regard to whether a policy clearly communicates is whether all of the people in the workplace understand exactly what types of behavior, conduct, or work rules are being prohibited. A company must tell them in no uncertain terms. There is no good business purpose in being evasive, and evasive language can only result in an inadequate policy. If an employer makes it clear that the examples given are just examples and that prohibited conduct can take many forms, there will be no problem with workers thinking that they have a comprehensive list of what can't be done and that everything else is fair game.

Retaliation

A policy should specifically point out that retaliation is a violation of the law and company policy and will be dealt with as a separate violation. As stated in the legal requirements chapter, this is an area in which employers can find themselves facing even more liability as retaliation claims are on the increase.

The case study policy does not mention retaliation as prohibited conduct, and workers could claim that they were unaware that this was not allowed. Making it clear will solve that problem.

Discuss the Time Frames for Filing Charges

Recently, the EEOC noted that an anti-harassment policy needs to contain information about the time frames for filing charges of unlawful harassment with the EEOC or state fair employment practice agencies. Also, it requires that the policy further explain that the deadline for filing runs from the last date that harassment occurred, not from the date that the complaint is resolved by the employer.

Using Understandable Language and Terms

It is a good idea to begin with the EEOC's definition of sexual harassment. A mistake made by many companies, however, is to think that this, by itself, is adequate. No one, including lawyers, can gain a good understanding of sexual harassment merely from reading the very legalistic and convoluted language contained in the guidelines. Employees should not be expected to do so either. Certainly, it is clear that sexual harassment has a legal definition and lawyers will continue to use it as the basis for lawsuits; however, a company's policy is not written for lawyers or judges. It is written for people of varying intellectual abilities and educational backgrounds, and all of them need to understand it.

The case-study policy does contain the EEOC definition but nothing further. How likely are the members of the workforce to understand this legalese? Does the coldness of the definition take away from an encouraging tone?

The policy ordered by the court in *Robinson* used the following language: "The management of Jacksonville Shipyards, Inc. considers the following conduct to represent some of the types of acts that violate JSI's Sexual Harassment Policy." The policy then goes on to list a series of examples under headings ranging from physical assaults of a sexual nature to sexual or discriminatory displays or publications anywhere in the workplace to retaliation for sexual harassment complaints. As stated previously, it is vital that specific examples of each be given and that retaliation be specifically singled out as a form of harassment and, thus, prohibited conduct. Retaliation, in the *Robinson* policy's definition of the term, can take many forms, including pressuring someone to drop a complaint, refusing to cooperate with an investigation, or falsely denying a complaint. It may, in fact, be better described to employees as retaliation or obstruction of an investigation.

What is missing from the *Robinson* policy is a listing of conduct that, although not sexual in nature, is still a form of gender harassment. This would include demeaning comments, general statements about the inadequacy of people of certain genders to perform certain tasks, and joking about the difficulty a person of one gender may have performing certain duties (for example, a woman who must exert more effort to lift a required weight). This type of behavior is what has recently been specifically included in the EEOC's definition of sexual harassment or, as it really should be termed, harassment on the basis of one's gender.

Explaining the Concept of "Unwelcome"

A business should help its employees differentiate between a socially acceptable, polite compliment or overture for a date and sexual harassment by reinforcing that the basis of a finding that conduct is harassment is that it is unwelcome. It should be carefully noted, however, that this is not always easy to determine and that silence or the fact that someone appears to be joining in should not necessarily be taken to mean that a particular conduct is welcome. A statement should be included that makes clear that it should be presumed that any sexual or demeaning comments, behavior, displays, and so on are unwelcome and also that, once a polite compliment or overture for a date has been turned down or any manifestation given that they are not wanted, the overtures should immediately cease.

The policy in the case study uses the term "unwelcome" yet does not explain it. This may not be helpful to the workers, who may not understand what it means or how it may be manifested.

Prohibiting Harassment Regardless of the Source

It is now fairly certain that an employer will be liable no matter who is involved in the harassing conduct. It should be made clear to the employees that they need not endure unwelcome overtures, comments, glances, or any other harassing behavior whether it is from a coworker, supervisor, manager from another department, customer, client, supplier, or salesperson. They should be assured that any violation of the policy, no matter who is involved, will be dealt with in a serious manner and appropriate action will be taken. A policy should state specifically that no one, no matter how highly placed in the organization, is exempt from these requirements or from being disciplined accordingly for violations.

Describing the Process for Reporting Violations

Because the policy and procedures should be designed both to prevent and to remedy harassment, a system must be put into place that will make employees feel comfortable in reporting problems. As previously stated, the courts and the EEOC continue to demand that the procedures be designed to encourage victims to come forward, not merely to allow them to report.

Creating "Fail-Safe" Procedures

The best advice with regard to deciding who should receive reports about sexual harassment is to give ultimate responsibility to someone who has authority and the respect of other workers. A business should make this a "fail-safe" system, however, by giving the employees alternates for reporting. These alternatives may include the employee's own supervisor, but, for several reasons, courts and the EEOC have stated that procedures that *require* complaining first to the next person in command will be deemed ineffective. The supervisor may be the offending party or may not be someone with whom the employee feels comfortable. In fact, if many employees tend to opt to report elsewhere, a prudent employer will use this as evidence that a particular manager may not be handling sexual harassment appropriately and should take steps to handle the problem. Although a requirement that employees go through specific channels is appropriate in the workplace in most respects, it is not advisable in sexual-harassment situations. An employer can best get a handle on any problems by making it as easy as possible to come forward.

Because it has been proven that talking about sexual harassment is difficult, especially for women, some thought should be given to naming at least one woman who has the authority to receive complaints. As with all parties involved in the process, the responsible people must be given adequate authority to go forward with complaints and training to receive them sensitively.

The case study policy does provide that behavior be reported to the supervisor and the director of Personnel. If this were an alternate reporting procedure, it would be much better. As written, this "chain of command" requirement is a major flaw in the policy. The policy also has not identified a woman who is authorized to receive complaints. This may be seen as allowing rather than encouraging reports.

Specifying Complete Complaint Procedures

A policy should not just give the title of the people, beyond the employee's own supervisor, who are designated to handle complaints. Although top managers may be well aware of the identity of the director of human relations in large companies, especially, those employees who are at the lower echelons may only know that he or she exists in some office at the other end of the building. The company should specifically list the person who is in charge of the policy and to whom complaints may be addressed, giving the name, contact information, and office location. In addition, a statement should be included assuring anyone who wishes to speak to these people that they should feel comfortable requesting an interview and that they will be accommodated, as much as possible, with regard to work or other scheduling considerations.

How would someone find Donner, in the case study company? Does everyone know who he is or where to find him? Probably not.

Reports by Anyone

It must be made clear that providing a universally conducive workplace is everyone's responsibility and that everyone has a right to feel comfortable in their work environment. Thus, a worker need not be the direct focus of harassing behavior to come forward and report the problem. Third parties should be urged to file a report, even if they are unsure about the potential victim's feelings about the behavior. A policy should state that an investigation will be undertaken to determine whether there is a problem and that a determination of whether the conduct was welcomed need not be made before reporting. It must be remembered, however, that conduct that is determined to be welcomed by the employee who is the focus of the harassment may still be contributing to a hostile environment for the third party and may have to be dealt with in any case.

Oral or Written Reports

Although it is preferable to have a written report by the person lodging the complaint, some workers do not feel comfortable expressing themselves in writing. It is also possible that some workers may not be able to read or write or have some learning disability that does not allow them to file written reports. (This is why it is advisable to go over the policy orally with all workers and explain it to them.) Thus, to encourage reporting, oral reports should be allowed. The person to whom the report is given orally may take notes about the situation during the interview. This can be reviewed for accuracy with the person making the complaint.

Anonymous Complaints

There are certainly some problems involved in allowing reports of harassing behavior without requiring the identity of the person making the complaint. As businesses find when they use suggestion boxes, however, they often learn a great deal more about the real situation when a specific individual need not be associated with the report. This is to the employer's benefit with regard to sexual harassment, when remedying problems and preventing escalation is paramount in avoiding extensive liability and legal costs. Anonymous complaints encourage reporting.

Anonymous reports can be carefully handled to minimize the possibility of them being used for vindictive or other purposes. If anonymous reports are allowed, a company may want to state that the anonymous reports might be handled differently from identified reports. The investigations may be undertaken if they are deemed to be credible, but the investigations may be more informal. In addition, remedies could be different, as dismissal without an identified report, for example, would be unlikely.

A company should encourage people to give their names, and, if too many anonymous complaints come in, try to determine why. Is there something about the workplace or the procedures that makes people afraid to give their names? This must be remedied. Anonymous complaint procedures will be discussed again in chapter 5.

Describing the Investigation Process

It is always more encouraging to become involved in a process when the potential participant understands what the process entails. Fear of the unknown can discourage reporting. Every workplace will have its own way of handling complaints based on its structure, the size of its staff, and other considerations, but an explanation of the process— whatever it is—is important. Certain elements should be involved in every process.

Employees should be assured that reports will be taken seriously and that an investigation will be undertaken promptly by someone trained to handle such situations. Then the promise must be carried out. It is not good to delay or put off an investigation for any reason other than the request of the complaining party. The courts and the EEOC mean it when they say that immediate action is required. This requires that, within a few days of receiving a report, the process should begin and a final report and remedial action be undertaken within a week or two, at the most. Unremedied situations have a way of getting out of hand, and this is something that should be avoided at all costs.

It is also important to ensure confidentiality as much as possible. Employees must believe, with good basis, that once a report is made, it will not become the subject of workplace gossip. The procedures should be designed to maintain secrecy and the employees should be made aware of that. This requires that those involved in the investigation be made aware of the need to keep all information as confidential as possible. Anyone who is informed of the complaint or any part of the investigation must only be told on a "need-to-know" basis. Separate locked files should be kept for records on complaints and investigations, with the keys carefully controlled. Everyone who is at all involved, from the investigator to the secretary who types the reports to the clerk who files them, should be trained to keep the information secret and told that any violations will be deemed and handled as very serious matters.

Employees must be told that it will be impossible to keep the report totally secret because there will have to be interviews with the alleged harasser and with any witnesses identified by either party. The policy should note, however, that in every way possible the confidentiality of the report will be paramount in the process. Investigators should look carefully at all parts of the process to be sure that this promise is kept. Are there soundproof, separate rooms for investigations and interviews? How will the company ensure that gossip doesn't center around who entered that room? Who will be involved in the investigation, and have they been adequately trained with regard to confidentiality? These and other questions must be carefully examined because the courts and the EEOC will be looking not just at what a company says it will do but also whether, in fact, it does it.

Complainants must believe that they will be treated with respect and in a serious manner. A trained investigator would not joke or make lighthearted comments during an interview. She or he should not address a complainant by their first name (unless invited to do so), wander in and out of the interview room, or smile inappropriately. Employees should be told that they should expect a serious investigation and that this is what will happen. They will be treated with respect and should expect nothing less.

The case study policy does not adequately describe the process for investigation. The employees at the company do not know what to expect if they file a complaint and may not be encouraged to do so.

Ensuring Follow-up Procedures

Once the investigation is completed and remedial measures taken, if appropriate, the complainants should not feel that they are on their own. They must be reassured by a description of the follow-up procedures. These procedures should involve, at a minimum, inquiries to make sure that harassment has not resumed and that the complainant has not suffered any retaliation. As always, it is vital not just to say that a follow-up will occur but, rather, to actually carry this out in every case.

Describing Penalties and Discipline

It is important to assure workers that the process is designed to "make them whole," a legal term that means they should not suffer any lasting consequences from the harassment. They must not be transferred without their consent; they must not be required to take an unwanted leave, and the company should inform them that it will take care of any adverse results of the harassment. This may require such actions as crediting sick leave banks for time taken as a result of the harassment, giving extra time and/or paying for counseling, reevaluating personal evaluations that could reflect bias, or taking any necessary steps to ensure that harassed employees are put back in the position they would have been in had the harassment not occurred.

A vital part of any policy and procedures tells the workers what the possibilities are if they choose to violate the rules. Discipline should be quickly handed out once the investigation is complete and should reflect both the severity of the incident and the perpetrator's history in this regard.

As the EEOC has stated, discipline should be designed to end the harassment and prevent the misconduct from occurring. Often this will require not only handing out the appropriate discipline but also reminding the harasser that the policy provides for stricter penalties, up to and including dismissal, for continued misbehavior.

A policy should describe the disciplines that are possible and make clear that discipline will be based on the individual situation but can include dismissal. The policy should also state that continuation or further instances of harassing behavior after an employee has been found guilty of a violation of the policy will result in much more severe penalties. Specific examples should be given of possible discipline, whether that is dismissal, transfer of the harasser, a demotion, pay increase denials or pay reductions, adverse performance evaluations, or formal reprimands in the worker's file.

Many courts have found that a procedure that allows for merely asking the offending employee to stop the behavior is inadequate. If the policy has been clearly communicated to employees, such behavior should be viewed as breaking a company rule and treated accordingly. At a minimum, if the employer believes that a verbal reprimand is adequate because of the relatively minor content of the behavior, the harassed employee should be consulted as to her or his feelings on the matter. Do they think this is adequate? Why or why not?

Interestingly, at least one court has stated that, in certain situations, the mere presence of a harasser may create a hostile environment and, if transfer to another location is not possible, the harasser may have to be dismissed, even though it may be a first offense. Each situation, including the past history of the harasser and the seriousness of the allegations, must be judged on its own merits. It has been noted, for example, that "in some cases the mere presence of an employee who has engaged in particularly severe or pervasive harassment can create a hostile working environment."[2] The investigator can only make the determination of what each situation requires, after consultation with the complainant.

Consultation with the employee who has been harassed is vital with regard to any discipline decision. Studies show that most employees simply want the harassment to stop and the matter to be forgotten, rather than wanting "revenge." They can be helpful in deciding how that can best be accomplished.

The case study policy merely states that an employee will be subject to appropriate sanctions. What does that term mean? The ambiguous word would be clearly inadequate, and the company needs to be more specific.

EFFECTIVE COMMUNICATION OF THE POLICY

Once it is put together, a company's sexual harassment policy must be clearly and regularly communicated to the employees. At the least, businesses should have their policies sent to all employees; posted in prominent locations throughout the workplace using graffiti-resistant paper for the posters; and pointed out to and included in any materials given to new employees. The responsibility for communicating the policy must be made a part of the job description of anyone with authority in the workplace. If the poster is taken down, it should be replaced and an investigation undertaken to determine the source of the removal, as it may be an indication of a potential hostile environment problem already in existence. To be absolutely sure that the policy is being adequately communicated, it might be advisable to have employees sign a sheet that they have been given a copy of the policy and procedures and that they understand it (some companies do this only for new employees, although to be completely careful everyone should be included). This signing should be done only after the employee is asked if there are any questions he or she would like answered and should be done in a noncoercive manner, probably by a supervisor or the head of personnel. Anyone who is going to be involved in presenting the policy and procedures to other employees should be carefully trained to do so in an appropriately serious manner and to answer any questions that might come up.

It is also a good idea for the policy to be accompanied by a letter from someone highly placed and respected at the company, preferably the CEO, expressing the company's serious commitment to the policy and to providing a workplace that is conducive to the success of all employees. It does not hurt for this letter to include an invitation to employees to approach the CEO (or whoever signs the letter for the company), if the employee feels that inadequate or inappropriate attention is being paid to complaints.

COMPLIANCE AS EVERY MANAGER'S RESPONSIBILITY

Compliance with the policy and a managerial approach that pays close attention to the workplace environment should be required of all supervisory personnel. A manager's efforts with regard to ensuring a nondiscriminatory workplace and in investigating and dealing with situations that occur should be a well-known part of all managers' performance evaluations. It should be made clear to all managers that the company views broadly its managers' responsibility in this regard. Merely investigating complaints is inadequate. The manager should also make it his or her continual duty to know what is going on in the workplace and to personally handle any situations that occur, whether reported or observed. This may include the responsibility to inquire sensitively as to the welcomeness of observed sexual advances, even if there is no outward indication of a problem. Of course, this also includes the duty to remove any and all demeaning materials and to make clear that they will not be tolerated.

The case study policy makes this important element clear. This is a strong point in its favor if it is challenged.

AFFIRMATIVE DIAGNOSTIC PROCEDURES

When an employee leaves a company, an exit interview is always a good idea. When it includes questions designed to find out about possible sexual harassment problems, it is even a better idea. Sensitively inquiring as to a person's reason for leaving the employment and also about any problems that were not the cause of the employee's leaving will help the company do a better job of controlling harassing behavior. Assuring them that reports of inappropriate conduct will not result in adverse consequences and will be subject to the same confidentiality any such complaint would receive (hopefully the program is so seriously conducted that this will not elicit laughter from the employee) will help in encouraging honest responses. If the exit interviewer is well trained and the interviewee is really comfortable as to his or her protection, an employer may find out vital information and can deal with situations before they get out of hand.

If the interviewer finds that sexual harassment is the *cause* of the employee's exit, she or he should immediately alert the company, and every effort should be made to keep the employee from leaving, including offers of a different job location, adequate measures to halt the problem, and discipline of the offender. Some businesspeople are under the false assumption that if any employee voluntarily leaves, the company cannot be liable for damages caused by the sexual harassment. This is not the case. Under the doctrine of constructive discharge, an employee can receive any or all of the remedies provided by law even if they resign, and in some states they have up to 3 years to bring a lawsuit. The courts feel that when conditions are intolerable, the situation should be viewed as if the employee was fired. This allows an award of back pay. Of course, attorney fees and pain and suffering damages may also be available.

IN BRIEF

Beth Ann Faragher v. City of Boca Raton
U.S. Supreme Court
1998

Issue: What is the standard of employer liability when the acts of a supervisor have created a hostile work environment for subordinates?

Facts: Between 1985 and 1990, while attending college, Beth Ann Faragher worked part time and during the summers as an ocean lifeguard for the City of Boca Raton. During this time, her supervisors were Bill Terry, Chief of the Marine Safety Division, David Silverman and Robert Gordon, Marine Safety lieutenants and later captains, who reported directly to Terry. During the five years that she worked for the City, Terry subjected Faragher to repeated touching and crude demeaning references to women. In addition, he stated that he would never promote a woman to the rank of lieutenant. Silverman behaved in similar ways, once tackling Faragher, telling her that he would have sex with her except for a characteristic that he found unattractive, pantomimed an act of oral sex, made vulgar references to women and sexual matters, and commented on the bodies of female lifeguards and beachgoers. Faragher did not complain to higher management, but did discuss the situation with Gordon, who did not take further action or inform other city officials.

Decision: Employers are subject to vicarious liability for "hostile" environment sexual harassment created by a supervisor with immediate (or successively higher) authority over the victimized employee. When no tangible employment action is taken, an employer may raise an affirmative defense to liability or damages. This requires that the employer prove, by a preponderance of the evidence, that the employer exercised reasonable care to prevent and correct promptly any sexually harassing behavior, and that the employee unreasonably failed to take advantage of any preventive or corrective opportunities provided by the employer or to avoid harm otherwise.

Ultimate conclusion for the plaintiff: Because the District Court had found that the elements for a "hostile environment" sexual-harassment case had been satisfied and the Supreme Court could find no facts in the opinion that would show that the City had exercised reasonable care, the District Court's award of one dollar in minimal damages was reinstated.

In addition, when an employee reports that she or he is leaving because of sexual harassment, the company should reexamine its anti-harassment program. Why did this employee not feel that the situation could be handled adequately while they were in the company's employ? Why did she or he feel it necessary to leave rather than report? This signals the possibility that the policy and procedures have flaws, which might render them ineffective as defenses to a sexual harassment charge.

A business should not wait for people to leave before questioning them. Periodic questionnaires should be sent out promising confidentiality. Consideration should also be given to making the responses anonymous. A variety of questions should be asked that will help the company perform better, but it is important to make sure that they are carefully designed to find out about harassment problems. It is not enough to ask: Have you been sexually harassed at the company? Many people would not label certain behavior as harassment (although programs should be helping them do so). Instead, questions should be designed to elicit the necessary information, even if the person filling out the questionnaire does not understand the legal terminology: How comfortable are you in your workplace—very—moderately—not very—very uncomfortable? What causes you stress on the job: supervisor's unreasonable demands—coworkers' behavior—production demands—long hours—and so on? Carefully crafted surveys can be invaluable in searching out all sorts of workforce problems but especially in locating the source of potential sexual harassment situations.

SUMMARY

In conclusion, a legally adequate policy for getting to the heart of harassment problems in the workplace requires more than a general statement against the behavior. It requires the efforts and support of management at all levels and continual training of all workers, as well as a procedure that *encourages* not just allows complaints. The next two chapters will discuss the legal and psychological considerations once the policy works and complaints come forward. With both a policy and the procedure for carrying it out in place, not only will the business be on stronger footing in any legal action, it will find that, human relations–wise, the entire workforce benefits from an environment of cooperation and respect. This can only reap benefits for the employer.

FOR REFLECTION

1. Discuss the difference between a policy that allows victims to come forward and one that *encourages* them.

2. Analyze why a separate sexual harassment policy is required.
3. Discuss some examples of types of behavior that could be viewed as sexual harassment and the discipline that would be appropriate for each.
4. Explain why it is important to explain the investigation procedures to employees.
5. Explain what the term "fail-safe" means with regard to a sexual harassment policy.

Notes

1. 760 F.Supp. 1486 (M.D. Fla 1991).
2. *Ellison v. Brady*, 924 F.2d at 883.

CHAPTER 5

Legal Requirements for Investigating and Remedying Sexual Harassment

Case Study

As you will recall from chapter 2, Victoria Janus and Marjorie Mattis had a problem with a pinup poster that was placed in the workplace. Victoria finally quit her job, but Marjorie stayed. After a few weeks, she began to notice that the men were excluding her from work discussions and that her tools were being taken while she was away from her work space. One day she came in and found herself surrounded by four men who began grabbing at her and asking if she wanted to "show that she was a real woman right here." When they finally went away laughing, Marjorie decided to take her complaint

to the human resources department. When she told them of her problem, they asked her to type out the complaint and sign it. She did this and then was told to go back to work, and they would contact her if they needed anything further.

After six weeks of hearing nothing and being subjected to continued behavior that she found offensive, Marjorie overheard one of the men talking about her complaint. "Yeah, HR put a note in Fred's file about the complaint. Someone's got to pay for that, right?" Marjorie then went to the HR office and was told that the complaint had been taken care of, but they couldn't discuss the details with her as it involved information about another employee.

Has the company done all it is required to do in this situation and, if not, where does it fall short?

INTRODUCTION

Because the Supreme Court and the EEOC have continually maintained their focus on the need for remedying sexual harassment as quickly and effectively as possible, the law has ventured into an area usually left only to human-resource profession-als—deciding what does and does not constitute an adequate investigational procedure and proper remedial action. The next chapter will outline considerations that should be considered with regard to the psychological aspects of an investigation and remedy. This chapter discusses what the courts and the EEOC have had to say in this regard. For ease of discussion, the term *resolution process* will be used to refer to investigating and remedying harassment.

Businesses often mistake their role in sexual-harassment procedures as one in which a decision is made as to whether the situation is serious enough to meet the level of legal liability. This means that remedies are often only applied in the most egregious cases, in essence, in those that are at the courthouse's door. This misinterprets the requirements of the law completely. As the EEOC confirmed in its policy guidance issued after *Ellerth:*

> The policy should encourage employees to report harassment *before* it becomes severe or pervasive. While isolated incidents of harassment generally do not violate federal law, a pattern of such incidents may be unlawful. Therefore, to discharge its duty of preventive care, the employer must make clear to employees that it will stop harassment before it rises to the level of a violation of federal law.

The Fifth Circuit also noted in a recent case:

> First, when a plaintiff promptly complains about . . . inappropriate sexual actions, she can thwart the creation of a hostile work environment. To the extent redress is sought, is justified, and is adequately provided by the company, the complained-of incidents will not likely have become severe or pervasive enough to create an actionable Title VII claim. This result effectuates the purpose of Title VII, which cannot guarantee civility in the American workplace but, at its best, inspires prophylactic measures to deter unwanted sexual harassment. By promptly invoking a company's grievance procedures, a plaintiff has received the benefit Title VII was

meant to confer. In such cases, an actionable hostile environment claim will rarely if ever have matured.[1]

Policies and procedures must be designed to solve all harassing conduct, whether or not it "affects a term, condition, or privilege of employment." Anything less is foolhardy, as a fire avoided is far better for the bottom line than a fire extinguished. Although there are no absolute rules as to how best to "avoid the fire," EEOC Guidelines and cases in which businesses claimed to have adequately investigated and dealt with harassment help guide business as to what considerations are vital to be able to use the affirmative defense, should an outside complaint be filed. You may recall that this defense requires that the employer exercised reasonable care to prevent and correct promptly any sexually harassing behavior and that the plaintiff unreasonably failed to take advantage of any preventive or corrective opportunities provided by the employer or to avoid harassment otherwise. It must be remembered, though, that this defense is only available in a hostile environment situation and a *quid pro quo* situation will not be absolutely settled by any type of policy, investigation, or internal remedy.

The EEOC first discussed what it would be looking for in a resolution process in 1980. Since then, it has refined the criteria with a policy guidance in 1990[2] and an enforcement guidance in 1999,[3] in response to the Supreme Court's decision in the *Ellerth* case. Taken as a whole, these offer great assistance to businesses on how to carry out an investigation and appropriately remedy conduct that is found to have occurred.

In 1980, the EEOC responded to the Supreme Court's *Vinson* decision by specifying that prevention is the best tool for the elimination of sexual harassment and that employers should take all steps necessary to prevent it from occurring. The 1990 guidance stated that an employer's responsibility is to investigate promptly and thoroughly, take immediate and appropriate corrective action by doing what is necessary to end the harassment, make the victim whole by restoring lost employment benefits or opportunities, and prevent the misconduct from recurring.

With regard to its role, the EEOC has noted that, when a complaint is filed, if the commission finds that harassment has been eliminated, all victims made whole, and preventive measures instituted, it will normally close the administrative complaint file. Although the employee may still file a lawsuit in federal court, it is highly likely that the EEOC's determination of adequate response will result in the judge dismissing the case before it can go to trial. In essence, a determination by the EEOC, which is in charge of Title VII, that the employer has satisfied the elements for the affirmative defense will be very persuasive in all legal arenas.

WHEN AN INVESTIGATION MUST BE UNDERTAKEN

It is clear that an investigation must be undertaken when a formal complaint of alleged sexual harassment is filed. In addition, an employer is required to investigate when a supervisor or manager is told of harassment, even if that person is not officially designated to receive complaints and even if the complaint is not made in an "official" manner. In other words, once the employer knows, the requirement of responsive action begins, and an employer knows when someone with workplace authority is made aware of it.

Awareness can come through various means, including seeing clearly unwelcome conduct. An example of this would be the requirement of removing demeaning or sexual graffiti or displays without waiting for a complaint.

The responsibility to undertake a resolution process is not changed even if a union grievance or arbitration process is under way that deals with the harassing behavior. According to the EEOC, the union proceeding deals with the collective interests of a bargaining unit under the contract, which may or may not focus on an individual's rights under the anti-harassment policy.

Promptness

Once the employer is made aware of an alleged incident of sexual harassment, an investigation must be undertaken as quickly as possible, preferably within no more than a few days. In fact, unless there are extenuating circumstances, the process should begin as soon as the complaint is received. The process itself should be finished in days or a few weeks, but certainly not in months. It must be remembered that, during the time of the investigation, the potential for further problems is great and the stress level of those involved will be high. Thus, it is in the best interests of the employer, as well as the employees, that the EEOC's term "immediate corrective action" be viewed as meaning exactly what it says.

Recall the case study that began this chapter. Was the investigation prompt?

Confidentiality

To the greatest extent possible, sexual-harassment complaints and investigations should be kept confidential. A separate filing system for investigation files (except for those involving discipline) should be kept and all persons involved routinely reminded about their duties in this regard. In one case, a court even noted that the showing of an employee's sexual harassment complaint to the alleged harasser added to ineffectiveness of the investigation.[4]

In the case study, do you have some indication that the company did not maintain the confidentiality requirements?

Impartiality

It is vital that a neutral party carries out the investigation. Though any-one working for the employer could conceivably be viewed as "partial" to the employer's interests, there has never been a requirement that someone outside of the company handle the investigation. In fact, third parties may create even more problems than they solve. These may include privacy concerns and the interplay of other laws. One such situation recently arose when the Federal Trade Commission issued an opinion letter that outside investigators would be considered "consumer reporting agencies" and, thus, were subject to the Fair Credit Reporting Act, which places extensive requirements on those who are paid to assemble and evaluate information on consumers. In addition, an internal person, if well-trained and clearly supported by the employer, will bring a unique understanding of the business that may be important to a good investigation, no matter what action must be taken.

It is important, however, that the people who will be in charge of the investigation not be linked to either party. In fact, anyone in the direct chain of command could be seen to be partial to either the employee making the complaint or the person against whom the complaint has been filed. If there is any possibility that a claim of partiality can be made, it would be best for the employer if another person is involved.

There are reasons, however, that the employees' supervisor may be helpful as a part of the investigation team. If both parties are comfortable with such involvement, supervisors can show their concern and will be made keenly aware of their responsibilities for nonretaliation, confidentiality, and impartiality. They may also be able to add insight, due to their day-to-day interactions with the parties that a person who is not always in the workplace may not grasp. Of course, if the supervisor is involved in any way with the harassment or if there is any concern on the part of either party about their presence, they should not be included. Reminding them of their duties of nonretaliation, confidentiality, and impartiality should be reinforced, no matter whether they are involved or not, both throughout the process and afterward.

The issue of whether an attorney should perform the investigation is often debated. On one hand, there is a feeling that a lawyer will know the law and what can and can't be done and that any documents could be protected in a lawsuit under the concept of attorney-client privilege. On the other hand, it is obvious that attorneys could bring a feeling of excessive formality to the process that may inhibit the free exchange of information and a desire for parties and even witnesses to bring attorneys as well.

Although it is certainly a decision that each business should make, it is probably best to have people well-trained in the psychological and human aspects of personnel matters (see the next chapter) perform the investigation, fully supported by the availability of an attorney should questions occur. Investigations usually involve issues of deciding facts and determining credibility, areas that attorneys are not uniquely trained for (in court this is left to a judge or jury). In addition, it can be argued that attorneys have a strong partiality toward the employer, especially if they will be called on to defend the employer if a lawsuit is filed. Documents involving the complaint, investigation, and remedial action will most likely be necessary if the employer is to prove the affirmative defense, so privilege will be of limited value in most circumstances.

Many sources advise using two people to perform the investigation—one male and one female. This will allow the possible differences in perception by gender to be taken into account. Also, having two people will allow one to take notes while the other asks questions. The comfort of the witness should be paramount, however, as a business does not want its process to be a problem itself, either in creating a hostile environment or in taking away the opportunity to use the affirmative defense.

Training of the people who will be doing the investigation is vital, however, no matter who is involved. This will include education on all of the legal requirements, as well as the psychological considerations, that are very important in carrying out a process that will not inhibit further complaints. The EEOC has stated that a process that is reasonably believed to be ineffective or unnecessarily intimidating or burdensome will negate the ability of an employer to claim the affirmative defense if an employee fails to report internally.

A sense of impartiality is important throughout the process. There should be no opinions expressed by those carrying out the investigation to anyone during the process and most certainly not offered during interviews with the parties or witnesses. An "I'm here to get to the truth no matter what that means" approach is important. Even the slightest comment can be taken as partiality and come back to haunt the company if a lawsuit is filed.

CARRYING OUT THE INVESTIGATION

The EEOC has stated that when detailed fact finding is necessary (when there is a dispute about what really happened or if anything happened), interviews should be done of the complainant, the alleged harasser, and any third parties who could reasonably have relevant information. General character witnesses, especially those who may be able to speak only to the party's personal lives, will rarely be useful. In addition, witnesses from the workforce who may only be able to state that they have not been harassed by this person will be of limited (if any) usefulness. As the chapter on the psychological aspects of sexual harassment made clear, harassers don't harass everyone.

Once the list of people to be interviewed has been determined, preparation for the interview is essential. Interestingly, the EEOC, which usually does not deal with specifics in areas of personnel administration, has been quite clear about what questions should be asked during the investigation. Though they are stated as examples of appropriate questions, they signal what the EEOC and probably a court will be looking for to determine if the employer can use the affirmative defense. These questions are designed to get at the truth of a situation in the most effective manner possible.

Of course, these questions must be tailored to each situation and not all will be relevant in every investigation. They do, however, show that a complete picture of the situation is what is required, however that can be attained.

Once all possible facts have been gathered, the investigator will sometimes have to determine credibility: Who is telling the truth? This is never an easy task, but there are many hints that will be helpful.

- Some testimony may just make more sense than others when considered in the individual situation. For example, we are more likely to believe that a person who has regular access to another's desk would be more likely to have been involved in placing something on it than someone who does not. This is called *inherent plausibility* by the EEOC.
- People often show by their demeanor whether they are telling the truth.
- Sometimes there is a motive that would make it more likely that someone would lie. For example, does someone appear to have a need to seek revenge for something that occurred earlier?
- When witnesses or physical evidence can corroborate what a party had to say, it is often strong evidence of what was stated. This must be balanced, however, with a consideration that there may be bias that causes a witness to perceive events in line with what they already believe or that they may have some motive to lie. Also, it is important to remember that harassers are not known to "look for an audience," so no witnesses to conduct is not an uncommon occurrence.
- When there is a past record of this type of conduct, it is also strong evidence of credibility, but a rush to judgment should not be done just because the person has been charged with sexual harassment previously. All parties have the right to have their stories heard impartially before a decision is made.

In this chapter's case study, how well does the company do in following the rules of investigating a complaint?

Once the investigation is completed, a determination must be made as to whether harassment occurred and what should be done. This can be done by the investigator or by a management official who reviews the report. It must be remembered, however, that those who did the investigation will, in most cases, be best able to determine credibility, having talked with all parties.

If no determination can be made because, even considering credibility and motive, the evidence is inconclusive, the EEOC recommends that training and monitoring be the proposed action. It must be remembered that an inconclusive determination is different than a determination that a complaint is false. Taking punitive action against complaints that are clearly false is acceptable. Punitive action against someone because the investigation is inconclusive can cause any number of legal problems in the future.

If it is determined that the harassing conduct did occur, then the law requires that remedies be designed to stop the harassment, correct its effects on the employee, and ensure that the harassment does not recur. Though consideration should be given to the remedies desired by the employee who filed the complaint, it is not necessary to institute them as long as the action taken is effective.

When harassment is found to have occurred and there is no disciplinary action taken, it may be difficult for the employer to prove that it did what was necessary to stop the harassment. One court noted that an investigation that revealed harassment and a remedy that included a small amount of training was not adequate. The court stated that "while we do not suggest that disciplinary action is always required to establish the adequacy of the employer's response, it obviously is relevant to our analysis of the adequacy of that response."[5]

An important consideration in determining the type of remedy is the seriousness of the offense. The EEOC agrees that, if it was "minor," such as an off-color joke by an individual with no prior history, then counseling and an oral warning might be all that is necessary. Severe or persistent harassment or a history of harassing conduct may require suspension or discharge. There are a number of intermediate remedies available to an employer, ranging from reduction in wages to demotion. Tailoring the remedy to the requirement that it effectively stop the harassment and prevent its recurrence is key.

Sometimes, the fact that harassment did or did not stop may be evidence of the effectiveness of the remedy, but it is not the only consideration. As one court noted: "Sometimes . . . an employer's reasonable attempt to prevent future harm will be frustrated by events that are unforeseeable and beyond the employer's control. The law requires an employer to be reasonable, not clairvoyant or omnipotent."[6]

Any remedial measures should not adversely affect the employee who was subjected to the harassment. This could be perceived as retaliation and ineffective handling of the complaint. If a party needs to be moved, it should be the party found to have been involved in harassment, unless the employee who filed the complaint prefers to be moved. A retaliation claim may be available to any employee who makes a complaint and then suffers any adverse consequences.

Measures should also be taken to make sure that the employee who was subjected to the harassment is "made whole," the law's term for being put into the position they would have been had the harassment not occurred. This may mean merit increases, reinstating vacation or sick time taken due to the harassment, restoring lost benefits, reinstatement to a previous position, removing negative evaluations, or, in some cases, reimbursing the cost of professional assistance the employee required due to the conduct. This often means paying for counseling that the employee sought to help handle the harassment.

Once the remedy is undertaken, it is vital that the employee who was harassed know that her or his employer will be continuing to monitor the situation and pay attention to actions taken with regard to his or her employment situation. The employee should be encouraged to report any further problems immediately, as this will ensure that no further harassment retaliation is allowed.

Recall the case study. How well were Marjorie's interests protected by the company's investigation process?

Employers are often concerned about the possibility of lawsuits by employees who are discharged for sexual harassment. These lawsuits will rarely be successful as long as the employer is careful to do what is necessary to avoid liability. First, it is vital to make clear in the anti-harassment policy that discharge is a possible punishment. Second, the investigation must have been done in an impartial manner, and adequate evidence must be shown to exist that the person was involved in severe or continuing harassment. In other words, a correct policy and procedure will also be a defense should the discharged employee decide to sue the business. As in all cases, proper documentation will be the best evidence.

THE "PAYOFF"

Although putting together and carrying out an adequate anti–sexual harassment program will take time and effort, the benefits with regard to lessening potential liability and increasing the morale of the workforce are extensive. In addition to quickly resolving any government agency investigations, businesses are finding that judges, even if cases are brought to court, are more open to dismissing complaints quickly when the defendant has followed the policy and procedure requirements carefully.

In the case of *Saxton v. American Telephone & Telegraph*,[7] for example, a lower court found it easy to dismiss the claim because of the company's process and their response to the woman's complaint. AT&T had a strong policy in effect, and it had begun an investigation the day after it was advised of the problem. A detailed report was completed within 2 weeks, and the perpetrator was transferred to another department within 5 weeks. The employee who was involved in the harassment was the complainant's supervisor, who had made unwelcome advances. The court realized that the plaintiff had wanted even more in response but it stated:

> No doubt from Saxton's perspective, AT&T could have done more to remedy the adverse effects of Richardson's conduct. But Title VII requires only that the employer take steps reasonably likely to stop the harassment. . . . In another context, transfer of the wrongdoer to a different department might amount to an ineffectual slap on the wrist; but in this case, it served to terminate all contact between Richardson and Saxton and bring a definitive end to any harassment.[8]

Several cases after the Supreme Court decided *Ellerth* also show the parameters of an appropriate response to sexual harassment complaints.

LAWSUITS BY FIRED EMPLOYEES

There have been some recent cases that have dealt with lawsuits by employees who have been discharged for sexual harassment. Many companies have made a commitment to fight the return of a harassing employee in court, if necessary, and are finding, on the whole, that courts are not sympathetic to such lawsuits. This is especially true if the employees knew about the penalties for violations of the sexual harassment policy, the investigation by the company was properly carried out, and the discipline deemed appropriate in light of the seriousness of the conduct. Companies that make such a commitment and follow it up with actions should find that the workers are reassured about the seriousness of their employer's desire to ensure a comfortable work environment.

The case study policy in the last chapter, by not specifying specific expected discipline, may be leaving the business open to lawsuits by any employee who may be discharged for sexual harassment.

UNION CONSIDERATIONS

Another area of concern for unionized workplaces would, of course, be the interplay of the contract, arbitration, and discipline for sexual harassment. Recently, a conflict has arisen in the lower courts over the handling of cases in which an arbitrator has ruled that dismissal of a union member for sexual harassment is unduly harsh and ordered the return of the offending employee. Some companies have gone to court requesting that the judge overturn the arbitrator's decision. Such a decision by a judge is highly unusual, as any labor-relations person knows. Courts usually give great deference to an arbitrator's decision, but in this circumstance, many of the federal appeals courts are more willing than usual to grant the employers' requests. They are doing so on the grounds that public policy against sexual harassment weighs more heavily than the usual arbitration deference.

The Supreme Court has so far refused to accept a case that would finally decide this issue (it has denied appeals both in cases where the decision of the arbitrator was upheld and where it was overturned). This leaves employers in somewhat of a difficult position but not one that is entirely unworkable. Getting the union involved in the policy and procedure formulation and making them part of the contract will alleviate later problems. It is vital, however, that the company not bargain away the rights of employees to a policy and procedures that are as effective as the EEOC requires. Labor organizations are included in Title VII's antidiscrimination requirements, so they should also be willing to work with the employer in this regard to lessen their own potential liability.

SUMMARY

To be legally adequate an investigation of a sexual-harassment complaint requires more than a cursory look at what happened, a "chat" with the parties, and an informal settlement of problems found. Specifics must be adhered to if the employer is going to be able to use the affirmative defense provided by the Supreme Court in hostile environment cases. Proper training and preparation for the investigation are invaluable in carrying out a process that will handle the situation appropriately and that will adequately remedy any problems that are uncovered.

FOR REFLECTION

1. When does the employer have a responsibility to investigate a potential sexual-harassment situation?

2. Explain why an outside agency or person might not be a good source for investigating potential sexual-harassment situations.
3. What is inherent plausibility?
4. What should be considered when a company undertakes remedial action?
5. When an employer takes remedial action but the harassment continues, is the employer liable for not doing enough to stop the harassment?

Notes

1. *Indest v. Freeman Decorating,* 164 F.3d 258, 265 (5th Cir. 1999).
2. Available online at www.eeoc.gov/docs/currentissues.html.
3. Available online at www.eeoc.gov/docs/harassment.html.
4. *Dees v. Johnson Controls World Services, Inc.,* No. 96–9079 (11th Cir. 1999).
5. *Baty v. Williamette Industries* (Kansas U.S. District Court, 1999).
6. *Brown v. Perry,* 184 F.3d 388, 396 (4th Cir. 1999)
7. 10 F.3d 526 (7th Cir. 1993).
8. *Saxton,* at 536.

CHAPTER 6

Implementing Procedures for Resolving Complaints of Sexual Harassment

INTRODUCTION

In chapter 3 we introduced you to a case study that describes an employee's experience with a senior-level supervisor. This case study is reprinted here:

Mary has just arrived at her first job. Upon her arrival she is met by a supervisor who shows considerable interest in her work and experience in college. Mary is flattered by his interest and agrees to discuss her work-related ideas over lunch in a restaurant downtown. After a few lunches where the conversation is general and social rather than focused on professional issues, Mary finds that the supervisor is touching her—rubbing his knees against hers, placing his hand on her back and arms, and once patting her on the bottom. He asks Mary to meet him outside of work for early dinners. She declines, offering various excuses, and tries to maintain a polite but distant tone in her conversations with him. One day the supervisor asks Mary to come into his office to discuss a project. Once she is inside the office, he closes the door, moves toward her, and puts his arms around her. Mary tries to push him away, but he holds her tighter and tries to kiss her. There is a knock on the door, he releases Mary, and she opens the door and hurries out of the office.

In chapter 3 we asked you to decide whether sexual harassment had indeed occurred in this scenario. We also asked you to identify when in the account of Mary's experiences you believe sexual harassment occurred. Now, after rereading this case study, let's address Mary's experiences from her own perspective.

Let's first consider the following addition to the scenario:

Three days after the occurrence in her supervisor's office, Mary makes an appointment to speak with you because she knows you are an investigator of sexual-harassment complaints for your company.

How would you then answer the following questions?

1.   What would you say when Mary comes into your office?
2.   Where would you sit vis-à-vis Mary?
3.   How would you answer the following questions she asks of you?
     a.   What is sexual harassment?
     b.   What did I do to encourage his behavior?
     c.   Why did he do this to me?
     d.   Am I naive?
     e.   What can you do to help me?
     f.   How many people here will know that I've come to talk with you?
     g.   I'm not thinking too clearly. What information should I have so I can make a decision about what to do from here?
     h.   Can you give me some suggestions about what I can do when I see him in the hall or in a meeting?
4.   What would you do to end the meeting with Mary?
5.   Mary phones you later in the week and tells you she's decided to file a formal written complaint.
     a.   What would you do next?
     b.   After you've received her written complaint, what would you do?
     c.   What would you say and do with the person complained about?
6.   Outline the rest of the process you would follow.
7.   The investigation indicates that sexual harassment had occurred; a written reprimand is recommended.
     a.   What do you do next?
     b.   How will you communicate the outcome of the investigation to Mary?
     c.   How will you communicate the outcome of the investigation to the supervisor?
8.   What follow-up work would you recommend to this investigation?

In this chapter we will address each of the issues raised by these questions, for example, how to maintain confidentiality in the grievance process; how to interview witnesses, the complainant, and the accused; how to maintain records for your organization's purpose; and how to determine what sanctions to impose should a sexual-harassment complaint be sustained. In a previous chapter we discussed many of these issues from a legal perspective. In this chapter we will focus our discussion around the importance of the complaint procedures, taking into account the psychological issues involved in the victimization process, including individual feelings of powerlessness, isolation, changes in social-network patterns, and desire to gain control over their personal and professional lives. We begin with a discussion of the characteristics required of investigators of complaints of sexual harassment.

Who Should Investigate Complaints of Sexual Harassment?

Each company will select the individual who will be responsible for hearing and investigating charges of sexual-harassment. At some companies, this role is often given to the human-resource department or sexual-harassment committees or panels. Conducting investigations of sexual-harassment complaints requires two important requirements: sensitive, skilled individuals to conduct the grievance process and a supportive management.

Investigator Characteristics

Investigators must be aware that their presence at the organization is cause for discomfort for most employees.[1] Sexual harassment is an uncomfortable issue for employees, as we have discussed throughout this text. By extension, individuals responsible for implementing sexual-harassment policy statements, grievance procedures, and training programs often make employees uncomfortable; these individuals are a constant reminder about the topic and about the organization's position statement.

Furthermore, no matter what the outcome of a grievance procedure, employees may be disappointed and even angry with the investigator.[2] Investigators frequently get blamed for not doing enough work or for encouraging a "witch hunt." They must take comfort in knowing that they did their best in each complaint process.

Based on empirical research in psychology and human-resource management, we recommend that investigators meet the following criteria:

They must

1. have sufficient credibility in the area of sexual harassment, including knowledge and formal training in the legal, psychological, and physical aspects of sexual harassment;

2. be readily accessible for employees and administrators;
3. have skill in relating to people and eliciting information from them;
4. not be uncomfortable in discussing matters of sexuality and sexual victimization, including incest, battering, and rape;
5. be fluent in languages in addition to English;
6. report directly to the individual who will determine the company's response (i.e., administer sanctions);
7. not permit any of the individuals in the complaint procedure to pressure them to reveal confidential information, to become their advocate, or to take sides in the final report of the investigation;
8. be honest and candid, without permitting personal feelings to interfere with effectiveness;
9. be sensitive to civil-service rules, collective-bargaining agreements, and other personnel rules;
10. be prepared for discussions to be very emotional, and be prepared to be a calming force for these emotional discussions;
11. set up a safe atmosphere for the complainant, alleged harasser, and witnesses to discuss their perspectives without the fear of being ridiculed or judged;
12. maintain a distance from all individuals involved in the complaint process so that (a) a reasoned judgment can be made about whether to sustain the charge of sexual harassment and (b) the investigator can be upheld as objective by individuals such as hearing officers, judges, and parties involved in the complaint process;
13. not use tape recorders or video recorders during interviews as part of the investigative process because these machines create unnecessary added stress for individuals;
14. ask parties not to discuss the complaint with others (this is essential to lessen the probability of retaliation and influence on other witnesses);
15. know that the organization has a legal as well as ethical obligation to make the workplace an environment free of sexual harassment and free of the fear of retaliation for speaking about sexual harassment;
16. work well with the company president and not be viewed as adversarial.

We recommend *behavioral rehearsal techniques* (see exhibit 6.1) for investigators to practice nonverbal as well as verbal communication. As is indicated in exhibit 6.1, this rehearsal must include being in tune with individuals' other psychological responses to sexual harassment.

EXHIBIT 6.1

Behavioral Rehearsal of Verbal and Nonverbal Communication

When making general statements about women (or any other group), be sure that the statements are based on accurate information, not on stereotypes.

Avoid humor or gratuitous remarks that demean or belittle people because of their sex, sexual orientation, race, religion, or physical characteristics.

Avoid using generic masculine terms to refer to people of both sexes. Although the effort to do this may involve some initial discomfort, it will result in more precise communication and understanding.

When using illustrative examples, avoid stereotypes, such as making all victims of sexual harassment women and all harassers men.

Try to monitor your behavior toward women and men. For example:

Do you give more time to men than to women?

Do you treat men more seriously than women?

Are you systematically more attentive to questions, observations, and responses made by women victims than by men victims?

Do you direct more of your own questions, observations, and responses to individuals of one sex?

Do you assume a heterosexual model when referring to human behavior?

Do you maintain eye contact when you are listening to individuals involved in a complaint procedure? Or do you shift your gaze away from them?

Are you someone who smiles even when hearing sad or discomforting information? An employee may interpret your smiling to mean that you believe her or his complaint or position on sexual harassment is silly or is without merit.

Do you let people know you are listening to them? Do you nod and say "hm hm"? How do you convey your interest and concern?

Adapted from M.A. Paludi and R.B. Barickman, *Academic and Workplace Sexual Harassment: A Resource Manual* (Albany: State University of New York Press, 1991). By permission of the State University of New York Press. © 1991.

Management Characteristics

Management must support its investigators of complaints of sexual harassment. Management must give its investigators the autonomy and power they require to undertake an effective investigation.[3] It can't ignore the knowledge of a sexual harassing situation, even if no complaint has been filed, and should never tell investigators to squash a complaint or find in favor of the accused or the complainant. Simply put, management must stay out of the way of an investigation until it is needed to institute sanctions (discussed later in this chapter). No retaliation against the investigator must be exhibited.[4] Should an investigator experience an unresponsive or hostile management, we recommend that he or she seek new employment.

WOMEN OR MEN AS INVESTIGATORS

It is common for investigators to report gender comparisons in employees discussing their sexual-harassment experiences with them.[5] For example, men may be more comfortable talking with women investigators. This is especially the case when the men have been sexually harassed by other men. Women may be reluctant to discuss their experiences with male investigators because of the sometimes explicitly sexual nature of many complaints of sexual harassment. We thus recommend having a team of investigators—both a woman and a man.

The team of investigators can rely on each other for support. For women complainants, the team approach offers a safer environment than talking about sexuality with an unknown man. It is also important to have a second investigator should a complaint be filed against the other. In this case, the complainant will have an opportunity to file a complaint at the organization. Without two investigators, the complainant has no option. Of course, if the complainant files against one member of the investigative team, the accused must exclude herself or himself from the investigatory process.

PSYCHOLOGICAL ISSUES INVOLVED IN THE VICTIMIZATION PROCESS: MAKING THEM CENTRAL TO THE INVESTIGATORY PROCESS

As we pointed out in chapter 3, research has suggested that individuals who experience sexual harassment frequently exhibit the following responses to it:[6]

Confusion and/or embarrassment

Am I overreacting? Have I misinterpreted the situation? Have I done something to lead him/her on?

Helplessness

No one is going to believe me. It's his or her word against mine.
If I complain, it will make matters worse.

Anger

> I'm being cheated out of a job. Why isn't anyone doing something about his or her behavior?

Worry

> I'll never get a good recommendation from him or her if I don't go along with him or her. All the other managers will know if I file a complaint.
>
> Everyone will say I'm too sensitive.

These responses center around individuals' feelings of having no control over the situation. This is especially true because of the humiliating and disorienting impact of sexual harassment, in which the victim may experience the sort of self-doubt, self-blame, and sense of degradation common to victims of rape, incest, and battering.[7] It is important, therefore, that the means of hearing and resolving complaints of sexual harassment take into account individuals' psychological responses and offer an investigatory procedure that will ease the burden of discussing their experiences. Unless employees feel they will have this protection of confidentiality, they will seldom report the sexual harassment they have experienced.[8] And, of course, individual complaints cannot be resolved and the pervasive injury done to the organization by sexual harassment cannot be remedied unless complaints are actually reported.

We therefore recommend that the investigative process take into consideration the emotional responses to sexual harassment to assist the complainant's path to recovery from the trauma of sexual harassment. For example:

Complainant's Response: Confusion
Investigator's Response: Help with labeling of experiences, provide behavioral definitions of sexual harassment
Complainant's Response: Helplessness
Investigator's Response: Discuss complainant's power in handling case, focus on ways individual is powerful in other aspects of her or his life
Complainant's Response: Anger
Investigator's Response: Discuss confidentiality of investigative process; focus on ways to rebuild career; offer support systems
Complainant's Response: Worry
Investigator's Response: Discuss due process, sanctions against retaliation, confidentiality of investigative process

Research has documented that the experience of participating in an investigative process is as emotionally and physically stressful as the victimization itself.[9] It is important to build in several support systems to help complainants and alleged harassers cope with the process of the complaint procedure. Investigators who must make a determination whether to sustain the complaint also must not be a counselor to either party who clearly needs support during the complaint process. Referrals for support groups and therapists in the community must be made readily available for complainants and alleged harassers.

Part of an Employees Assistance Program (EAP) in a company may be devoted to dealing with individuals involved in a sexual-harassment complaint procedure. Counselors in an EAP must be trained in the psychological issues involved in sexual harassment. It is important not to convey too early to any of the individuals involved in an investigation that they are perceived to be in need of psychological help. Complainants, for example, may interpret such a referral as the investigator telling them they are "crazy" and that they "made up" the whole experience. A sample handout for these purposes is presented in exhibit 6.2.

SUPPORTIVE TECHNIQUES FOR WORKING WITH INDIVIDUALS INVOLVED IN A SEXUAL HARASSMENT INVESTIGATORY PROCESS

All individuals involved in an investigation of a sexual harassment complaint must be treated sensitively in the investigatory process. We recommend that counselors, peer-support staff, and the EAP offer the following supportive techniques to the complainant, accused, and witnesses:

1. Acknowledge individuals' courage by stating how difficult it is to label, report, and discuss sexual harassment.
2. Encourage individuals to share their feelings and perceptions.
3. Provide information about the incidence of sexual harassment. Also share the symptoms associated with sexual-harassment trauma syndrome.
4. Assure complainants that they are not responsible for their victimization.
5. Work with individuals in their search for the meaning in their victimization; support them while they mourn their losses.
6. Work with individuals in monitoring their physical, emotional, and interpersonal responses to sexual harassment and to the investigatory process.
7. Provide a safe forum for individuals' expression of anger and resentment.
8. Work with individuals on ways to validate themselves so as to feel empowered.

9. Suggest a peer-counseling group for individuals who need support for dealing with their experiences. See exhibit 6.3 for information about support groups on sexual harassment.
10. Work with individuals and the organization in their investigation of complaints of sexual harassment.

EXHIBIT 6.2

Referrals for Therapeutic Support

Many individuals who have participated in an investigation of a sexual-harassment complaint have reported that they wanted some neutral party to be a sounding board for them, someone to help them sort out all the emotions they were experiencing during the investigatory process.

We at _____ (name of company) have prepared the following list of therapeutic support systems for individuals who are involved in an investigation of sexual harassment. We have prepared this list to serve as a reference guide for individuals and support groups who may be contacted by employees here at _____.

We have also presented some national organizations from which employees may request written information concerning sexual harassment in general and therapeutic support in particular.

National Organizations

9 to 5
614 Superior Avenue, NW
Cleveland, OH 44113
800-522-0925

Coalition of Labor Union Women
15 Union Square
New York, NY 10003
212-242-0700

NOW Legal Defense Fund
9 Hudson Street
New York, NY 10013
212-925-6635

Equal Rights Advocates
1663 Mission Street
Suite 550
San Francisco, CA 94103
415-621-0672

Federally Employed Women
14001 I Street NW
Washington, DC 20005
202-898-0994

Women's Legal Defense Fund
1875 Connecticut Avenue, NW
Washington, DC 20009
202-986-2600

Local Organizations

. . .

EXHIBIT 6.3

Suggestions for Support Groups on Sexual Harassment

Goals

Listen to and respect individuals' reactions to being sexually harassed.

Sort out sound choices with respect to dealing with sexual harassment.

Be aware of the commonality of themes in group members' lives.

Define *quid pro quo* and hostile environment sexual harassment.

Discuss psychological issues involved in dealing with sexual harassment.

Discuss the physical and emotional reactions to being sexually harassed.

Provide a psychological profile of sexual harassers.

Discuss peer sexual harassment.

Discuss means of resolution for complaints of sexual harassment.

Assess our own perceptions of the definition, incidence, and psychological
dimensions of sexual harassment.

Responsibilities

Support-group members agree to avoid judging and to focus on giving support and making positive statements to each person, even when making a
difficult comment.

Time arrangements (both beginning and end) are agreed upon and honored
by all members.

Any confrontation is clear, gentle, and nurturing.

Members agree to come every time unless it is impossible to do so.

Confidential information must never be relayed to others outside a support
group.

Privacy must be respected at all times.

An atmosphere of safety and security must be maintained at all times.

Each individual has the responsibility of taking care of herself or himself.

Therapists must know that they may be asked to provide information regarding their treatment of an individual involved in an investigatory process.[10] Victims of sexual harassment suffer long-term after
effects because (1) sexual harassment is a trauma; (2) sexual harassment is a violation of trust, especially when the harasser is in a position of authority; and (3) sexual harassment causes secondary losses,
including the lack of support and comfort from family and friends and
retaliation because of filing charges (e.g., being fired).[11]

It is important that the therapist understand that his or her role is
not to judge whether sexual harassment as legally defined has

occurred. In addition, the support system is not an attorney. Counselors must only help individuals with their options, not advise them on their civil rights. Understanding the psychological impact of sexual harassment must include an awareness that the victim's perceptions and cognitive appraisals of her or his experiences activates negative self-images.[12] Frequently, victims of sexual harassment view themselves as needy, frightened, weak, and out of control. For the victimization caused by sexual harassment to be resolved, shattered beliefs must be reformulated to assimilate the experience of sexual harassment. This process has been called *cognitive readjustment.*[13] Successful cognitive readjustment of beliefs includes a discovered ability to cope, learn, adapt, and become self-reliant. Cognitive readjustment produces a greater sense of self-confidence, maturity, honesty, and sense of strength.[14]

RESPONDING TO A COMPLAINT
OF SEXUAL HARASSMENT

Allegations of sexual harassment are accompanied by decreased productivity in the workplace, morale problems among employees, adverse publicity, and perhaps the filing of EEOC charges. It is most important, therefore, to treat sexual harassment complaints seriously and sensitively. Furthermore, we recommend that investigators follow a consistent plan for all complaints of sexual harassment. This plan includes the following stages for formal complaints that are filed in the workplace:

1. Prepare the materials needed for a formal complaint procedure.
2. Review the legal and psychological issues involved in sexual harassment in general and investigatory procedures specifically.
3. Identify all information the complainant will have to address in the formal complaint.
4. Investigate the complaint filed.
5. Prepare a report of the investigation.
6. Discuss the investigation with the company president or CEO.
7. Assist the president or CEO with possible recommendations for remedial action.
8. Institute remedial action and write a response to all parties involved in the investigatory process.

Each of these steps is described in detail in the following section.

Prepare the Materials Needed
for a Formal Complaint Procedure

The materials needed for conducting a formal investigation are the following:

1. standard notification form for complainant
2. standard notification form for accused
3. standard notification forms for witnesses
4. standard note-taking form

Examples of each notification form are presented in exhibit 6.4. These forms must be prepared on the company's stationery. Copies should be sent via certified mail to all parties involved in the investigation. We recommend that notification letters be sent to the individuals' home addresses, not work addresses.

EXHIBIT 6.4

Standard Notification Forms

Example of Standard Notification Letter for Witnesses
Date

Name
Home Address

Dear ___ :

I am writing to inform you that I was given your name by ___ (either complainant or accused) to contact you regarding being a witness in a sexual-harassment complaint filed by ____ against ____. This is in following the investigative procedures of sexual harassment at (name of organization).

In accordance with these procedures, I would like to meet with you in person to discuss your evidence. I am available to meet with you at one of the following times: ___. Will you please call me this week to set up a meeting time? Or, if you wish, you may leave a message for me at ___ . You may write to me in care of ___.

Your name or other identifying information will not be made known to ___. I have enclosed a copy of our policy statement and procedures.

Sincerely,

_____
Sexual Harassment Investigator

EXHIBIT 6.4, continued

Standard Notification Forms

Example of Standard Notification Letter for Complainant
Date

Name
Home Address

Dear _____:

I am writing to inform you that I am in receipt of your written formal complaint of sexual harassment against _____, under the procedures of sexual harassment at _____ (name of organization).

In accordance with these procedures, I would like to meet with you to discuss your complaint. I am available to meet with you at one of the following times: _____. Will you please call me this week to set up a meeting time? Or, if you wish, you may leave a message for me at _____. You may write to me in care of _____.

I am interested in resolving this matter as quickly as possible. Our first priority will be to attempt to resolve the problem through a mutual agreement of the complainant and the person complained against. I have enclosed another copy of our policy statement and procedures.

Sincerely,

_____
Sexual Harassment Investigator

Review the Legal and Psychological Issues Involved in Sexual Harassment in General and Investigatory Procedures Specifically

We recommend a review of the following materials:

1. legal definition of sexual harassment
2. interviewing techniques for use with complainant and accused
3. sexual-harassment trauma syndrome symptoms
4. suggested questions to ask during interviews

A summary of resources for this review is presented in exhibit 6.5. In addition, we recommend reviewing chapters 2 and 3 in this

---

EXHIBIT 6.4, continued

Standard Notification Forms

Example of Standard Notification Letter for Accused
Date

Name
Home Address

Dear _____:

I am writing to inform you that I am in receipt of a formal complaint of sexual harassment against you made by _____, under the procedures of sexual harassment at _____ (name of organization).

In accordance with these procedures, I would like to meet with you to discuss the complaint and your responses to it. I am available to meet with you at one of the following times: _____. Will you please call me this week to set up a meeting time? Or, if you wish, you may leave a message for me at _____. You may write to me in care of _____.

I am, of course, interested in resolving this matter as quickly as possible. Our first priority will be to attempt to resolve the problem through a mutual agreement of the complainant and the person complained against. I have enclosed another copy of our policy statement and procedures. In addition, I have enclosed a copy of _____'s formal complaint.

I welcome any questions you have about the policy and procedures and will be pleased to discuss them with you when you contact me to set up an appointment.

Sincerely,

_____
Sexual Harassment Investigator

---

book for the legal and psychological issues involved in sexual harassment.

Identify All Information the Complainant Will Have to Address in the Formal Complaint

The content of a formal complaint of sexual harassment should include the following components:

Part 1: Information concerning verbal and/or nonverbal behavior; dates, time, witnesses present

Part 2: How complainant felt and still feels; impact on work performance

Part 3: What complainant wants for resolution of complaint

The complaint must be signed, dated, and addressed to the sexual-harassment investigator, care of the investigator working with the complainant.

Investigate the complaint filed.

We recommend the following process for investigators to follow from the time a written formal complaint has been received:

1. Send standard notification letter to complainant via certified mail to her or his home address.
2. Send standard notification letter to accused via certified mail to his or her home address. With this notification letter also send

    copy of complaint
    copy of organization's policy statement and investigatory procedures.

3. Notify the company president or CEO about the formal complaint received and investigation pending. Start file of correspondence for the president/CEO, as well as for investigators.

EXHIBIT 6.5

Resources for Investigators

Psychological Issues of Sexual Harassment

Fitzgerald, Louise F. "Sexual Harassment: Violence against Women in the Workplace." *American Psychologist* 48 (1993): 1070–76.

Gutek, Barbara, and Mary Koss. "Changed Women and Changed Organizations: Consequences of and Coping with Sexual Harassment." *Journal of Vocational Behavior* 42 (1993): 28–48.

O'Donohue, William (Ed.). *Sexual Harassment: Theory, Research, and Practice.* Boston: Allyn & Bacon, 1997.

Paludi, Michele, and Richard Barickman. *Sexual Harassment, Work and Education: A Resource Manual for Prevention.* Albany, New York: State University of New York Press, 1998.

Bowes-Sperry, Lynn, and Jasmine Tata, "A Multiperspective Framework of Sexual Harassment," in *Handbook of Gender and Work,* edited by Gary Powell, et al. Thousand Oaks, California: Sage, 1999.

4. Use standard note-taking form for meetings with complainant and accused (see exhibit 6.6 for a sample note-taking form). Complete the information following the meeting because it is distracting to the individuals involved to have the investigator constantly with her or his head lowered and taking notes. Investigators must respond to the individuals physically as well as psychologically. Sample questions to be asked of both parties are presented in exhibit 6.7.

EXHIBIT 6.6

Note-Taking Form

Date of meeting or call: _____

Individual's name: _____

Telephone numbers: _____

Description of sexual-harassment problem (nature of incident, time, dates, description of alleged harasser, health- and work-related consequences):

Symptom checklist (please ask individual whether or not the following symptoms have been experienced since the harassment started. Circle or check off those experienced.)

Career Effects
- Changes in work habits
- Drop in work performance because of stress
- Absenteeism
- Withdrawal from work
- Changes in career goals

Emotional Reactions
- Shock, denial
- Anger, frustration
- Guilt
- Shame, powerlessness
- Insecurity, embarrassment

Physical Reactions
- Headaches
- Inability to concentrate
- Sleep disturbances
- Lethargy
- Gastrointestinal distress

- Respiratory problems
- Phobias, panic reactions
- Nightmares
- Eating disorders
- Dermatological reactions

Changes in Self-Perception
- Poor self-concept or self-esteem
- Powerlessness
- Isolation
- Lack of competency

Social Effects
- Withdrawal
- Fear of new people
- Lack of trust
- Change in physical appearance
- Change in social networks

EXHIBIT 6.6, continued

Other symptoms:

Additional critical facts:

Verbal objection:

Written objection:

Consultation with therapist or support group:

Consultation with physician:

Date of receipt of written complaint:

Date of notification of receipt of complaint:

Date of notification of alleged harasser:

Date of meeting(s) with alleged harasser:

Outcome of meeting:

Outcome of subsequent meetings with complainant:

Date of meeting(s) with witnesses:

Follow-up contacts:

Date: Who called: Content:

---

5. Use standard notification letters for witnesses for each party. Send the letter via certified mail to the witnesses' home addresses.
6. Notify parties involved that witnesses have been contacted. The identity of the witnesses should not be disclosed in this correspondence.
7. Review any correspondence sent between the parties involved in the investigation. Where necessary, and with permission from the individual involved in the investigation, review any company files (e.g., supervisor's performance evaluations).

EXHIBIT 6.7

Questions to Ask During Interviews

With Complainant

Tell me what happened that made you decide to come see me.

What specifically was said, done to you, etc.?

When did this behavior occur—date, time, etc.?

How did this behavior make you feel?

Did you or are you now experiencing any of the following symptoms after this incident occurred? (Show Sexual Harassment Trauma Syndrome symptoms.)

Tell me what you want the sexual harassment committee to do to help you with the issue you told me about today.

With Accused

Now that you've had an opportunity to review the complaint, tell me about your perspective on the incidents described in the report.

The behaviors described in this report are unacceptable here. Do you know that?

How did you think your comments/touch (fill in the behavior) made (the complainant) feel?

Were you surprised by what ___ (the complainant) said about how your behavior impacted on her/him?

With Witnesses

Tell me what you observed with respect to the incident under investigation.

What did the people involved say or do?

Prepare a report of the investigation.

A report of the investigation should be prepared directly from the note-taking form used throughout the entire investigation. This report should include the findings of the allegation and the following decisions made by the investigator:

Should the complaint be sustained?

If no, this information and the reasons believed to substantiate this decision must be explained.

If yes, this information and the reasons for the decision and recommendations for corrective action must be identified.

If the investigator believes there is insufficient information on which to offer an answer to this question, we recommend that the investigator interview parties again,
following the procedures that have been outlined here.

Discuss the Investigation With the President or CEO.

Assist the President or CEO with recommendations for remedial action.

Institute Remedial Action and Write a Response to All Parties Involved in the Investigatory Process.

Send a copy of this full report to the president; keep a copy in
your office for the time being. No other copies should be kept from
this point on. The company president will now have to initiate corrective action. Letters should be sent from the president's office concerning the outcome of the investigation to all individuals—complainant,
accused, and witnesses.

Types of sanctions include the following:

Verbal and/or written reprimands concerning the harasser's
behavior and how the workplace will not tolerate any further behavior of this type. Written reprimands may be placed
in the individual's personnel file. These reprimands must also
make clear that further sustained complaints will result in
more severe sanctions, including dismissal.

Dismissal when more severe sexual harassment has occurred.
Should the president accept this recommendation from the
investigator, then any collective-bargaining agreements procedures must be followed. Investigators should be used as
expert witnesses in any subsequent hearings related to the
charges of sexual harassment against an employee.

Suspension may be an option when the recommendation
involves counseling or other rehabilitation processes. This
suspension should not be viewed as a reward; the suspension
must not include paid salary.

Transfers for one or both individuals to other positions within
the workplace may be appropriate. This type of remedial
action helps with potential retaliation.

Demotions of supervisory employees to nonsupervisory positions
may be a sanction considered prior to suspension or dismissal.

Requiring attendance at a sexual-harassment training program.

Apologizing to the victim.

Should a complaint be determined to be totally fabricated, the
organization may want to take steps to restore the reputation of the

accused if she or he was damaged by the proceedings. Such steps may include a statement read at a manager's meeting or note in a newsletter or other appropriate action.

FROM THE LABORATORY TO THE REAL WORLD

As a summary of the procedures we recommend be followed for conducting a formal investigation of sexual harassment, let us return to the case study involving Mary and her supervisor. (You may want to reread the case study at the beginning of this chapter.)

We asked you to consider that Mary makes an appointment to speak with you in your role as an investigator of sexual-harassment complaints. We now offer some suggested responses to the questions posed at the beginning of the chapter. Our responses take into account the empirical research we reviewed in this chapter and in chapter 3. We invite you to compare our responses to the ones you gave.

What would you say when Mary comes into your office?

Thank her for coming.

Acknowledge the difficulty in coming to speak with an investigator.

Explain that your role in this first meeting is to listen to her and work with her in identifying her concerns.

Where would you sit vis-à-vis Mary?

Ask Mary to choose between two seats—one across from you, the other next to you. Recall the importance of putting control into individuals' lives.

How would you answer the following questions she asks of you?

What is sexual harassment?

Provide behavioral examples of sexual harassment.

Then fill in with legal terms (e.g., *hostile environment*)

Show Mary a handout you will give to her with all of the terms and examples clearly defined.

What did I do to encourage his behavior?

Explain that behaviors on the part of others may not be elicited.

Indicate it is common to blame oneself when these things happen.

Why did he do this to me? Am I naive?

Suggest that individuals who engage in this type of behavior often do so with a variety of people. Mary probably wasn't singled out because she was naive, attractive, single, or other such reasons.

Tell her that because she was relatively new to the company and didn't know the politics of the place yet, she might have been targeted for the behavior.

What can you do to help me?

Discuss the policy statement and grievance procedures.

Highlight the points you are making on the materials for Mary to keep.

Review the procedures at least three times.

Remind Mary that it is entirely her choice to file a complaint.

Alert Mary to your legal obligation to investigate a complaint when a situation is brought to your attention, even if the individual does not wish to file a complaint.

How many people here will know that I've come to talk with you?

For a formal complaint, only the investigator and the president will know.

I'm not thinking too clearly. What information should I have so I can make a decision about what to do from here?

Discuss the policy statement and grievance procedures step by step.

Can you give me some suggestions about what I can do when I see him in the hall or in a meeting?

Tell Mary she doesn't have to talk with the supervisor. She may leave the situation if she can. If she feels she has no choice but to say something—like hello—tell Mary she can get by with the minimum conversation. Tell her to report any incident to you.

Engage in some behavioral rehearsal with Mary; take turns playing both roles.

What would you do to end the meeting with Mary?

Remind Mary about her choices. Tell her you are obligated to investigate once the matter is brought to your attention.

Thank her again for coming to talk with you. Set up another meeting prior to her leaving. Be sure she has your phone number.

Mary phones you later in the week and tells you she's decided to file a formal complaint. What would you do next?

Remind Mary about the three parts to a formal complaint: (1) what was done and said, (2) how she feels, and (3) what she wants to happen.

Ask Mary to address the complaint to you as the investigator.

After you've received her written complaint, what would you do?

Send Mary the standard notification form for complainants.

Send the supervisor the appropriate standard notification form.

Alert the company president that there is a formal complaint under investigation.

Meet with Mary and the supervisor individually.

If there are witnesses, use standard notification forms to notify them; interview them.

The outcome is that sexual harassment had occurred; a written reprimand is suggested. What do you do next?

Prepare a full report of the investigation, including your suggestions for corrective action.

Give this report to the president.

How will you communicate with Mary the outcome of the investigation?

Send a letter telling her that the investigation is completed and that she will be hearing from the president shortly.

Put letter in file for the president.

How will you communicate with the supervisor about the outcome of the investigation?

Send a letter telling him that the investigation is completed and that he will be hearing from the president shortly.

Put letter in file for the president.

INFORMAL COMPLAINTS OF SEXUAL HARASSMENT

Using a formal complaint procedure can be intimidating to individuals. These procedures take time and can cause considerable embarrassment and stress for all those involved in the process. We recommend providing individuals with an option of filing an informal complaint of sexual harassment in addition to the formal procedures we outlined above.[15]

If the individual bringing the complaint is willing to be identified to the person against whom the complaint is made and wishes to attempt informal resolution of the problem, the investigator will make a confidential record of the circumstances (signed by the complainant) and undertake appropriate discussions with the person or people involved.

This type of complaint procedure works best with certain types of hostile environment sexual harassment, especially gender harassment (see chapter 3). Should complainants not be satisfied with the outcome of the informal procedure, they should be offered the option of using the formal complaint process; the steps to follow would be identical to those already discussed. However, organizations cannot take disciplinary action using informal procedures; disciplinary action requires a formal complaint. Informal complaints are aimed at stopping the behavior in an immediate way rather than determining culpability or intent.

Record keeping of informal complaint procedures must be adequately maintained to determine whether the same offender may be part of several informal resolutions.

MEDIATION AS A PROCEDURE FOR RESOLVING COMPLAINTS OF SEXUAL HARASSMENT

Recently, some institutions have built into their grievance procedures a mediation technique, whereby complaints can be resolved informally between the individuals involved.[16] In a mediation procedure, the complainant and accused typically meet together with a mediator to attempt to resolve the sexual harassment. In this session, both parties tell their side of the story to the mediator in the presence of the other party.

It has been proposed that employees may prefer mediation to a formal complaint process for the following reasons: faster resolution, preservation of confidentiality, and avoiding the stress of a formal process. However, such sessions often become volatile. Individuals have very powerful emotions associated with the situation. Furthermore, such a procedure assumes both individuals are of equal power in the organization.[17] Research has suggested, however, that most victims of sexual harassment hold less organizational power and/or sociocultural power than their harassers.[18] Perhaps most important, most individuals who have experienced sexual harassment want to flee the harasser, not sit face-to-face with this person. They fear that the mediation session will become an extension of the sexual harassment.[19]

We thus recommend against mediation as a technique for resolving complaints of sexual harassment. In the informal complaint process we discussed above, the investigator does serve as a mediator. However, this investigator will listen to each party individually and summarize their statements for the other party. The parties never have to meet face-to-face.

ADDITIONAL ISSUES IN INVESTIGATING COMPLAINTS OF SEXUAL HARASSMENT

Individuals may be unable to file a formal complaint of sexual harassment within a short time frame following their experiences. They may not want to take this assertive response (see chapter 3) or they may be worried about a pending performance appraisal and possible retaliation. The statute of limitations should therefore not be too restrictive. We recommend 60 days from realization of the discomfort of the situation. For individuals who want to file a complaint but hold off for a few weeks until the investigation begins (e.g., because they have a performance review scheduled), this request must be granted by the investigator, who must make note of this for the investigation.

Informal complaints of sexual harassment can usually be dealt with within a couple of days of the investigator's hearing about the situation. Formal complaints can take much longer, depending on the schedule of individuals involved, the number of witnesses involved, and other factors. Because the grievance procedure is an emotionally laden process, we recommend conducting the investigation within a 2-week time period, not to exceed 1 month from receipt of the formal complaint. This time frame must be articulated to all parties involved in the grievance procedure; it will help provide a sense of closure for them.

Closure must also be provided at the completion of the investigation with a letter of apology sent to the complainant from the president or CEO should the complaint be sustained.

SUMMARY

Whereas each company will set up a complaint procedure that fits the unique needs of that business, the following general guidelines identified in this chapter should apply for all investigations of sexual harassment:

1. Clearly state to all parties involved in the investigative procedure that the company has an obligation to maintain a workplace free of sexual harassment and free of the fear of being retaliated against for filing a complaint of sexual harassment. Investigators must also state that they cannot ignore any complaint of sexual harassment.
2. Take every complaint seriously.
3. Keep every complaint confidential. The need for confidentiality is essential to protect the rights of those who filed the complaint, those against whom the complaint has been filed, and witnesses.
4. Do not make any conclusions about the veracity of the complaint until the investigation is completed. Investigators must not make determinations about the complaint based on the reputations of the individuals involved.
5. The investigation must be thorough and fair. The workplace's policy statement and procedures must be followed at all times.

There must be provisions, for example, for hearing complaints against the investigator. New procedures should not be developed during the course of an investigation.

6. Document every step of the investigation completely and accurately in a form that can be defended to others. This procedure should be maintained for the in-house investigation and for subsequent lawsuits, for which all notes, reports, and written materials will be subpoenaed and be made part of the court record.

7. Complete investigations in a timely fashion. A prompt investigation is necessary to obtain accurate and complete statements from all individuals involved in the complaint. A quick time frame also assists in the complainant's coping with the victimization. Time deadlines for individuals to respond to charges of sexual harassment must be rigorously observed.

8. Interview the complainant in detail. The following information must be obtained from the complainant in writing:

   detailed description of the behavior about which the individual is complaining (i.e., approximate dates, times, frequency, location, circumstances, identity of alleged harasser)

   names of potential witnesses

   impact of behavior on complainant in terms of emotional, physical, or work productivity

   whether individual has voiced her or his concern to alleged harasser and, if so, the outcome of such objection

   the type of resolution the individual is seeking for herself or himself and for the alleged harasser.

9. Interview the person complained about in detail. The person must be shown the written complaint and the documents given to the investigator. The following information must be obtained in writing from the individual against whom the complaint was filed:

   reaction to complaint

   interpretation of events mentioned in complaint

   understanding of the impact of his or her behavior on complainant.

10. Interview all witnesses. Witnesses identified by the complainant and by the alleged harasser should be invited to meet with the investigator. Witnesses should discuss only information related to the incidents about which they are assumed to have knowledge with respect to the complaint at hand. They must not be interviewed about information they may have about previous victims, for example. The identity of the witnesses for the complainant must not be provided for the alleged harasser. Similarly, the identity of the witnesses for the alleged harasser must

not be made known to the complainant. This confidentiality will ensure that witnesses will come forth and participate in the investigative process without fear of retaliation.

11. Review all documents presented by the complainant, alleged harasser, and witnesses. Documents include, but are not limited to, performance appraisals, letters, and notes sent to an individual involved in the complaint process. Investigators must not seek out any additional records without the prior written consent from the individual(s) involved, and only when these materials are deemed absolutely necessary to conduct the investigation.

12. Handle each complaint against the same individual independently. The outcome of the investigation should never be based on knowledge that the alleged harasser has had other complaints filed against him or her. Similarly, knowledge that the complainant has filed complaints against other employees must not enter into the investigative process. Such information may be helpful in determining sanctions, however.

13. Make provisions for individuals who wish to wait until they receive a performance appraisal prior to filing a complaint. This need may be met by instituting an anonymous complaint procedure whereby individuals do not have to sign the complaint for it to be investigated. This complaint procedure works best when one or several employees file a complaint against a manager. Another way to meet this need is to provide more lenient time frames for filing complaints, for example, not 5 days or 2 weeks when 1 month would be better for the complainant.

14. Provide closure for all parties involved in the complaint procedure. Information regarding the status of the investigation and the completion of the investigation must be provided to all individuals involved in the complaint process. Contact the complainant periodically for at least 1 year to determine whether the resolution of the complaint is satisfactory, whether she or he has experienced any retaliation, and whether there has been any recurrence of the sexual harassment. The individual who has engaged in sexual harassment should also be contacted periodically for 1 year to determine whether the investigator can provide any subsequent assistance, such as referrals for therapeutic support.

FOR REFLECTION

1. Identify the reasons why investigatory procedures are important in dealing with sexual harassment in any organization.
2. Identify several characteristics of a good investigator of sexual-harassment complaints.

3. Outline the responsibilities of management with respect to empowering its investigators.
4. What are the benefits to having both a woman and man as a team of investigators?
5. Give an example of relating the grievance procedure to a psychological response of being victimized by sexual harassment.
6. Discuss ways therapeutic support can be beneficial to individuals who are going through a grievance procedure.
7. Identify the steps investigators should take to deal with a formal complaint of sexual harassment.
8. Distinguish between an informal and a formal complaint of sexual harassment.
9. Offer some objections for using mediation as a technique in the investigative process.

Notes

1. H. REMICK et al., *Investigating Complaints of Sexual Harassment*, in SEXUAL HARASSMENT ON COLLEGE CAMPUSES: ABUSING THE IVORY POWER (M. Paludi, ed., 1996). I. MCQUEEN, *Investigating Sexual Harassment Allegations: The Employer's Challenge,* in SEXUAL HARASSMENT: THEORY, RESEARCH, AND TREATMENT (W. O'Donohue, ed., 1997).
2. H. REMICK et al., *Investigating Complaints of Sexual Harassment*, in SEXUAL HARASSMENT ON COLLEGE CAMPUSES: ABUSING THE IVORY POWER (M. Paludi, ed., 1996). I. MCQUEEN, *Investigating Sexual Harassment Allegations: The Employer's Challenge,* in SEXUAL HARASSMENT: THEORY, RESEARCH, AND TREATMENT (W. O'Donohue, ed., 1997). M. PALUDI & R. BARICKMAN, SEXUAL HARASSMENT, WORK, AND EDUCATION: A RESOURCE MANUAL FOR PREVENTION (1998).
3. H. REMICK et al., *Investigating Complaints of Sexual Harassment*, in SEXUAL HARASSMENT ON COLLEGE CAMPUSES: ABUSING THE IVORY POWER (M. Paludi, ed., 1996).
4. H. REMICK et al., *Investigating Complaints of Sexual Harassment*, in SEXUAL HARASSMENT ON COLLEGE CAMPUSES: ABUSING THE IVORY POWER (M. Paludi, ed., 1996). I. MCQUEEN, *Investigating Sexual Harassment Allegations: The Employer's Challenge,* in SEXUAL HARASSMENT: THEORY, RESEARCH, AND TREATMENT (W. O'Donohue, ed., 1997).
5. L. GRAUERHOLZ, H. GOTTFRIED, C. STOHL, and N. GABIN, *There's Safety in Numbers: Creating a Campus Adviser's Network to Help Complainants of Sexual Harassment and Complaint Receivers,* VIOLENCE AGAINST WOMEN 5, at 950–977.
6. B. DANSKY & D. KILPATRICK, *Effects of Sexual Harassment,* in SEXUAL HARASSMENT: THEORY, RESEARCH, AND TREATMENT (W. O'Donohue, ed., 1997).
7. See M. PALUDI, PSYCHOLOGY OF SEXUAL VICTIMIZATION: A HANDBOOK (1999).
8. I. MCQUEEN, *Investigating Sexual Harassment Allegations: The Employer's Challenge,* in SEXUAL HARASSMENT: THEORY, RESEARCH, AND TREATMENT (W.

O'Donohue, ed., 1997). M. PALUDI & R. BARICKMAN, SEXUAL HARASSMENT, WORK, AND EDUCATION: A RESOURCE MANUAL FOR PREVENTION (1998).

9. I. MCQUEEN, *Investigating Sexual Harassment Allegations: The Employer's Challenge,* in SEXUAL HARASSMENT: THEORY, RESEARCH, AND TREATMENT (W. O'Donohue, ed., 1997).

10. J. SALISBURY & F. JAFFE, *Individual Training of Sexual Harassers,* in SEXUAL HARASSMENT ON COLLEGE CAMPUSES: ABUSING THE IVORY POWER (M. Paludi, ed., 1996). J. SALISBURY, A. GINORIO, & D. STRINGER, *Counseling Victims of Sexual Harassment,* in PSYCHOTHERAPY: RESEARCH AND PRACTICE 23, at 316–324.

11. B. DANSKY & D. KILPATRICK, *Effects of Sexual Harassment,* in SEXUAL HARASSMENT: THEORY, RESEARCH, AND TREATMENT (W. O'Donohue, ed., 1997).

12. V. MAGLEY, C. HULIN, L. FITZGERALD, & M. DENARDO, *Outcomes of Self-Labeling Sexual Harassment,* JOURNAL OF APPLIED PSYCHOLOGY 84, at 390–402.

13. S. TAYLOR, *Adjustment to Threatening Events: A Theory of Cognitive Adaptation,* AMERICAN PSYCHOLOGIST 38, at 1161–1173. M. P. KOSS, *Changed Lives: The Psychological Impact of Sexual Harassment,* in IVORY POWER: SEXUAL HARASSMENT ON CAMPUS (M. Paludi, ed., 1990).

14. M. P. KOSS, *Changed Lives: The Psychological Impact of Sexual Harassment,* in IVORY POWER: SEXUAL HARASSMENT ON CAMPUS (M. Paludi, ed., 1990).

15. H. REMICK et al., *Investigating Complaints of Sexual Harassment,* in SEXUAL HARASSMENT ON COLLEGE CAMPUSES: ABUSING THE IVORY POWER (M. Paludi, ed., 1996).

16. M. PALUDI & R. BARICKMAN, ACADEMIC AND WORKPLACE SEXUAL HARASSMENT: A MANUAL OF RESOURCES (1991).

17. M. PALUDI & R. BARICKMAN, SEXUAL HARASSMENT, WORK, AND EDUCATION: A RESOURCE MANUAL FOR PREVENTION (1998).

18. S. TANGRI & S. HAYES, *Theories of Sexual Harassment,* in SEXUAL HARASSMENT: THEORY, RESEARCH, AND TREATMENT (W. O'Donohue, ed., 1997). E. PERRY, J. SCHMIDTKE, & C. KULIK, *Propensity to Sexually Harass: An Exploration of Gender Differences,* SEX ROLES 38, at 443–460.

19. M. PALUDI & R. BARICKMAN, SEXUAL HARASSMENT, WORK, AND EDUCATION: A RESOURCE MANUAL FOR PREVENTION (1998).

CHAPTER 7

The Role of the EEOC in Sexual Harassment Situations

Case Study

Jennifer Jones has been working in an environment that has intermittently been very uncomfortable for her. When she first came into the shop, she was constantly the focus of sexual innuendos and comments and belittling statements about her ability to do the job. For the past 7 months, however, the shop has been rather quiet, until one morning when the supervisor brings in a new pinup calendar from one of the suppliers. The men call her over and show her the calendar, asking why she isn't on it. They continue ridiculing her because she didn't "make it" into the pictures until the supervisor grows tired of the joke and tells everyone to get back to work.

Jennifer is crushed because she thought the problem was over. She knows that her company has a sexual-harassment policy and procedure, but it requires that she report the problem to her supervisor first.

Finally, after talking to a friend on the phone, she takes a long lunch and walks over to the EEOC office, where she files an official complaint. When her supervisor hears about her complaint, he is furious and wants to fire her for not using internal procedures. Can Jennifer do this? What is the best way for the company to handle the situation? Can it ask the EEOC to back off because the company has its own policy?

INTRODUCTION

As has been previously stated, the Equal Employment Opportunity Commission is the federal agency that is granted the authority to carry out the requirements of Title VII. A basic understanding of how the EEOC operates and the process for dealing with complaints is important in a complete picture of the law and sexual harassment. In this chapter, we will discuss the EEOC's procedures, but note that many employees will be involved with local rather than federal agencies. Whereas many follow much the same procedures of complaint filing and conciliation, it is important to check with any applicable local agencies. A list showing examples of such agencies is included in appendix 2. Usually, they will have booklets available that will describe the agencies' procedures and help in understanding what to expect.

THE AUTHORITY OF THE EEOC

The EEOC was created by the Civil Rights Act of 1964, in which the EEOC was granted the authority to investigate and conciliate complaints that alleged a violation of the law of employment discrimination. In 1972, Title VII was amended to grant the EEOC the power to bring court actions in certain cases on behalf of victims of discrimination.

The EEOC has been instrumental in a variety of ways in shaping the law of sexual harassment. It has issued guidelines and policy statements to help employers understand the ever-changing law in this area. For example, its *Guidelines for Discrimination on the Basis of Sex*[1] provides the basic definition that is usually quoted in regard to sexual harassment. In addition, the EEOC has brought a number of lawsuits that were pivotal in developing the law and has filed *amicus* briefs[2] in many lawsuits and appeals brought by private individuals. The EEOC was quoted several times by the U.S. Supreme Court in its decisions in *Meritor Savings Bank v. Vinson* and *Harris v. Forklift Systems*, the sexual-harassment cases discussed in chapter 2.

The EEOC has authority under Title VII to pursue complaints for parties who feel that they have had their equal-employment rights violated. Although Title VII does not prohibit lawsuits by private parties, it requires that employees first file a charge of discrimination with the EEOC before they are allowed to go to court for themselves. Charges may be filed with the EEOC in person, by mail, or by telephone. In states or localities where there is an antidiscrimination law and an agency authorized to grant or seek relief, a charge must be presented to that state or local agency. If the complaint is filed with the EEOC, the agency will forward it to the appropriate agency and defer its investigation until the state makes a determination on the complaint. If the complaint is filed with the state agency, a request may be made that it also be forwarded to the EEOC, or the employee may wait to file with the EEOC within the timeline discussed in the next section.

STATUTES OF LIMITATIONS

There are strict statutes of limitations, or time periods, in which complaints must be filed. Title VII specifies that a charge must be filed within 180 days of the alleged discriminatory act. In situations wherein a claim is required to be brought to the state or local agency first, the EEOC complaint may be filed within 300 days of the discriminatory act or 30 days after receiving notice that the state or local agency has terminated its processing of the charge, whichever is earlier. A party may also request that a charge be forwarded by the state agency to the EEOC.

In certain situations, courts will allow a charge for acts that occurred outside the time periods. This would occur when the EEOC and the courts decide that the situation involves what is called a *continuing violation.* Often, a sexual-harassment claim involves several acts of discrimination (such as the belittling comments in the case study), but only one of the acts is within the statutory limits. Under the continuing violation doctrine, despite the fact that only one act occurred in the time limit, all of the conduct can become part of the claim.

In the case study, the behavior that occurred 7 months before her complaint may become part of Jennifer's case if the EEOC and/or a court feels that they are part of the same pattern of discrimination.

An inappropriate response to a sexual-harassment claim may be the one act within the time frame that brings in all the other discriminatory acts. Once again, it is vital that the employer's process or lack of process not itself be part of the problem.

THE EEOC INVESTIGATION

The EEOC, after receiving the complaint, may begin an investigation to determine whether there is merit to the claim. First, the potential plaintiff will be interviewed to determine as much information as possible and to find out whether all of the legal jurisdictional requirements, such as the statutes of limitations, have been met. The charge will then be properly prepared and the investigation procedure explained to the person making the complaint.

Next, the EEOC notifies the employer about the charge. The EEOC will usually request that a fact-finding conference be held at which an EEOC specialist will try to work out a settlement. Whereas the advice of the company's attorney is probably appropriate at this time, resistance or anger is usually not a useful or beneficial response. After all, a company that has exercised good business sense should have nothing to hide, and if there is a problem, this may be the last possible point at which to control liability costs. The courts are clear that, even if the employer had no notice before the charge is filed, there *is* notice once the EEOC informs the company. If the problem was not adequately handled before, it should be handled at this point to minimize a much greater potential expense later.

In the investigation, the EEOC may try to solve the problems informally using what Title VII calls methods of "conference, conciliation, and persuasion." If the evidence has shown that there is reasonable cause to believe that discrimination has occurred, the agency will attempt to persuade the employer to eliminate or remedy the problem voluntarily. Among other remedies, it may seek reinstatement of the employee, back pay, and/or restoration of lost benefits. A business that digs in its heels and refuses to acknowledge that it has not done what it should in this situation can only increase its liability and cost. If the situation wasn't handled correctly before, it should be done at the conciliation stage.

During these informal proceedings, Title VII provides protection for the employer who is working with the EEOC to try to resolve the situation. The law provides that "nothing said or done during and as a part of such informal endeavors may be made public by the Commission . . . or used as evidence in a subsequent proceeding." Thus, materials revealed to the EEOC or statements made during this time could not be admitted as evidence against the company should the case end up in court.

If conciliation fails, the EEOC considers the case for a lawsuit in the federal courts. This case would be filed by the agency on behalf of the complaining party or parties, and the EEOC would bear the cost of the litigation. This process could take many years, and the potential for appeals and the legal costs to the employer could be extensive. ·

RIGHT TO SUE

At any stage of the investigation, the EEOC may determine, for a variety of reasons, that it is not going to pursue the complaint. In addition, after 90 days has elapsed from the filing of the complaint, the complainant may ask the agency for the right to take the case to court.

For a private lawsuit to be filed under Title VII, the EEOC must issue what is called a "right to sue" letter to the employee who made the complaint. The employee then has 90 days in which to file a private lawsuit in federal or state court. Even though the EEOC chooses not to pursue the complaint, this does not necessarily mean that there is no merit to the claim. An employer should not automatically assume that the matter is then concluded. Many such claims are decided in favor of the complaining parties; the EEOC's refusal to pursue may be based merely on the agency's budgetary constraints.

Once a private party has filed a federal lawsuit under Title VII, the EEOC is usually no longer involved with the claim. In a few instances, it may intervene as an *amicus,* as discussed before, but usually it will have no further dealings with either party.

LAWSUITS

Whereas the resolution of the claim in an agency proceeding is probably better for minimizing costs, the increasing number of complaints filed with the EEOC these days makes it likely that the agency will not be involved and that the plaintiff will end up in court. At this point, if the employer has done all that can be expected, a request to the judge for a summary judgment may be in order. A summary judgment means that the judge has determined from the pleadings, the written declarations by the plaintiff and defendant, that a trial is unnecessary and one party is entitled by law to win.

Recent studies of current practice in sexual-harassment cases show that a defendant is most likely to be granted a summary judgment only in cases where there is a legally defensible policy and appropriate responses. Rarely will a judge step in before trial for other possible defenses. For example, a claim that this behavior was welcomed or that it did not affect a term or condition of employment—that the behavior was not serious enough—is unlikely to result in a summary judgment. Judges are too aware of the expanding and amorphous nature of sexual harassment to make a decision before all of the facts, witnesses, and evidence have been presented. Most likely, under current law, this presentation will be before a jury, and as every lawyer can tell you, juries are usually involved when huge damages are awarded.

WHEN AN EMPLOYEE TURNS TO THE EEOC

After putting together and carrying out an extensive sexual-harassment policy and program, any problems should have been dealt with internally and without government intervention. There is always the potential, however, even if a company adopts a strong policy and procedure, that an employee will not take advantage of the opportunity to handle the problem internally. She or he may choose, for whatever reason, to go directly to a government agency, such as the EEOC or a local agency, and file a complaint. There is nothing to prevent this from happening, and a company need not become defensive if it does. A request from an agency for a fact-finding conference is not a challenge, and no determination has been made that the complaint is valid. It must be remembered that, in the beginning, the EEOC is most interested in finding out exactly what happened and conciliating or settling the matter amicably between the two parties.

If the employer has done what is expected, there is probably little to worry about if a complaint is filed. There is every possibility that the EEOC will find no merit in the complaint, and that will be the end of the matter as far as the agency is concerned. Of course, an employee has an option to file a lawsuit, but from all the cases being decided today, there is every indication that an employer would win a case when it can show that it has done all that was required: its policy and procedures are seriously carried out; it encourages reporting and handles complaints in an effective and efficient manner; harassed employees do not suffer adverse consequences; discipline is designed to prevent any recurrences; retaliation is not allowed; and training is provided and required on an ongoing basis. The company meant what it said in its policies and procedures and indicated this in no uncertain terms from the CEO on down. There is nothing more that the law can ask with regard to removing the opportunity for a hostile environment to exist—and, in fact, it does not ask more.

However, there is always the possibility that something did go amiss with regard to the policy or that this is a *quid pro quo* situation, in which even the most extensive internal program may not be a defense.

In the case study, it is evident that the company's policy did not contain a fail-safe provision, which led to Jennifer turning to the EEOC. Once the company hears about the complaint from the government agency, it should immediately figure out how to solve the problem to Jennifer's satisfaction. Then it should solve the problem with the policy so that other employees don't feel the need to go outside the internal procedures.

SUMMARY

It should be apparent that there are many stages at which complaints may be handled and that as it progresses through these stages, a complaint becomes more and more expensive. Once again, the smartest course for a company is to "take care of business" at the earliest possible point. Adopt a process that handles any sexual-harassment situation appropriately right from the start. If the process doesn't do so, handle the situation when the agency gives notice. If the situation goes beyond that point, the costs can be staggering, both economically and in terms of public relations.

There are three possible scenarios, then, that are satisfactory for an employer dealing with sexual harassment. The first and best is that the EEOC or a state or local agency will never call because the business's employees are satisfied and happy with the internal program and procedures, which are handling complaints before the point of legal liability is ever approached. The second best is that the EEOC gives notice of a complaint, and the employer responds calmly and confidently because it has done everything that is necessary to minimize liability, and it knows the process has worked correctly. The third is that an agency gives notice and the employer, after responding calmly and confidently, determines that a problem has occurred, despite its best efforts, and remedies the problem immediately. Any other scenario evidences an attitude that is foolish, time consuming, and costly, reflecting bad business judgment.

Take a final look at the case study. The supervisor wants to fire Jennifer for going to the EEOC, an angry reaction to what he may view as insubordinate behavior. Doing so, however, could be viewed as retaliation for Jennifer's exercising rights granted to employees under Title VII, a clear violation of the law. By firing Jennifer, the supervisor not only may get the company into some possibly heavy damages but also may allow all of the previous months' behavior to become part of the case on the continuing violation doctrine. Such a response makes no business sense.

FOR REFLECTION

1. Discuss why a company's response to the EEOC is so important.
2. Discuss why you think the law sets up statutes of limitations. What is gained by them? What is lost? What do you think about the 180 days requirement?
3. Why do you think that the courts began using the continuing violation doctrine? Do you agree that it is a good idea? Why or why not?

4. Why do you think the "right to sue" letter is required by the law? Why can plaintiffs not go directly to court? What role did the law expect for the EEOC?

5. Some employers believe that a complaint from the EEOC means that a lawsuit is imminent. Discuss why that is not necessarily true.

6. Why do you think the law restricts the use of information gained during an EEOC investigation? Do you think that this is a good policy? Why or why not?

Notes

1. 29 CFR Sec 1601.

2. An *amicus curiae* brief is a written presentation of a point of view that is filed with a court when the party is not a plaintiff or a defendant in the case. The court must approve a request to file an *amicus* brief and usually does so when it feels that the individual or organization making the request has some relevant information or an important perspective to add to the issue(s) being decided.

Resources for Conducting Training Programs on Sexual Harassment

An organization's policy statement and grievance procedures must be communicated to all employees. Employees must know their rights and responsibilities with respect to being a complainant, an accused, or a witness. The most effective way to communicate the grievance procedure and policy statement is through training programs. Effective training programs send a clear message to all employees that the sexual-harassment policy must be taken seriously and that sexual harassment will not be tolerated by management.

There are several steps to designing and implementing a training program on sexual harassment. We identify and discuss each of these steps in this appendix.

ISSUES TO CONSIDER BEFORE TRAINING

Conduct a Needs Assessment.

There are several topics to be discussed in any training program on sexual harassment (e.g., legal definition, sexual-harassment trauma syndrome, the organization's policy and investigatory procedures). We also recommend conducting a needs assessment (see exhibit 1) with the administrative staff of an organization to identify additional issues they expect to be covered in a training session. Examples of these additional topics include (1) the interface of racial harassment and sexual harassment,[1] (2) the role the Employees Assistance Program plays in counseling individuals involved in a sexual-harassment complaint procedure, and (3) the interface of homophobia and sexual harassment.[2] The topics are typically suggested to a trainer based on the organization's prior complaints.

We recommend the following needs assessment for determining training programs on sexual harassment.

1. Identify groups and individuals to be involved in needs assessment (e.g., managerial staff).
2. Ask individuals to provide answers to questions regarding sexual harassment in the workplace via an anonymous mail survey.
3. Facilitate 2-hour focus groups or roundtable discussions with randomly selected employees (20 per session) to elicit in-depth

```
                        ┌─────────────────────┐
                        │      EXHIBIT I       │
                        └─────────────────────┘
```

Needs Assessment

Introduction

We are seeking assistance with advancing the understanding of sexual harassment. As part of our effort, you are being asked to complete the following brief survey based on your needs for and expectations of future training sessions on issues related to sexual harassment.

Your participation in this survey will help me in my role as a consultant to more fully understand the organizational climate and culture in your company and best represent your needs.

This is an anonymous survey. All replies will be kept confidential. Any information used from this survey will be used in aggregate form with no reference to individual responses.

I appreciate the time you are taking to complete and return this important survey.

Part I: Demographic Information

1. What is your age?

   (Please circle appropriate category)

20–25	46–50
26–30	51–55
31–35	56–60
36–40	61–65
41–45	65+

2. What is your racial/ethnic background?

   (Please circle the appropriate category)

   African American

   Asian American

   Euro-American

   Hispanic/Latino

   Native American

   Multiracial

   Other   (please specify) _____

3. What is your sex?

   Female

   Male

4. Are you physically challenged?

   Yes

   No

   Please specify:

Part 2: Needs Associated with Training in Sexual Harassment

1. Some of the goals of training in issues related to sexual harassment are

   defining sexual harassment

   providing incidence rates

   providing a profile of a sexual-harassment victim

   providing a profile of harassers

   how to file a complaint of sexual harassment

   Which of these goals do you consider most important? Why? Are there other goals you would add to this list? If so, please identify them and indicate why you believe they are important. Use the space below to write your answer. Should you need more space, please use the reverse side of this sheet.

2. Which of the following activities would be most important to the future of dealing with sexual harassment in your company?

   educating managers

   educating employees

   revising the policy

   revising the investigatory procedures

   having a new investigator

3. In your opinion, what indications are there that individuals in your company are not trained in issues related to sexual harassment?

4. In your opinion, how can the need for training individuals be met most effectively?

5. In your opinion, what is the state of readiness for a training program on sexual harassment?

6. Please complete the following sentences:

   Things I would like to understand better about sexual harassment are . . .

   Things I would like to learn how to do better with respect to dealing with sexual harassment in my company are . . .

   Feelings I have in my company regarding sexual harassment that I would like to change or improve are . . .

---

 responses (see exhibit 2). Structured interview questions for individuals who participate in the focus groups center around employees' goals for training sessions, including their needs with regard to better understanding victims of sexual harassment and individuals with viewpoints different from their own.

EXHIBIT I, continued

7. Indicate below (using check marks) whether you would like the information to be included in a training session on sexual harassment:

Topic	Yes—Include in Training	No—Don't Include in Training
sexual orientation	_____	_____
ethnicity and race	_____	_____
racism	_____	_____
homophobia	_____	_____
abuses of power	_____	_____
verbal communication styles	_____	_____
nonverbal communication styles	_____	_____
empowerment of diverse populations	_____	_____
reporting techniques	_____	_____
profiles of harassers	_____	_____
impact of sexual harassment on victims	_____	_____

Additional comments you wish to make:

I welcome your comments about any of the items in the survey
and additional information about the training programs being developed for your company that you would like to share with me. Thank
you again.

---

4. Analyze responses from steps 2 and 3 using qualitative and
   quantitative statistical analyses.
5. Prepare a written report that summarizes the needs assessment,
   including suggestions for the following:

   How to increase awareness

   Ways to examine attitudes

   Alternatives to stereotyping

   Methods of supportive action
6. Make recommendations for post-training evaluations.

Thus, the major goal of the proposed needs assessment is to
obtain information concerning the manner in which sexual harassment is addressed in the organizational climate of the company,
including such topics as empowerment, establishment of mutual trust

EXHIBIT 2

Sample Interview Questions
for Roundtable Discussions with Managers

(Total Time Required per Focus Group: 2 Hours)

Part 1: Introduction and Overview
of Focus Group
(10–15 minutes)

Verbal Overview

As you know, this company is seeking assistance with advancing the understanding and management of sexual harassment. A few weeks ago, you were asked to complete a brief anonymous survey regarding the issues you would like to see addressed in training sessions on sexual harassment.

Today, you are being asked to participate in a focus group/ roundtable discussion to help me in my role as a consultant to more fully understand the organizational climate and culture in your company and best represent your needs (in aggregate form, not to be singled out in any way) for planning training sessions.

Introduction of trainer

Introductions of individuals participating in focus groups

Part 2: Focus Group Structured Questions
(10–15 minutes per question; participants offer viewpoints.)
(Responses will be written on flip chart for all participants to see.)

What specifically do you want to accomplish in your company in the next two years?

How will training programs on sexual harassment in the workplace help facilitate achieving these goals?

What specifically do you want to cover in training sessions in order to help you achieve your goals?

Identify two things you need to help you feel more empowered as a manager in your company.

Identify two things you hope the training programs will help you to identify and manage.

What do you believe is the state of readiness for a training program on sexual harassment in your company?

Part 3: Summary

Trainer reviews comments generated from managers in focus groups.

Trainer asks for additional comments related to future training sessions.

Trainer allows time for individuals to discuss their concerns with her or him individually.

---

and respect, methods of inclusion or exclusion, verbal and nonverbal communication, and empowerment of employees in the process.[3] The process of the assessment will be consistent with the goal of the training programs in which the employees will subsequently participate.

Identify the Goals and Objectives of the Training Session.

The goals for sexual-harassment training for most employers are:

1. to provide all members of the company with a clear understanding of their rights and responsibilities;
2. to enable individuals to distinguish between behavior that is sexual harassment and behavior that is not sexual harassment;
3. to provide individuals with information concerning the policy statement against sexual harassment and investigatory procedures set up by the organization;
4. to set up an environment that is free of sexual harassment and free of the fear of being retaliated against for speaking about sexual harassment.

Once the goals have been established, the following steps *must* be taken prior to the beginning of the training sessions:

1. Develop or revise the company's policy statement against sexual harassment. Because the policy statement is part of the training session content, it must be completed prior to training.
2. Develop or revise investigatory procedures for handling complaints of sexual harassment. Investigatory procedures are part of the content of the training and thus should be developed prior to training.

The CEO Should Invite All Employees to Participate in a Training Session.

The most important feature of effective investigative procedures for any company is the training programs designed to implement this policy. If the company wants to demonstrate its determination to stop sexual harassment, the CEO must actively participate in the training session and not give the verbal or nonverbal message that she or he is simply going through the motions. The CEO must set a tone that suggests that the company will not tolerate sexual harassment and that training is needed for all members of the company, including those individuals who hold the organizational power.

All employees must be informed about their rights and responsibilities with respect to sexual harassment. Their participation in a training session should be mandatory. Optional attendance at a training session conveys management's belief that it is not worth devoting 3 or 4 hours to the topic of sexual harassment. The commitment to addressing sexual harassment must be put in writing to all members of the organization by the CEO. This administrator must also demand every employee's participation at training sessions. The letter or memo must be written in a straightforward and nonthreatening manner. Flexibility in accommodating work schedules must be maintained. We suggest that the CEO maintain a record of all employees who fail to participate in a training session. A letter to this effect should be placed in an employee's personnel file.

Design Training Sessions for Groups of Individuals Working Together in a Department or Organization.

Training sessions can be established for individuals within certain departments because they each have unique responsibilities. Training sessions for investigators of complaints of sexual harassment should be separate from other training programs. In exhibit 3, we present a sample outline for training investigators of complaints.

In addition, some organizations request training programs for their employees who have been selected to provide the training programs for the entire company. These programs are referred to as "train-the-trainer" seminars. A sample outline of the issues to be presented in a train-the-trainer seminar is presented in exhibit 4.

Develop Resources for Participants in Training Sessions.

Training sessions are areas for disseminating information about the organization's policy against sexual harassment, as well as for discussing sexual harassment in general. We advise trainers to distribute pamphlets or handouts describing the following information to the participants in the training session:

legal definition of sexual harassment
behavioral definitions of sexual harassment
policy statement against sexual harassment
investigatory procedures at the organization
name and phone numbers/office numbers of investigators
locations where information on sexual harassment may be
    obtained
information regarding stress effects of sexual harassment

EXHIBIT 3

Sample Outline of Training Program for Investigators

The goals of the training program are to

> provide information concerning liability,
>
> define *quid pro quo* and hostile environment sexual harassment,
>
> discuss psychological issues involved in dealing with sexual harassment,
>
> discuss the physical and emotional reactions to being sexually harassed,
>
> discuss means of resolution for complaints of sexual harassment.

At the conclusion of this training program, investigators will be able to

> assess their own perceptions of the definition, incidence, and psychological dimensions of sexual harassment;
>
> adequately label behaviors as illustrative of sexual harassment or not illustrative of sexual harassment;
>
> assess why individuals choose to report or not report sexual harassment;
>
> identify peer sexual harassment;
>
> identify employees' rights and responsibilities under Title VII;
>
> design educational programs to deal with sexual harassment, including peer sexual harassment;
>
> adequately interview complainants and individuals about whom complaints have been filed.

Topics for Presentation and Discussion

Part 1   Introduction to training session and goals of seminar/workshop

Part 2   The complainant's perspective

Part 3   Psychology of the victimization process

Internally and externally focused strategies

Psychology of reporting incidents of sexual harassment

Part 4   The accused's perspective

Part 5   Differential evaluations of identical behavior

Part 6   Keeping investigative process consistent with responses to sexual harassment by individuals involved

Break

Part 7   Interviewing techniques

Part 8   Note taking and record keeping

Part 9   Case studies

Part 10 Summary and general discussion

Break

Part 11 Role-play exercises

EXHIBIT 4

Sample Outline of Training Program
for "Train the Trainers"

Content Training

The goals of the training program are to

> provide information concerning liability,
>
> define *quid pro quo* and hostile environment sexual harassment,
>
> discuss psychological issues involved in dealing with sexual harassment,
>
> discuss the physical and emotional reactions to being sexually harassed,
>
> provide a psychological profile of sexual harassers,
>
> discuss peer sexual harassment,
>
> discuss means of resolution for complaints of sexual harassment at this company.

At the conclusion of this training program, trainers will be able to

> assess their own perceptions of the definition, incidence, and psychological dimensions of sexual harassment;
>
> adequately label behaviors as illustrative of sexual harassment or not illustrative of sexual harassment;
>
> assess why individuals choose to report or not report sexual harassment;
>
> identify peer sexual harassment;
>
> identify employees' rights and responsibilities under Title VII.

Topics for Presentation and Discussion
Part 1   Introduction to Training Session and Goals of Seminar/Workshop

(20 minutes)

> Trainer welcomes participants to seminar.
>
> Trainer introduces herself or himself to participants and indicates responsibility in establishing a climate free of sexual harassment.
>
> Participants introduce themselves and state their goals for the training session.
>
> Trainer writes these goals on the flip chart or chalkboard for all participants to see.
>
> Trainer summarizes goals.
>
> Trainer lectures on the major components of the training session.

Part 2   Perceptions versus Realities in Sexual Harassment

(20 minutes)

> Trainer summarizes individuals' responses to questions concerning sexual harassment.
>
> Trainer makes summary comments from this unit.

Part 3   Definition of Sexual Harassment

(30 minutes)

> Trainer lectures and leads guided discussion of sexual harassment:
>> summary of case law on *quid pro quo* and hostile environment sexual harassment
>>
>> behavioral examples of sexual harassment
>>
>> peer sexual harassment
>
> Trainer makes summary comments from this unit.

Part 4   Incidence of Sexual Harassment

(20 minutes)

> Trainer lectures on the incidence of workplace sexual harassment:
>> measurement considerations
>>
>> underreporting of incidences
>>
>> individuals at risk for sexual harassment
>>
>> relationship between incidence and reporting
>
> Trainer makes summary comments from this unit.

Break—10 Minutes

Part 5   Impact of Sexual Harassment on Individuals and Workplace

(25 minutes)

> Trainer lectures on the impact of sexual harassment on employees.
>
> Trainer lectures on the cost of sexual harassment for the workplace.
>
> Trainer makes summary comments from this unit.

Part 6   Causes of Sexual Harassment

(20 minutes)

> Trainer lectures on explanatory models of sexual harassment.
>
> Trainer lectures on psychological profiles of harassers.
>
> Trainer makes summary comments from this unit.

Part 7   Preventing Sexual Harassment in the Workplace

(45 minutes)

Trainer lectures on the components of an effective policy statement for employees.

Trainer discusses grievance procedures.

Trainer makes summary comments from this unit.

Part 8   Summary Comments and Review

(30 minutes)

Trainer lectures on myths and realities of sexual harassment.

Trainer leads general discussion of sexual harassment.

Trainer asks participants to reread case study and answer questions.

Trainer reviews participants' goals that were generated at the beginning of the session.

Question and answer period.

Lunch Break—1½ Hours

Pedagogy Training

The goals of the training program are to

provide information concerning creating an atmosphere conducive to training employees;

discuss use of role-playing, case studies, and scenarios in training employees;

discuss use of pretraining and posttraining surveys.

At the conclusion of this training program, trainers will be able to

assess their own perceptions of their ability to provide training for employees,

adequately address questions concerning content,

administer surveys to assess attitudes and prevalence regarding sexual harassment.

Topics for Presentation and Discussion

Part 1 Introduction to Pedagogy Training

(20 minutes)

> Discuss attitudes of employees in attending training sessions on sexual harassment.
>
> Discuss ways to empower employees who are participating in sexual-harassment training.
>
> Trainer summarizes goals.

Part 2 Notifying Employees That They Will Participate in Training Sessions

(20 minutes)

Part 3 Presenting Material on Sexual Harassment to Employees

(60 minutes)

> Definitions of sexual harassment
>
> Impact of sexual harassment on individuals and workplace
>
> Effective verbal and nonverbal communication strategies
>
> Explanatory models of sexual harassment

Break—10 Minutes

Part 4 Dealing with Anger, Frustration, and Anxiety on the Part of Employees Participating in Training Sessions

(60 minutes)

Part 5 How to Discuss Policy Statement and Grievance Procedures in Training Session

(30 minutes)

Part 6 Summary Comments and Review

(30 minutes)

Assess the Participants' Concerns About Sexual Harassment Prior to the Training Session.

Frequently, participants in training sessions question the high incidence reported with respect to victims of sexual harassment in the workplace. They also commonly state that "it's not that bad here where we work." Such comments made in the training session inhibit individuals from speaking about their own concerns and subsequently filing a complaint. To address the incidence and dimensions of sexual harassment at a particular company, it is helpful to disseminate an anonymous questionnaire that asks employees about sexual harassment—either their knowledge or their experiences with this form of discrimination. Results from such surveys can be used as part of the training session. The trainer should develop and analyze responses from these surveys. Sample questions that tap participants' knowledge of sexual harassment include:

TRUE OR FALSE?

Sexual harassment is similar to flirtation.

Sexual harassment may occur even if the harasser and the individual being harassed are the same sex.

Sexual harassment only occurs between a manager and a subordinate.

If the harasser's intent is not to harass, then her/his behavior doesn't constitute sexual harassment.

An employee is sexually harassed only when they have been sexually assaulted.

These questions may be used as a pretest prior to the training program. Suggestions regarding surveys related to incidence of sexual harassment may be found in Fitzgerald, et al., and Paludi and Barickman.[4]

ISSUES TO CONSIDER DURING TRAINING

Specific Objectives

The specific goals of sexual-harassment training programs are to:

1. educate employees about the legal definitions and behavioral examples of *quid pro quo* and hostile environment sexual harassment;
2. discuss the physical and emotional reactions to being sexually harassed;
3. provide employees with a clear understanding of their rights and responsibilities;
4. encourage employees to examine their personal feelings and those of others;

5. dispel myths about sexual harassers;
6. explore responsible behavior in dealing with sexual harassers;
7. examine the effects of sexual harassment on employees, their families, and coworkers;
8. empower employees to take control of their behavior;
9. discuss female and male verbal and nonverbal communication styles;
10. discuss the company's central role in preventing sexual harassment.

We recommend that training sessions must be at least 2.5 to 3 hours in length and provided for the entire organization within a short time period. Training programs for investigators of sexual-harassment complaints and trainers take considerably longer periods of time. Sexual-harassment training involves much more than just a recitation of individuals' rights and responsibilities and what the law and company policy require. Training also requires dealing with individuals' assumptions and misconceptions about sexual harassment and their anxieties about the training itself. Thus, training sessions must devote ample time to dealing with the participants' feelings, misconceptions, and questions. It is best to schedule a maximum of 30 to 35 individuals per training session so as to have ample discussion and contribution from all participants.

Training Sessions Must Build in Time for Questions From Individuals Who Wish to Speak Privately to the Trainer.

Frequently, individuals in training sessions want to discuss their concerns with the trainer alone, without hearing any comments from other participants. Because sexual harassment involves sexuality, it is not like other forms of discrimination. Individuals often view sexual harassment as intimate and sexual and therefore difficult to discuss in public.[5]

Training programs should include both women and men as participants. One of the consistent research findings in sexual harassment concerns the different perceptions of the same event by women and men.[6] Women tend to perceive sexual harassment as an abuse of power; men tend to view sexual harassment as flirtation and flattery. In training sessions, many women are pleased that the issue finally will be addressed; many men are worried that they can't joke or have fun with women anymore. It is helpful to have women and men included in the same training sessions so that these different perceptions can be identified and discussed. Separate sessions for women and men may perpetuate stereotypes that all men are guilty of sexual harassment and all women are victims. This latter type of training is also divisive. Both women and men have the same rights and responsibilities with respect to sexual harassment and must be provided the same information concerning these rights and responsibilities.

Additional Issues.

The following considerations must be well thought out before the initiation of any training program:

1. What provisions does the company have for employees who are prompted by the training to report an experience?
2. Does the company have trained therapists available during and following the training session to assist any employee who has a "flashback" or is visibly upset after the training?
3. What means of reinforcing the information from the training program has the company instituted?

Issues to Consider after Training

Conduct Follow-up Surveys.

We recommend that 3- and 6-month follow-up surveys be disseminated to all employees in order to determine

1. whether they have noticed a difference in the climate since the training sessions,
2. whether they feel the training sessions helped them feel better about the organization,
3. whether they believe the training sessions made it possible to discuss sexual harassment without fear of retaliation,
4. whether they believe the company continues to take the issue of sexual harassment seriously.

Hold Training Sessions Annually.

We recommend that organizations hold training sessions on sexual harassment annually as well as at new employee orientations. Training programs following the distribution of a revised policy statement are necessary to instruct employees in any new components of the policy statement and investigatory procedures. Materials on sexual harassment must also be included in employee handbooks. We also recommend a statement from the CEO outlining the organization's policy against sexual harassment be reissued annually.

EDUCATIONAL QUALIFICATIONS OF TRAINERS

There are several recommended characteristics of good trainers of sexual-harassment programs.[7] We can recommend the following educational qualifications that should be evaluated by any company seeking training in sexual harassment:

1. Knowledge of psychological theories of sexual harassment and of power is helpful when training employees. Trainers must be able to explain psychological terms in nontechnical terms for employees.
2. Knowledge of the psychology of work and careers.
3. Knowledge of research and theories on gender-role socialization. This knowledge must include socialization agents (i.e., parents, peers, media, teachers, music), theories of gender-role acquisition, and research on verbal and nonverbal communication skills;
4. Knowledge of recent case law and legislation is mandatory for trainers.
5. Fluency in languages in addition to English (or presence of a co-trainer who can meet this need).

We recommend that trainers be interviewed in person by a few individuals who represent the group of employees for whom the training will be provided. Areas of inquiry include:

1. education or training in the psychological issues involved in sexual harassment;
2. education or training in the legal issues involved in this area;
3. publications or presentations on the topic;
4. list of previous training seminars or workshops and individuals who can give recommendations about previous training programs;
5. outlines or videotapes of previous training seminars or workshops;
6. familiarity with companies of the size of the present one;
7. ability to work with administrators, including human-resource specialists;
8. education or training in psychological issues involved in facilitating a training program.

Personality Characteristics of Trainers

One of the repeated findings from research and education and training programs at companies concerns the resistance to talking about sexual harassment.[8] These experiences are difficult to discuss, the topic taps the experiences of many individuals, resolutions may seem out of reach and burdensome, and the behaviors are occurring to someone we know or ourselves at the time we are participating in a training program. Although we may want to avoid discussing sexual harassment, we have no choice: Sexual harassment is illegal.

Questions that dominate the training sessions tend to be classified into two major types: those that deal with the nature of sexual harassment and abuse and those that reflect a frustration about the topic.

Employees' questions reflect fear and confusion surrounding sexual harassment. The topic of sexual harassment arouses discomfort and defensiveness. Employees may want to joke about abuse. Would they joke that way in a training program on racial relations or AIDS? Most likely not. Training sessions on sexual harassment inevitably challenge widely held assumptions about female-male relationships and power that are not easy to change. Some employees may joke during the training session as a coping strategy.

It is important to give legitimacy to the anxieties, confusion, and fears raised by participants in the training programs.[9] In addition, it is necessary to establish rapport and a respectful atmosphere in the training session. It is also important to talk up front about the attitudes individuals brought with them to the session, perhaps using the issues raised in national media accounts of an example of sexual harassment as a starting point.[10]

It is imperative that trainers know that some employees may be experiencing sexual harassment, and that the anger they feel toward the perpetrator may be expressed to the trainer. We recommend that therapeutic support staff (e.g., EAP personnel) be present during training programs to assist in this regard.

Sample Outline of Training Programs

In exhibit 5 we present a sample outline of a training program on sexual harassment for employees.

Note that we include in this outline the following topics we have discussed in detail throughout this book:

legal definition of sexual harassment

behavioral examples of sexual harassment

impact of sexual harassment on individuals and the organization

theoretical models to explain the occurrence of sexual harassment

the organization's commitment to preventing sexual harassment.

In addition to this technical information, we also included some pedagogical techniques, for example, welcoming the employees to the training program, asking them to state a goal they have for the training session, and spending time with employees individually following the training program. We believe these pedagogical techniques are important; they help foster a sense of trust, commitment to the prevention of sexual harassment, and respect of individuals' dignity. The pedagogical techniques thus model for the employees appropriate behavior in the workplace.

EXHIBIT 5

Sample Outline of Training Programs
on Sexual Harassment For Employees

The goals of the training program are to

provide information concerning liability,

define *quid pro quo* and hostile environment sexual harassment,

discuss psychological issues involved in dealing with sexual harassment,

discuss the physical and emotional reactions to being sexually harassed,

provide a psychological profile of sexual harassers,

discuss peer sexual harassment,

discuss means of resolution for complaints of sexual harassment at this company.

At the conclusion of this training program, individuals will be able to

Assess their own perceptions of the definition, incidence, and psychological dimensions of sexual harassment;

Adequately label behaviors as illustrative of sexual harassment or not illustrative of sexual harassment;

Assess why individuals choose to report or not report sexual harassment;

Identify peer sexual harassment;

Identify employees' rights and responsibilities under Title VII.

Topics for Presentation and Discussion

Part I   Introduction to Training Session and Goals of Seminar

Trainer welcomes participants to seminar.

Trainer introduces herself or himself, qualifications, background, etc.

Trainer summarizes goals of seminar.

Trainer asks each employee to state goals he or she has for the program.

Trainer writes each response on flip chart or chalkboard for all participants to see.

Trainer summarizes the goals of the participants in the training program.

EXHIBIT 5, continued

Part 2   Definition of Sexual Harassment

Summary of case law on *quid pro quo* and hostile environment sexual harassment.

Behavioral examples of sexual harassment.

Peer sexual harassment.

Trainer makes summary comments from this unit.

Part 3   Impact of Sexual Harassment on Individuals and Workplace Environment

Trainer discusses the impact of sexual harassment on employees.

Trainer discusses the cost of sexual harassment for the workplace.

Trainer makes summary comments from this unit.

Part 4   Causes of Sexual Harassment

Trainer highlights explanatory models of sexual harassment.

Trainer discusses psychological profiles of harassers.

Trainer makes summary comments from this unit.

Part 5   Preventing Sexual Harassment

Importance of policy statement, grievance procedures, and training.

Trainer makes summary comments from this unit.

Trainer distributes copies of policy statement and grievance procedures.

Trainer introduces individual who is responsible for investigating complaints.

Part 6   Summary Comments and Review

Trainer summarizes major points from training program.

Trainer leads general discussion of sexual harassment.

General question and answer period.

Individual meetings with interested employees.

We recommend that the following additional issues be considered when implementing training programs:

1. The trainer should not use notes or read from any written material. Instead, she or he must maintain eye contact with the participants.
2. It is best for companies to hire an outside consultant who meets the educational qualifications and has the personality charac-

teristics we outlined in this chapter. Human-resource specialists at most companies cannot afford the time and commitment it takes to conduct the kind of in-depth sessions we have recommended.

3. Trainers can use case studies (ones we have discussed in this book work well) to stimulate discussion and to assist employees in understanding their responsibilities and sexual harassment in general.[11]

4. A post-training evaluation is helpful. The trainer should keep in mind that she or he may not get the highest marks from individuals in the training session who are angry that they had to take this program in the first place. Trainers must not get discouraged but understand the psychology of the process of participating in a training session. In exhibit 6 we present a sample post-training evaluation form. A summary of the comments should be presented to the CEO of the company at which the training was held.

EXHIBIT 6

Sample Posttraining Evaluation Form

Thank you for completing this posttraining evaluation form. Your responses are anonymous and will be kept confidential. Your responses will be helpful to me in developing future programs.

Please use the following scale in answering the questions:

3: Agree   2: Don't know/undecided   1: Disagree

I. About the Trainer

1.	(Trainer's name) is knowledgeable about the issues.	3	2	1
2.	(Trainer's name) has an effective communication style.	3	2	1
3.	(Trainer's name) respected the participants in the session.	3	2	1
4.	(Trainer's name) answered questions in a respectful manner.	3	2	1
5.	(Trainer's name) treated participants as colleagues.	3	2	1
6.	(Trainer's name) raised my awareness about the issues.	3	2	1

II. About the Content

1.	The training program was organized.	3	2	1
2.	The resource material will be helpful to me.	3	2	1
3.	I learned the legal definition of sexual harassment.	3	2	1
4.	I learned some behavioral examples of sexual harassment.	3	2	1

| | EXHIBIT 6, continued | | |

5. I was given some examples on how to monitor my own behavior with respect to sexual harassment.   3 2 1

6. I learned about power issues involved in sexual harassment.   3 2 1

7. I learned about my company's policy statement and investigatory procedures.   3 2 1

III. About the Program in General

1. The objectives of the program were clearly identified.   3 2 1
2. The utilization of handouts enhanced the training.   3 2 1
3. Audiovisual equipment needs to be used in the training.   3 2 1
4. The acoustics and physical aspects of the room were sufficient.   3 2 1
5. The training increased my awareness of the issues.   3 2 1

IV. About Myself

1. I believe there is a commitment here to work on respecting the dignity of all people.   3 2 1
2. I feel that I benefited from participating in this training program.   3 2 1
3. I believe we need more training on these issues.   3 2 1

V. Overall Rating of Training Program

Please circle one of the following:

  Good   Fair   Poor

VI. Additional Comments You Wish to Make

Thank You!

Notes

1. A. BARAK, *Cross-Cultural Perspectives on Sexual Harassment,* in SEXUAL HARASSMENT: THEORY, RESEARCH, AND TREATMENT (W. O'Donohue, ed., 1997). K. ROSPENDA, J. RICHMAN, & S. NAWYN, *Doing Power: The Confluence of Gender, Race, and Class in Contrapower Sexual Harassment,* GENDER AND SOCIETY 12, at 40–60. E. DESOUZA, J. PRYOR, & C. HUTZ, *Reactions to Sexual Harassment Charges between North Americans and Brazilians,* SEX ROLES 39, at 913–928. S. MECCA & L. RUBIN, *Definitional Research on African American*

Students and Sexual Harassment, PSYCHOLOGY OF WOMEN QUARTERLY 23, at 813–817.

2. A. CULBERTSON, P. ROSENFELD, S. BOOTH-KEWLEY, & P. MAGNUSSON, ASSESSMENT OF SEXUAL HARASSMENT IN THE NAVY: RESULTS OF THE 1989 NAVY-WIDE SURVEY, Navy Personnel Research and Development Center (1992). B. SCHNEIDER, *Consciousness about Sexual Harassment among Heterosexual and Lesbian Women Workers,* JOURNAL OF SOCIAL ISSUES 38, at 75–97. D. BROGAN, et al., *Harassment of Lesbians as Medical Students and Physicians,* JOURNAL OF THE AMERICAN MEDICAL ASSOCIATION 282, at 1290, 1292.

3. M. PALUDI & R. BARICKMAN, SEXUAL HARASSMENT, WORK, AND EDUCATION: A RESOURCE MANUAL FOR PREVENTION (1998).

4. M. PALUDI & R. BARICKMAN, SEXUAL HARASSMENT, WORK, AND EDUCATION: A RESOURCE MANUAL FOR PREVENTION (1998). L. FITZGERALD, et al., *The Incidence and Dimensions of Sexual Harassment in Academia and the Workplace,* JOURNAL OF VOCATIONAL BEHAVIOR 32, at 152–175.

5. L. FITZGERALD, C. HULIN, & F. DRASGOW, *The Antecedents and Consequences of Sexual Harassment in Organizations: An Integrated Model,* in JOB STRESS 2000: EMERGENT ISSUES (G. Keita & S. Sauter, eds., 1993).

6. L. HURT, R. WIENER, B. RUSSELL, & R. MANNEN, *Gender Differences in Evaluating Social-Sexual Conduct in the Workplace,* BEHAVIORAL SCIENCES AND THE LAW 17, at 413–433.

7. J. WILKERSON, *The Impact of Job Level and Prior Training on Sexual Harassment Labeling and Remedy Choice,* JOURNAL OF APPLIED SOCIAL PSYCHOLOGY 29, at 1605–1623. R. CAMBELL, S. RAJA, & P. GRINING, *Training Mental Health Professionals on Violence against Women,* JOURNAL OF INTERPERSONAL VIOLENCE 14, at 1003–1013. B. GUTEK, *Sexual Harassment Policy Initiatives,* in SEXUAL HARASSMENT: THEORY, RESEARCH, AND TREATMENT (W. O'Donohue, ed., 1997).

8. B. GUTEK, *Sexual Harassment Policy Initiatives,* in SEXUAL HARASSMENT: THEORY, RESEARCH, AND TREATMENT (W. O'Donohue, ed., 1997). M. PALUDI & R. BARICKMAN, SEXUAL HARASSMENT, WORK, AND EDUCATION: A RESOURCE MANUAL FOR PREVENTION (1998).

9. M. PALUDI & R. BARICKMAN, SEXUAL HARASSMENT, WORK, AND EDUCATION: A RESOURCE MANUAL FOR PREVENTION (1998). B. GUTEK, *Sexual Harassment Policy Initiatives,* in SEXUAL HARASSMENT: THEORY, RESEARCH, AND TREATMENT (W. O'Donohue, ed., 1997).

10. M. KIMMEL, *Clarence, William, Iron Mike, Tailhook, Senator Packwood, Spur Posse, Magic . . . And Us,* in CONFRONTING RAPE AND SEXUAL ASSAULT (M. Odem et al., eds., 1998). F. TRIX & S. SANKAR, *Women's Voices and Experiences of the Hill-Thomas Hearings,* AMERICAN ANTHROPOLOGIST 1, at 32–40. M. ROGERS, *Clarence Thomas, Patriarchal Discourse and Public/Private Spheres,* SOCIOLOGICAL QUARTERLY 39, at 389–308.

11. Also see M. PALUDI & R. BARICKMAN, SEXUAL HARASSMENT, WORK, AND EDUCATION: A RESOURCE MANUAL FOR PREVENTION (1998).

APPENDIX 2

Selected Excerpts
from the EEOC Guidelines

EQUAL EMPLOYMENT OPPORTUNITY COMMISSION'S GUIDELINES ON DISCRIMINATION BECAUSE OF SEX

Sec 1604.11 Sexual harassment

(a) Harassment on the basis of sex is a violation of section 703 of Title VII.[1] Unwelcome sexual advances, requests for sexual favors, and other verbal or physical conduct of a sexual nature constitute sexual harassment when (1) submission to such conduct is made either explicitly or implicitly a term or condition of an individual's employment, (2) submission to or rejection of such conduct by an individual is used as the basis for employment decisions affecting such individual, or (3) such conduct has the purpose or effect of unreasonably interfering with an individual's work performance or creating an intimidating, hostile, or offensive working environment.

(b) In determining whether alleged conduct constitutes sexual harassment, the Commission will look at the record as a whole and at the totality of the circumstances, such as the nature of the sexual advances and the context in which the alleged incidents occurred. The determination of the legality of a particular action will be made from the facts, on a case by case basis.

(c) Applying general Title VII principles, an employer, employment agency, joint apprenticeship committee or labor organization (hereinafter collectively referred to as "employer") is responsible for its acts and those of its agents and supervisory employees with respect to sexual harassment regardless of whether the specific acts complained of were authorized or even forbidden by the employer and regardless of whether the employer knew or should have known of their occurrence. The Commission will examine the circumstances of the particular employment relationship and the job functions per-

---

1. The principles involved here continue to apply to race, color, religion or national origin.

formed by the individual in determining whether an individual acts in either a supervisory or agency capacity.

(d) With respect to conduct between fellow employees, an employer is responsible for acts of sexual harassment in the workplace where the employer (or its agents or supervisory employees) knows or should have known of the conduct, unless it can show that it took immediate and appropriate corrective action.

(e) An employer may also be responsible for the acts of non-employees, with respect to sexual harassment of employees in the workplace, where the employer (or its agents or supervisory employees) knows or should have known of the conduct and fails to take immediate and appropriate corrective action. In reviewing these cases the Commission will consider the extent of the employer's control and any other legal responsibility which the employer may have with respect to the conduct of such non-employees.

(f) Prevention is the best tool for the elimination of sexual harassment. An employer should take all steps necessary to prevent sexual harassment from occurring, such as affirmatively raising the subject, expressing strong disapproval, developing appropriate sanctions, informing employees of their right to raise and how to raise the issue of harassment under Title VII, and developing methods to sensitize all concerned.

(g) Other related practices: Where employment opportunities or benefits are granted because of an individual's submission to the employer's sexual advances or requests for sexual favors, the employer may be held liable for unlawful sex discrimination against other persons who were qualified for but denied that employment opportunity or benefit.

EQUAL EMPLOYMENT OPPORTUNITY COMMISSION'S PROCEDURAL GUIDELINES

Sec 1601.6 Submission of information
(a) The Commission shall receive information concerning alleged violations of Title VII . . . from any person. Where the information discloses that a person is entitled to file a charge with the Commission, the appropriate office shall render assistance in the filing of a charge. Any person or organization may request the issuance of a Commissioner charge for an inquiry into individual or systematic discrimination. Such request, with any pertinent information, should be submitted to the nearest field office.

(b) A person who submits data or evidence to the Commission may retain or, on payment of lawfully prescribed costs, procure a copy of transcript thereof, except that a witness may for good cause be limited to inspection of the official transcript of his or her testimony.

Sec 1601.7 Charges by or on behalf of persons claiming to be aggrieved

(a) A charge that any person has engaged in or is engaging in an unlawful employment practice within the meaning of Title VII . . . may be made by or on behalf of any person claiming to be aggrieved. A charge on behalf of a person claiming to be aggrieved may be made by any person, agency, or organization. The written charge need not identify by name the person on whose behalf it is made. The person making the charge, however, must provide the Commission with the name, address, and telephone number of the person on whose behalf the charge is made. During the Commission investigation, Commission personnel shall verify the authorization of such charge by the person on whose behalf the charge is made. Any such person may request that the Commission shall keep his or her identity confidential.

Sec 1601.8 Where to make a charge

A charge may be made in person or by mail at the offices of the Commission in Washington, D.C., or any of its field offices or with any designated representative of the Commission. The addresses of the Commission's field offices appear in Sec. 1610.4.

Sec 1601.12 Contents of charge; amendment of charge

(a) Each charge should contain the following: (1) The full name, address and telephone number of the person making the charge except as provided in 1601.7; (2) The full name and address of the person against whom the charge is made, if known (hereinafter referred to as the respondent); (3) A clear and concise statement of the facts, including pertinent dates, constituting the alleged unlawful employment practices: See § 1601.15(b); (4) If known, the approximate number of employees of the respondent employer or the approximate number of members of the respondent labor organization, as the case may be; and (5) A statement disclosing whether proceedings involving the alleged unlawful employment practice have been commenced before a state or local agency charged with the enforcement of fair employment practice laws and, if so, the date of such commencement and the name of the agency.

Sec 1601.18 Dismissal: Procedure and authority

(a) Where a charge on its face, or as amplified by the statements of the person claiming to be aggrieved discloses, or where after investigation the Commission determines, that the charge and every portion thereof if not timely filed, or otherwise fails to state a claim under Title VII . . . the Commission shall dismiss the charge.

(b) Where the person claiming to be aggrieved fails to provide requested necessary information, fails or refuses to appear or to be available for interviews or conferences as necessary, fails or refuses to provide information requested by the Commission . . . or otherwise refuses to cooperate to the extent that the Commission is unable to resolve the charge, and after due notice, the charging party has had 30 days in which to respond, the Commission may dismiss the charge.

(c) Where the person claiming to be aggrieved cannot be located, the Commission may dismiss the charge.

(d) Where a respondent has made a settlement offer . . . which is in writing and specific in its terms, the Commission may dismiss the charge if the person claiming to be aggrieved refuses to accept the offer: *Provided,* That the offer would afford full relief for the harm alleged by the person.

Sec 1601.19 No cause determinations: Procedure and authority

(a) Where the Commission completes its investigation of a charge and finds that there is not reasonable cause to believe that an unlawful employment practice has occurred or is occurring as to all issues addressed in the determination, the Commission shall issue a letter of determination to all parties to the charge indicating the finding. The Commission's letter of determination shall be the final determination of the Commission. The letter of determination shall inform the person claiming to be aggrieved or the person on whose behalf a charge was filed of the right to sue in Federal district court within 90 days of receipt of the letter of determination.

Sec 1601.21 Reasonable cause determination: Procedure and authority

(a) After completing its investigation, where the Commission has not settled or dismissed a charge or made a no cause finding as to every allegation . . . the Commission shall issue a determination that reasonable cause exists to believe that an unlawful employment practice has occurred or is occurring.

Sec 1601.22 Confidentiality

Neither a charge, nor information obtained during the investigation of a charge of employment discrimination . . . nor information obtained from records required to be kept or reports required to be filed . . . shall be made matters of public information by the Commission prior to the institution of any proceeding . . . involving such charge or information.

Sec 1601.24 Conciliation: Procedure and authority

(a) Where the Commission determines that there is reasonable cause to believe that an unlawful employment practice has occurred or is occurring, the Commission shall endeavor to eliminate such practice by informal methods of conference, conciliation and persuasion. In conciliating a case . . . the Commission shall attempt to achieve a just resolution of all violations found and to obtain agreement that the respondent will eliminate the unlawful employment practice and provide appropriate affirmative relief.

(c) Proof of compliance with Title VII . . . in accordance with the terms of the agreement shall be obtained by the Commission before the case is closed.

Sec 1601.25 Failure of conciliation; notice

Where the Commission is unable to obtain voluntary compliance . . . and it determines that further efforts to do so would be futile or non-productive, it shall . . . so notify the respondent in writing.

Sec 1601.27 Civil actions by the Commission

The Commission may bring a civil action against any respondent named in a charge . . . after thirty (30) days from the date of the filing of a charge with the Commission unless a conciliation agreement acceptable to the Commission has been secured.

Sec 1601.28 Notice of right to sue: Procedure and authority

(a) Issuance of notice of right to sue upon request.

(1) When a person claiming to be aggrieved requests, in writing, that a notice of right to sue be issued . . . the Commission shall promptly issue such notice . . . to all parties, at any time after the expiration of one hundred eighty (180) days from the date of filing of the charge with the Commission.

(2) Issuance of a notice of right to sue shall terminate further proceeding of any charge . . .

(3) The issuance of a notice of right to sue does not preclude the Commission from offering such assistance to a person issued such notice as the Commission deems necessary or appropriate.

(b) Issuance of notice of right to sue following Commission disposition of charge.

(1) Where the Commission has found reasonable cause to believe that Title VII . . . has been violated, has been unable to obtain voluntary compliance . . . and where the Commission has decided not to bring a civil action against the respondent, it will issue a notice of right to sue.

Sec 1601.74 Designated and notice agencies

(a) The designated FEP agencies are:

Alaska Commission for Human Rights
Alexandria (Va.) Human Rights Office
Allentown (Pa.) Human Relations Commission
Anchorage (Alaska) Equal Rights Commission
Anderson (Ind.) Human Relations Commission
Arizona Civil Rights Division
Arlington County (Va.) Human Rights Commission
Austin (Tex.) Human Relations Commission
Baltimore (Md.) Community Relations Commission
Bloomington (Ill.) Human Relations Commission
Bloomington (Ind.) Human Relations Commission
California Department of Fair Employment and Housing
Charleston (W.Va.) Human Rights Commission
City of Salina (Kans.) Human Relations Commission and
   Department
Clearwater (Fla.) Office of Community Relations
Colorado Civil Rights Commission
Colorado State Personnel Board
Commonwealth of Puerto Rico Department of Labor
Connecticut Commission on Human Rights and Opportunity
Corpus Christi (Tex.) Human Relations Commission
Dade County (Fla.) Fair Housing and Employment Commis-
   sion
Delaware Department of Labor
District of Columbia Office of Human Rights
Durham (N.C.) Human Relations Commission
East Chicago (Ind.) Human Rights Commission
Evansville (Ind.) Human Relations Commission
Fairfax County (Va.) Human Rights Commission
Florida Commission on Human Relations
Fort Dodge–Webster County (Iowa) Human Rights Commis-
   sion
Fort Wayne (Ind.) Metropolitan Human Relations Commission
Fort Worth (Tex.) Human Relations Commission
Gary (Ind.) Human Relations Commission
Georgia Office of Fair Employment Practices
Hawaii Department of Labor and Industrial Relations
Hillsborough County, Florida, Equal Opportunity and Human
   Relations Department
Howard County (Md.) Human Rights Commission
Huntington (W.Va.) Human Relations Commission
Idaho Human Rights Commission

Illinois Department of Human Rights
Indiana Civil Rights Commission
Iowa Civil Rights Commission
Jacksonville (Fla.) Equal Employment Opportunity Commission
Kansas City (Kans.) Human Relations Department
Kansas City (Mo.) Human Relations Department
Kansas Human Rights Commission
Kentucky Commission on Human Rights
Lee County (Fla.) Department of Equal Opportunity
Lexington-Fayette (Ky.) Urban County Human Rights Commission
Lincoln (Nebr.) Commission on Human Rights
Louisiana Commission on Human Rights
Louisville and Jefferson County (Ky.) Human Relations Commission
Madison (Wis.) Equal Opportunities Commission
Maine Human Rights Commission
Maryland Commission on Human Relations
Mason City, Iowa, Human Rights Commission
Massachusetts Commission Against Discrimination
Michigan City (Ind.) Human Rights Commission
Michigan Department of Civil Rights
Minneapolis (Minn.) Department of Civil Rights
Minnesota Department of Human Rights
Missouri Commission on Human Rights
Montana Human Rights Division
Montgomery County (Md.) Human Relations Commission
Nebraska Equal Opportunity Commission
Nevada Commission on Equal Rights of Citizens
New Hampshire Commission for Human Rights
New Hanover (N.C.) Human Relations Commission
New Haven, Connecticut, Commission on Equal Opportunities
New Jersey Division of Civil Rights, Department of Law and
    Public Safety
New Mexico Human Rights Commission
New York City (N.Y.) Commission on Human Rights
New York State Division on Human Rights
North Carolina State Office of Administrative Hearings
North Dakota Department of Labor
Ohio Civil Rights Commission
Oklahoma Human Rights Commission
Omaha (Nebr.) Human Relations Department
Oregon Bureau of Labor
Orlando (Fla.) Human Relations Department

Paducah, Kentucky, Human Rights Commission
Pennsylvania Human Relations Commission
Philadelphia (Pa.) Commission on Human Relations
Pinellas County, Florida, Affirmative Action Office
Pittsburgh (Pa.) Commission on Human Rights
Prince George's County (Md.) Human Relations Commission
Prince William County (Va.) Human Rights Commission
Rhode Island Commission for Human Rights
Richmond County (Ga.) Human Rights Commission
Rockville (Md.) Human Rights Commission
St. Louis (Mo.) Civil Rights Enforcement Agency
St. Paul (Minn.) Department of Human Rights
St. Petersburg (Fla.) Human Relations Division
Seattle (Wash.) Human Rights Commission
Sioux Falls (S.D.) Human Relations Commission
South Bend (Ind.) Human Rights Commission
South Carolina Human Affairs Commission
South Dakota Division of Human Rights
Springfield (Ohio) Human Relations Department
Tacoma (Wash.) Human Relations Commission
Tampa, Florida, Office of Community Relations
Tennessee Commission for Human Development
Texas Commission on Human Rights
Topeka, Kansas, Human Relations Commission
Utah Industrial Commission, Anti-Discrimination Division
Vermont Attorney General's Office, Civil Rights Division
Vermont Human Rights Commission
Virgin Islands Department of Labor
Virginia Council on Human Rights
Washington Human Rights Commission
West Virginia Human Rights Commission
Wheeling (W.Va.) Human Rights Commission
Wichita Falls, Texas, Human Relations Commission
Wisconsin Equal Rights Division, Department of Industry,
   Labor and Human Relations
Wisconsin State Personnel Commission
Wyoming Fair Employment Practices Commission
York (Pa.) Human Relations Commission
Youngstown (Ohio) Human Relations Commission
(b) The designated Notice Agencies are:
Arkansas Governor's Committee on Human Resources
Ohio Director of Industrial Relations
Raleigh (N.C.) Human Resources Department, Civil Rights
   Unit

APPENDIX 3

Selected Excerpts from Title VII

SEC 2000E-2 UNLAWFUL EMPLOYMENT PRACTICES

Employer practices

(a) It shall be an unlawful employment practice for an employer—

(1) to fail or refuse to hire or to discharge any individual, or otherwise to discriminate against any individual with respect to his compensation, terms, conditions, or privileges of employment, because of such individual's race, color, religion, sex, or national origin; or

(2) to limit, segregate, or classify his employees or applicants for employment in any way which would deprive or tend to deprive any individual of employment opportunities or otherwise adversely affect his status as an employee, because of such individual's race or color, religion, sex, or national origin.

Employment agency practices

(b) It shall be an unlawful employment practice for an employment agency to fail or refuse to refer for employment, or otherwise to discriminate against, any individual because of his race, color, religion, sex, or national origin, or to classify or refer for employment any individual on the basis of his race, color, religion, sex, or national origin.

Labor organization practices

(c) It shall be an unlawful employment practice for a labor organization—

(1) to exclude or to expel from its membership, or otherwise to discriminate against, any individual because of his race, color, religion, sex, or national origin;

(2) to limit, segregate, or classify its membership or applicants for membership, or to classify or fail or refuse to refer for employment any individual, in any way which would deprive or tend to deprive any individual of employment opportunities, or would limit such employment opportunities or otherwise adversely affect his status as an employee or as an applicant for employment, because of such individual's race, color, religion, sex, or national origin; or

(3) to cause or attempt to cause an employer to discriminate against an individual in violation of this section.

SEC 2000E-3 OTHER UNLAWFUL EMPLOYMENT PRACTICES

(a) Discrimination for making charges, testifying, assisting, or participating in enforcement proceedings

It shall be an unlawful employment practice for an employer to discriminate against any of his employees or applicants for employment, for an employment agency, or joint labor-management committee controlling apprenticeship or other training or retraining, including on-the-job training programs, to discriminate against any individual, or for a labor organization to discriminate against any member thereof or applicant for membership, because he has opposed any practice made an unlawful employment practice by this subchapter, or because he has made a charge, testified, assisted, or participated in any manner in an investigation, proceeding, or hearing under this subchapter.

SEC 2000E-4 EQUAL EMPLOYMENT OPPORTUNITY COMMISSION

(a) Creation; composition; political representation; appointment; term; vacancies; Chairman and Vice Chairman; duties of Chairman; appointment of personnel; compensation of personnel

There is hereby created a Commission to be known as the Equal Employment Opportunity Commission, which shall be composed of five members, not more than three of whom shall be members of the same political party. Members of the Commission shall be appointed by the President by and with the advice and consent of the Senate for a term of five years. Any individual chosen to fill a vacancy shall be appointed only for the unexpired term of the member whom he shall succeed, and all members of the Commission shall continue to serve until their successors are appointed and qualified, except that no such member of the Commission shall continue to serve (1) for more than sixty days when the Congress is in session unless a nomination to fill such vacancy shall have been submitted to the Senate, or (2) after the adjournment *sine die* of the session of the Senate in which such nomination was submitted. The President shall designate one member to serve as Chairman of the Commission, and one member to serve as

Vice Chairman. The Chairman shall be responsible on behalf of the Commission for the administrative operations of the Commission, and, except as provided in subsection (b) of this section, shall appoint, in accordance with the provisions of Title V governing appointments in the competitive service, such officers, agents, attorneys, administrative law judges, and employees as he deems necessary to assist it in the performance of its functions and to fix their compensation in accordance with the provisions of chapter 51 and subchapter III of chapter 53 of Title V, relating to classification and General Schedule pay rates: *Provided,* That assignment, removal, and compensation of administrative law judges shall be in accordance with sections 3105, 3344, 5372, and 7521 of Title 5.

(g) Powers of Commission
The Commission shall have power—

(1) to cooperate with and, with their consent, utilize regional, state, local, and other agencies, both public and private, and individuals;

(2) to pay to witnesses whose depositions are taken or who are summoned before the Commissions or any of its agents the same witness and mileage fees are as paid to witnesses in the courts of the United States;

(3) to furnish to persons subject to this subchapter such technical assistance as they may request to further their compliance with this subchapter or an order issued thereunder;

(4) upon request of (i) any employer, whose employees or some of them, or (ii) any labor organization, whose members or some of them, refuse or threaten to refuse to cooperate in effectuating the provisions of this subchapter, to assist in such effectuation by conciliation or such other remedial action as is provided by this subchapter;

(5) to make such technical studies as are appropriate to effectuate the purposes and policies of this subchapter and to make the results of such studies available to the public;

(6) to intervene in a civil action brought under section 2000e-5 of this title by an aggrieved party against a respondent other than a government, governmental agency or political subdivision.

SEC 2000E-5 ENFORCEMENT PROVISIONS

(b) Whenever a charge is filed by or on behalf of a person claiming to be aggrieved, or by a member of the Commission, . . . the Commission shall serve a notice of the charge (including the date, place and circumstances of the alleged unlawful employment practice) . . . and shall make an investigation thereof. Charges shall be in writing under oath or affirmation and shall contain such information and be in such form as the Commission requires. Charges shall not be made public by the Commission. If the Commission determines after such investigation that there is not reasonable cause to believe that the charge is true, it shall dismiss the charge and promptly notify the person claiming to be aggrieved and the respondent of its action. In determining whether reasonable cause exists, the Commission shall accord substantial weight to final findings and orders made by state or local authorities in proceedings commenced under state or local law pursuant to the requirements of subsections (c) and (d) of this section. If the Commission determines after such investigation that there is reasonable cause to believe that the charge is true, the Commission shall endeavor to eliminate any such alleged unlawful employment practice by informal methods of conference, conciliation, and persuasion. Nothing said or done during and as a part of such informal endeavors may be made public by the Commission, its officers or employees, or used as evidence in a subsequent proceeding without the written consent of the persons concerned. Any person who makes public information in violation of this subsection shall be fined not more than $1,000 or imprisoned for not more than one year, or both. The Commission shall make its determination on reasonable cause as promptly as possible and, so far as practicable, not later than one hundred and twenty days from the filing of the charge or, where applicable under subsection (c) or (d) of this section, from the date upon which the Commission authorized to take action with respect to the charge.

(c) State or local enforcement proceedings; notification of State or local authority; time for filing charges with Commission; commencement of proceedings

In the case of an alleged unlawful employment practice occurring in a State, or political subdivision of a State, which has a State or local law prohibiting the unlawful employment practice alleged and establishing or authorizing a State or local authority to grant or seek relief from such practice or to institute criminal proceedings with respect thereto upon receiving notice thereof, no charge may be filed under subsection (b) of this section by the person aggrieved before the expiration of sixty days after proceedings have been commenced under the State or local law, unless such proceedings have been earlier terminated, provided that such sixty-day period shall be extended to one hundred and twenty days during the first year after the effective date of such State or local law. If any requirement for the commencement of such proceedings is imposed by a State or local authority other than a requirement of the filing of a written and signed statement of the facts upon which the proceeding is based, the proceeding shall be deemed to have been commenced for the purposes of this subsection at the time such statement is sent by registered mail to the appropriate State or local authority.

(d) State or local enforcement proceedings; notification of state or local authority; time for action on charges by Commission

In the case of any charge filed by a member of the Commission alleging an unlawful employment practice occurring in a State or political subdivision of a State which has a State or local law prohibiting the practice alleged and establishing or authorizing a State or local authority to grant or seek relief from such practice or to institute criminal proceedings with respect thereto upon receiving notice thereof, the Commission shall, before taking any action with respect to such charge, notify the appropriate State or local officials and, upon request, afford them a reasonable time, but not less than sixty days (provided that such sixty-day period shall be extended to one hundred and twenty days during the first year after the effective day of such State or local law), unless a shorter period is requested, to act under such State or local law to remedy the practice alleged.

(e) Time for filing charges; time for service of notice of charge on respondent; filing of charge by Commission with State or local agency; seniority system

A charge under this section shall be filed within one hundred and eighty days after the alleged unlawful employment practice occurred and notice of the charge (including the date, place and circumstances of the alleged unlawful employment practice) shall be served upon the person against whom such charge is made within ten days thereafter, except that in a case of an unlawful employment practice with respect to which the person aggrieved has initially instituted proceedings with a State or local agency with authority to grant or seek relief from such practice or to institute criminal proceedings with respect thereto upon receiving notice thereof, such charge shall be filed by or on behalf of the person aggrieved within three hundred days after the alleged unlawful employment practice occurred, or within thirty days after receiving notice that the State or local agency has terminated the proceedings under the State or local law, whichever is earlier, and a copy of such charge shall be filed by the Commission with the State or local agency.

(f)(1) If within thirty days after a charge is filed with the Commission or within thirty days after expiration of any period of reference under subsection (c) or (d) of this section, the Commission has been unable to secure from the respondent a conciliation agreement acceptable to the Commission, the Commission may bring a civil action against any respondent not a government, governmental agency, or political subdivision named in the charge. In the case of a respondent which is a government, governmental agency, or political subdivision, if the Commission has been unable to secure from the respondent a conciliation agreement acceptable to the Commission, the Commission shall take no further action and shall refer the case to the Attorney General who may bring a civil action against such respondent in the appropriate United States district court. The person or persons aggrieved shall have the right to intervene in a civil action brought by the Commission or the Attorney General in a case involving a government, governmental agency, or political subdivision. If a charge filed with the Commission pursuant to subsection (b) of this section is dismissed by the Commission, or if within one hundred and eighty days from the filing of such charge or the expiration of any period of reference under subsection (c) or (d) of this section, whichever is later, the Commission has not filed a civil action under this section or the Attorney General has not filed a civil action in a case involving a government, governmental agency, or political subdivision, or the Commission has not entered into a conciliation agreement to which the person aggrieved is a party, the Commission, or the Attorney General in a case involving a government, governmental agency, or political subdivision, shall so notify the person aggrieved and within ninety days after the giving of such notice a civil action may be brought against the respondent named in the charge (A) by the person claiming to be aggrieved or (B) if such charge was filed by a member of the Commission, by any person whom the charge alleges was aggrieved by the alleged unlawful employment practice. Upon application by the complainant and in such circumstances as the court may deem just, the court may appoint an attorney for such complainant and may authorize the commencement of the action without the payment of fees, costs, or security. Upon timely application, the court may, in its discretion, permit the Commission, or the Attorney General in a case involving a government, governmental agency, or political subdivision, to intervene in such civil action upon certification that the case is of general public importance. Upon request, the court may, in its discretion, stay further proceedings for not more than sixty days pending the termination of State or local proceedings described in subsection (c) or (d) of this section or further efforts of the Commission to obtain voluntary compliance.

(2) Whenever a charge is filed with the Commission and the Commission concludes on the basis of a preliminary investigation that prompt judicial action is necessary to carry out the purposes of this

Act, the Commission, or the Attorney General in a case involving a government, governmental agency, or political subdivision, may bring an action for appropriate temporary or preliminary relief pending final disposition of such charge. Any temporary restraining order or other order granting preliminary or temporary relief shall be issued in accordance with rule 65 of the Federal Rules of Civil Procedure. It shall be the duty of a court having jurisdiction over proceedings under this section to assign cases for hearing at the earliest practicable date and to cause such cases to be in every way expedited.

(g) If the court finds that the respondent has intentionally engaged in or is intentionally engaging in an unlawful employment practice charged in the complaint, the court may enjoin the respondent from engaging in such unlawful employment practice, and order such affirmative action as may be appropriate, which may include, but is not limited to, reinstatement or hiring of employees, with or without back pay (payable by the employer, employment agency, or labor organization, as the case may be, responsible for the unlawful employment practice), or any other equitable relief as the court deems appropriate. Back pay liability shall not accrue from a date more than two years prior to the filing of a charge with the Commission. Interim earnings or amounts earnable with reasonable diligence by the person or persons discriminated against shall operate to reduce the back pay otherwise allowable.

(k) In any action or proceeding under this subchapter the court, in its discretion, may allow the prevailing party, other than the Commission or the United States, a reasonable attorney's fee (including expert fees) as part of the costs, and the Commission and the United States shall be liable for costs the same as a private person.

SEC 2000E-7 EFFECT ON STATE LAWS

Nothing in this subchapter shall be deemed to exempt or relieve any person from any liability, duty, penalty, or punishment provided by any present or future law of any State or political subdivision of a State, other than any such law which purports to require or permit the doing of any act which would be an unlawful employment practice under this subchapter.

SEC 2000E-8 INVESTIGATIONS

Examination and copying of evidence related to unlawful employment practices

(a) In connection with any investigation of a charge filed under section 2000e-5 of this title, the Commission or its designated representative shall at all reasonable times have access to, for the purposes of examination, and the right to copy any evidence of any person being investigated or proceeded against that relates to unlawful employment practices covered by this subchapter and is relevant to the charge under investigation.

(e) It shall be unlawful for any officer or employee of the Commission to make public in any manner whatever any information obtained by the Commission pursuant to its authority under this section prior to the institution of any proceeding under this subchapter involving such information. Any officer or employee of the Commission who shall make public in any manner whatever any information in violation of this subsection shall be guilty of a misdemeanor and upon conviction thereof, shall be fined not more than $1,000 or imprisoned not more than one year.

SEC 2000-E12 REGULATIONS

(a) The Commission shall have authority from time to time to issue, amend, or rescind suitable procedural regulations to carry out the provisions of this subchapter. Regulations issued under this section shall be in conformity with the standards and limitations of subchapter II of chapter 5 of Title V.

Index

A

Administrative Procedures Act, 9
Affirmative defense, 19–20, 26, 91, 109, 117
Agency, law of, 45–47
Aggression and sexual harassment, 69
American Association of University Women, 76
Americans with Disabilities Act, 9
Amicus briefs, 148, 151, 154*n*2
Andrews v. City of Philadelphia, 33
Arbitration agreements, 9–10
Assault, lawsuit for, 12
"Assumption of risk" excuse, 44

B

Bailey, N., 77
Baker, Nancy, 66
Barnes v. Costle, 17–18
Battery, lawsuit for, 12
Blue-collar tradeswomen, incidence of harassment, 66
Broderick v. Ruder, 41
Burlington Industries v. Ellerth, 15, 16–17, 18–20, 91, 108–9, 116
Burns v. McGregor Elec. Indus., Inc., 33, 36–37

C

Certiorari, 4
Circuit courts, 4–5, 8
Civil Rights Act of 1964, 7, 9, 12, 148
Client/customer sexual harassment, 45
Clothing, "sexy," 11–12, 40
Colleges, sexual harassment of students, 75–79
Commerce Clause, 7
Common law, 5–6, 12, 13
Complaints
    correct and consistent handling of, 41–42, 129–38
    effective policy for reporting, 89–105
    false complaints, 114
    inconclusive, 114
    informal, 140–41
    investigating and remedying, 107–18
    resolving, 119–46
Confidentiality, 110
Consensual romantic relationships, 29
Constitutional law, 5
"Constructive discharge," 52–53, 102
Continuing violation, 149
Coping after harassment, 73–75
Court systems, 4–5, 8

D

Damages
    equitable, 52–53
    jury awards of, 54, 151
    in state common-lawsuits, 51
Discrimination, 4, 13, 149

Diversity jurisdiction, 4
Documentation, 115
Dziech, B., 77

E

EEOC v. Arabian American Oil Co., 7–8
"Effect" on a gender, 29
Effect *vs.* intent, 31–34
Electronic mail harassment, 40–41
Ellison v. Brady, 24, 32–33
Emotional distress, lawsuit for, 12
Empirical definition, 62–64
Employees
    complaint filed outside of employer, 152
    definition of, 13–14, 52
    "making them whole," 99–101, 115
    temporary help, 13–14
Employer liability
    effective policy/policies, 89–105
    statute definition of, 13–14
Employment agencies, under Title VII, 7
Employment, conditions of, 29–31
Employment discrimination, federal and state statutes, 5
Enabling act, 9
Equal Employment Opportunity Commission (EEOC)
    authority of, 148–49
    complaint filed outside of employer, 152
    conciliation stage with employer, 150
    defining sexual harassment, 14–15
    designated agencies, 182–84
    determining an employer/employee, 13–14
    examples of sexual harassment, 39–42
    excerpts from guidelines, 177–84
    excerpts from Title VII, 185–92
    Guidelines for Discrimination on the Basis of Sex, 148
    investigation of a complaint, 150
    "reasonable victim" perspective, 33–35
    recommended elements for policy/procedure, 92–100
    reports of charges filed, ix
    "right to sue," 151
    role in sexual harassment situations, 147–54
    statutes of limitations, 149
    summary judgment, 151
    Title VII cases, 9
"Equal opportunity harassers," 42–43
Equal Pay Act, 9
Equitable damages, 52–53
Ethnic/racial harassment, 76–79
Exit interviews, 102–4
Externally focused coping strategies, 73, 75

F

Faragher v. City of Boca Raton, 15, 26, 103
Federal court systems, 3–5, 8

193